DIVINE SOVEREIGNTY
AND HUMAN RESPONSIBILITY

DIVINE
SOVEREIGNTY
AND HUMAN
RESPONSIBILITY

Biblical perspectives in tension

D .A. CARSON

Wipf and Stock Publishers
EUGENE, OREGON

Wipf and Stock Publishers
199 West 8th Avenue, Suite 3
Eugene, Oregon 97401

Divine Sovereignty and Human Responsibility
Biblical Perspective in Tension
By Carson, D.A.
©1994 Carson, D.A.
ISBN: 1-57910-859-8
Publication date: January, 2002
Previously published by Baker Books, 1994.

To the memory of
MY PARENTS
who first taught me by precept and example
to love the Word of God
and
to my best friend and dear wife
JOY
this book is gratefully dedicated.

CONTENTS

ABBREVIATIONS

Note: The following list does not include abbreviations to biblical, apocryphal, pseudepigraphical and rabbinic material, nor to the works of Josephus, nor to the Dead Sea Scrolls. Titles of books and articles are sometimes abbreviated after their first appearance. Titles for all but the most common journals are written out and not abbreviated. When a commentary on the Gospel of John is first cited, its full title is provided; but thereafter, only the author's surname is given.

APAT   *Die Apokryphen und Pseudepigraphen des Alten Testaments,* ed. E. Kautzsch, 1900

APOT   *The Apocrypha and Pseudepigrapha of the Old Testament,* 2 vols., ed. R. H. Charles, 1913

BAG   W. F. Arndt and F. W. Gingrich (eds), *A Greek-English Lexicon of the New Testament and Other Early Christian Literature,* 1957

BDB   F. Brown, S. R. Driver and C. A. Briggs (eds), *A Hebrew-English Lexicon of the Old Testament,* (1907) 1955

BDF   F. Blass and A. Debrunner (eds), *A Greek Grammar of the New Testament and Other Early Christian Literature,* ed. and tr. R. W. Funk, 1961

CBQ   *Catholic Biblical Quarterly*

DJD   *Discoveries in the Judaean Desert, 1955-*

DPP   *Dictionary of Philosophy and Psychology,* 3 vols., ed. J. M. Baldwin, 1901-5

DSS   Dead Sea Scrolls

Ex.T   *Expository Times*

IDB   *The Interpreter's Dictionary of the Bible,* 4 vols., ed. G. A. Buttrick *et al.,* 1962

ISBE   *International Standard Bible Encyclopedia,* 5 vols., ed. J. Orr, rev. M. G. Kyle, 1930

JBL   *Journal of Biblical Literature*

JE	*Jewish Encyclopedia*, 12 vols., ed. I. Singer *et al.*, 1901-6
JTS	*Journal of Theological Studies*
LXX	Septuagint
MT	Masoretic Text
NBD	*New Bible Dictionary*, ed. J. D. Douglas, 1962
Nov.T	*Novum Testamentum*
NTS	*New Testament Studies*
OED	*Oxford English Dictionary*
PT	Palestinian Targum
RB	*Revue Biblique*
RGG	*Die Religion in Geschichte und Gegenwart: Handwörterbuch für Theologie und Religionswissenschaft*, 7 vols., ed. K. Galling *et al.*, 1957-65
SB	H. L. Strack and P. Billerbeck, *Kommentar zum Neuen Testament aus Talmud und Midrasch*, 6 vols., 1926-61
SM	*Sacramentum Mundi*
St.Ev.	*Studia Evangelica*
TDNT	*Theological Dictionary of the New Testament*, 10 vols., ed. G. Kittel and G. Friedrich; ET by G. W. Bromiley, of *Theologisches Wörterbuch zum Neuen Testament*, 1964-76
TJ_I	Pseudo-Jonathan Targum
TJ_{II}	Fragmentary Targum
TO	Targum Onkelos
UBS	United Bible Societies
VT	*Vetus Testamentum*

PREFACE
TO THE SECOND EDITION

More than a dozen years have passed since this book was published. I am grateful to HarperCollins and to Baker Book House for bringing it back into print.

The material found in these chapters began life as a doctoral dissertation at Cambridge University, defended in 1975. My supervisor, the Rev. Dr Barnabas Lindars, SSF (later the Rylands Professor of Biblical Criticism and Exegesis at the University of Manchester, and now deceased) offered steady advice, rigorous criticism, and generous friendship. Not least among his many gifts were a frank intellectual candour that never bluffed, and a patient willingness to allow a young student to disagree with his mentor. Such largeness of spirit is not found in all scholars, and I am grateful for the privilege of working with him. That this book does not contain more lapses in judgement than it does owes much to Professor Lindars.

In revising the dissertation for publication in this form, I eliminated about 25,000 words, comprising some of the more technical debates with the secondary literature, plus a chapter on the Hermetica, and a chapter on Philo. The latter eventually found its way into print elsewhere (*Novum Testamentum 23* [1981] 148-164). Foreign languages now appear in English – in official translations where such are available, and in my own translation in other cases.

When in 1978 I wrote the Preface for the first edition of this book, I had no idea that I would spend five of the next fifteen years in Cambridge. This longer perspective enables me all the more heartily to repeat my thanks to those who made the initial period of doctoral study so enjoyable and fruitful. Several individuals and organizations provided funds to meet some of my expenses: in particular I want to record my gratitude to the Tyndale Fellowship for Biblical Research, the trustees of the Bethune-Baker Fund, the trustees of the Thorpe Fund (Emmanuel College), and the trustees of the Mary Robinson Exhibition. The Rev Don cupitt, then Dean of Emmanuel College, helped me in some of these and other matters. The superb facilities of the University Library and of

Tyndale House were made accessible by competent and courteous staff. Professor C.F.D. Moule's New Testament seminars expanded my horizons as few discussions have done before or after. A great educational opportunity surrounds 'elevenses' and tea at Tyndale House. Many friendships first nurtured there or at Eden Baptist Church continue undiminished. Several colleagues proofread parts of the original dissertation and saved me from embarrassing errors: I am especially grateful to the Rev. Dr H.H.P. Dressler, Dr (now Professor) H.G.M. Williamson, and Dr Colin Hemer. Mr Paul Helm, then of Liverpool University (recently appointed to a chair at King's College, London) steered me through some of the philosophical minefields. Pat Warkentin (then Pat Doidge) contributed her skilful typing, at a time (now hard to remember!) when writers did not compose their own work on laptop computers.

I am grateful that there is still enough demand for this book to warrant reprinting it. If I had to write it today, its main arguments, I think, would remain intact, even if the bibliography and some of the discussions would be updated. Having more recently written a commentary on the Gospel of John, I suppose some of the lengthy section of John in this book would be more mature. I would revise a few minor judgements on the Septuagint and the Targums; my hesitant criticisms of how merit theology is treated by E. P. Sanders, whose *Paul and Palestinian Judaism* had not long appeared when I revised my work for publication, would be strengthened and buttressed, but not changed.

When this book first appeared, it was dedicated to my parents and to my dear wife Joy. The gratitude to my parents I acknowledge all the more, even if it must be expressed *in memoriam*. The gratitude to my wife I can, thank God, express to her personally.

Soli deo gloria.

D.A. Carson
Trinity Evangelical
Divinity School,
November 1993

CHAPTER ONE

INTRODUCTION

THE PROBLEM

Both theology and philosophy wrestle with the tension which
exists between God's sovereignty and human responsibility
(hereafter called the 'sovereignty-responsibility tension').
Although not restricted to monotheistic religions,[1] this tension is
particularly acute there because pure monotheism excludes
cosmological dualism and usually pictures God as both omnipotent and good. This monograph is concerned with the
sovereignty-responsibility tension as delineated within monotheism—indeed, within the christian form of monotheism—and
is more theological than philosophical.

The sovereignty-responsibility tension is almost impossibly
broad. It lies at the heart of questions about the nature of God,
and it poses difficult conundra about the meaning of human
'freedom'. The most common questions it raises are well known.
If God is absolutely sovereign, in what sense can we meaning-
fully speak of human choice, of human will? In what way are
we to relate passages which stress divine transcendence and
omnipotence with those which speak of divine repentance? How
does the shape of the sovereignty-responsibility tension affect
the problem of theodicy? Must God be reduced to accommodate
the freedom of human choice? Does significant human responsibility so lean on power to the contrary that God becomes
contingent?

Yet the tension is broader than the range of these standard
questions. At the heart of the Christian faith lies the
incarnation: God became man. What effect does this astounding
notion have on the relationship between God's sovereignty and
man's responsibility? Or, to reverse the question, how does this
tension affect christology? Moreover, since the message Jesus
preached is saturated with the theme of the reign of God, in
what sense, may we ask, does an absolutely sovereign God *begin*
to reign, or *promise* to reign? One might have thought that

divine sovereignty already presupposes a reign of God so
universal and eternal that ideas of an eschatological reign are
excluded.

To ask such questions is not to promise easy answers.
However, it is important at the outset to see that the tension
between divine sovereignty and human responsibility not only
embraces the well worn theme of how soteriological election is
to be construed, but also stands intertwined with christology and
eschatology. And because it deals comprehensively with the
nature of God and the nature of man, it cannot escape questions
of anthropology and of 'theo'-logy proper.

I frankly doubt that finite human beings can cut the Gordian
knot; at least, this finite human being cannot. The sovereignty-
responsibility tension is not a problem to be solved; rather, it is
a framework to be explored. To recognise this is already a
major advance, for it rejects those easy 'solutions' which impose
alien philosophical constructions upon the biblical data, or
which dismiss those elements of the biblical data not conducive
to the investigator's system. To explore this tension is to explore
the nature of God and his ways with men.

Yet although we must not too readily adopt simplistic
'solutions', neither must we too easily succumb to the viewpoint
that the tension is intrinsically illogical. To admit we do not
possess enough pieces of the puzzle to complete the picture is a
far cry from saying that the pieces belong to quite different
puzzles and therefore could not be related to each other even if
we were given the rest of them. In other words, part of the
purpose in exploring the sovereignty-responsibility tension
theologically and exegetically lies in the value of a mature
reflection on the problem, a reflection which deals fairly with
the data and is simultaneously resistant to charges of
irrationality and incoherence.

APPROACHING THE PROBLEM

Terms used in the debate do not possess the same meaning from
author to author, and so preliminary definitions are in order.
'Predestination' in this book refers to the fore-ordination of
events by God. 'Election' refers to soteriological predestination,
with the added caveat that no judgment as to the nature of the
salvation is presupposed by the terms themselves. Because

predestination, by this definition, has God as the one who predestines, it is to be distinguished from 'determinism', which supposes that all is in principle completely predictable according to the universal laws of nature, but which does not trace such fixedness to God.[2] 'Responsibility' here means a personal relationship of obligation and accountability toward (usually) God. That the relationship is personal and accountable presupposes some measure of real freedom; but possible approaches to 'free will' are best considered inductively. 'Freedom' and 'free will' may therefore be excluded from initial definitions.

Approaches to the biblical data have often adopted methods open to serious criticism. In the first place, the approach through systematic theology has often succumbed to the danger of constructing the 'system' too early and with insufficient controls, or to the danger of overlooking genuine variations of approach and emphasis within the biblical literature, or to the danger of forcing the biblical writers to respond to too many questions which do not interest them. Some writers draw every possible conclusion out of all passages which stress or presuppose God's unconditioned sovereignty, and then construct a system to filter out and explain any other evidence. Methodologically speaking, such an approach is no different from that of writers who focus on man, his responsibilities and choices, and conclude on the basis of their system that God's sovereignty is necessarily limited, perhaps self-limited, in some way.[3] Not a few adopt philosophical structures essentially alien to the biblical data. For example, I. T. Ramsey uses the corollaries of process theology to render the sovereignty-responsibility tension innocuous: 'all-powerful' becomes a 'qualified model' and the tension between God's sovereignty and human responsibility becomes a 'pseudo-problem'. W. S. Towner's book tells us more about how he wishes God would deal with evil than about the biblical data. And J. Farrelly, adopting primarily scholastic categories, ably pits the strong points of the Thomists (Banezians) against those of the Molinists, but is decidedly light-weight when it comes to the biblical text.[4]

The second methodologically weak approach to the sovereignty-responsibility tension concentrates on word studies. These can be invaluable, but they are open to serious abuse.[5] It is well known that Hebrew has no root for 'providence' (perhaps the closest approximation is in some uses of *pqd*: e.g.

Job 10.12); yet the concept itself is woven into all divisions of the Hebrew canon. In the Old Testament, election is not restricted to the roots *bḥr* and *yḏ'*; it lurks behind such motifs as covenant, marriage, Yahweh's people, and many more. The Gospel of John never uses the Greek word *proorizein*; but the concept of predestination is none the less present. Thus, even when carefully done, word studies, though an essential tool, are too restrictive for an adequate probing of the sovereignty-responsibility tension.

The third approach is the examination of some narrow theme which constitutes a part of the sovereignty-responsibility tension. For example, there are several important discussions of election in the Old Testament.[6] Such studies can prove very helpful; but they sometimes give the impression that once the election problem is resolved (at least to the writer's own satisfaction!) the tension has disappeared. In fact, as we have seen, election is only one aspect of the sovereignty-responsibility tension, and there are tighter connections between the whole and its part than is often realised. Moreover, the tension, precisely because it is so broad and so pervasive, can emerge in some literature which makes no reference to election or to some other particular aspect of the broader problem.

These three approaches, of course, are not necessarily mutually exclusive, and not necessarily bad. But the recognition of their limitations has prompted a rather different approach in this volume.

First, in the New Testament I have restricted myself to detailed consideration of the Gospel of John. Next to some of the Pauline literature, the fourth Gospel stands out as a New Testament focus for the sovereignty-responsibility tension. Paul has earned detailed comment and not a few monographs on the subject; but, despite the mushrooming literature on John during the last three decades, relatively little of it has been given over to this particular theme. So in a sense, this monograph is a contribution to the study of johannine theology.

Second, I have cast johannine theology against the backdrop of Jewish background, directing the attention of the first two parts of the book to the Old Testament and to the most readily available intertestamental Jewish literature. The latter include the Apocrypha and pseudepigrapha, the Dead Sea Scrolls (hereafter DSS), targums and rabbinic literature, and Josephus.

With regret I have excluded Samaritan sources: they do not change my main lines of argument, and appropriate consideration of them would unduly lengthen this volume.

Third, I have attempted to reflect the essence of the sovereignty-responsibility tension in each corpus of literature. Some ancient writers are interested in theodicy, others not at all. Some are captured by the prospect of God's invading reign at the end of history, and others are more concerned about responding to him now, or about determining the significance of the gracious call that brought Abraham out of Ur and the children of Israel out of Egypt. Again, the peculiar christology and eschatology of the fourth Gospel must be understood first of all on their own terms, within the framework of the Gospel itself. Such diversity of emphasis and interest calls forth an important principle: viz., in attempting to delineate the shape of the sovereignty-responsibility tension in each corpus of literature, we cannot insist on tracing narrow themes throughout. Rather, we must let the literature itself dictate, as much as possible, the shape of the sovereignty-responsibility tension within its pages.

Two corollaries follow. (1) This study must not be construed as an attempt to find the background of John, or to contribute to history-of-religions research. In one sense, of course, the study of the sovereignty-responsibility tension in any corpus must shed light on the study of the same theme in any other corpus, if only because of suggestive parallels and contrasts. But although I am interested in the extent to which, and the manner in which, John reflects his Jewish background, I am not attempting to trace out trajectories. (2) It now becomes clearer why this monograph largely restricts itself, canonically speaking, to the treatment of the theme in the Gospel of John, with some space for the Old Testament and less for the New Testament writers. To recognise that the sovereignty-responsibility tension needs to be unpacked in each corpus before proceeding to the attempt to systematise one's findings from the entire canon entails such a restriction—or else a very large volume!

Fourth, notwithstanding these limitations, the fourth part of this study seeks to apply the biblical data thus gleaned to the broader theological and philosophical dimensions of the tension between divine sovereignty and human responsibility. This is done, not in the hope that some comprehensive theology of the tension may emerge, but in the hope that careful application of one strand of the biblical treatment of the subject may provide helpful parameters within which the theology of the tension may fruitfully develop.

Fifth, in an effort to gain precision, some attention is paid to the *functions* to which various aspects of the sovereignty-responsibility tension are put in each corpus. For example: Granted that some men are graciously chosen, in what connection does a particular writer bring up the subject? What lessons does he draw from election? Again, what deductions follow, in different texts, from the predestinarian potter-and-clay model? Does the fact that men choose become an occasion for boasting or a stimulus to choose rightly? Answering such questions is in the first instance a descriptive undertaking. It often proves misleading to govern ontology by function.[7] Nevertheless the examination of how certain perspectives and concepts function in the writings here studied provides a useful guideline: viz., we ought to be cautious about drawing deductions from various concepts if those deductions are not explicitly or implicitly drawn by those who expound the concepts.

PART ONE

THE SOVEREIGNTY-RESPONSIBILITY TENSION IN THE HEBREW CANON

CHAPTER TWO

SELECTED OLD TESTAMENT PASSAGES

The present chapter and the next are given over to a survey of the sovereignty-responsibility tension in the Hebrew canon. This chapter focuses on a select list of twelve biblical passages in which some kind of tension between God's sovereignty and man's responsibility is woven into the fabric of the text, so much so that it can be avoided only by great exegetical ingenuity. These twelve passages have been chosen from a long list of potential candidates, primarily because they are particularly good examples, but also because they represent a fair cross-section of Old Testament literature.

The next chapter abandons close scrutiny of a small number of passages in favour of painting a picture with a large brush. It is divided into two main parts. The first surveys the ways in which the Old Testament portrays man as responsible and God as contingent; the second surveys the ways in which the Old Testament portrays God as so utterly sovereign as to exclude any limiting contingency. The aim of the chapter is not to provide a history of the development of the sovereignty-responsibility tension within canonical tradition, but to outline the tradition itself. Some care has been taken to avoid reading the Old Testament through monochromatic spectacles: after all, the parameters of the sovereignty-responsibility tension in wisdom literature are not precisely the same as those found in the prophets or in the Pentateuch, and there are smaller variations within each corpus; but over-simplifications no doubt occur. Some of the danger is alleviated by constantly asking how various themes function within their own context.

Genesis 45.5-8; 50.19f. (cf. Psalm 105.16-25)

The comfort Joseph offers to allay his brothers' fears turns on God's overruling in an event itself evil. To become vindictive now, Joseph reasons, would be to put himself in God's place (50.19). This is not a simple declaration of non-competence to

judge what is right and wrong. The meaning rather is that God
himself has acted with benevolent purposes in the entire event,
and, acknowledging these, Joseph is content to harbour no
grudge.[1] Joseph finds in Yahweh's good intentions sufficient
motive for imitative benevolence.

But to isolate the function of God's sovereignty in these verses
is not to resolve the tension between that sovereignty and man's
responsibility. On the one hand the words, 'so it was not you
who sent me here, but God' (45.8) are hyperbolic: Joseph does
not minimise the ugly fact that the brothers with evil intent
(50.20) did indeed sell him (45.5). The text will not allow the
brothers to be classed as puppets and thus to escape their guilt.
On the other hand, neither does it picture God as *post eventu*
deflecting the evil action of the brothers and transforming it into
something good.[2] To cite Joseph's words to his brothers: 'As for
you, you meant (*ḥašaḇtem*) evil against me; but God meant
(*ḥašaḇah*) it for good' (50.20). Both God and the brothers
entertain specific intentions in their respective roles in the same
event; but their intentions are disjunctive. 'God has himself
directed all for good: in deep hiddenness he has used all the
dark things in human nature to further his plans, that is, "to
preserve many people alive" (Gen. 45.5ff., 50.20).[3] While the
brothers contrive to rid themselves of Joseph, God contrives to
effect their (and others') deliverance.

Leviticus 20.7ff.; 22.31f.

The Holiness Code (Lev. 17-26) drums with the demand to
be holy. It is Yahweh himself who gives the highest motive for
such holiness: 'You shall be holy; for I the LORD your God am
holy' (Lev. 19.2). Unlike 19.2, the two texts which immediately
concern us, 20.7 and 22.31, do not explicitly posit the holiness
of Yahweh as the ultimate motive driving the people towards
holiness, although perhaps that is assumed in Yahweh's words,
'for I am the LORD your God' (20.7), 'I am the LORD' (22.31).
The new ingredient lies elsewhere: it is the last clause of 20.8
and 22.32: 'I am the LORD who sanctifies you' (NASB). It is
unwarranted to take this clause as a mere variation of the other
holiness-motive clauses:[4] rather, Yahweh himself is to be
credited with sanctifying the people. Clearly, that Yahweh is
the sanctifier does not relieve the Israelites of their respon-

sibility to sanctify themselves; and conversely, that responsibility does not entail Yahweh's passivity in their sanctification.

Judges 14.4a

The words of 14.4a must not be regarded as secondary additions. Not only do they provide the background to the displeasure of Samson's parents (14.3), but they provide the framework within which the playing out of his riddle takes on meaning.[5]

The portrait of Samson is scarcely salubrious. Samson's insistence on an illicit union, in this passage, is no exception. Yet the writer can still say that it was from Yahweh, because Yahweh[6] was seeking an opportunity against the Philistines. There is no obvious effort to whitewash Samson; nor is Yahweh's character impugned. In some mysterious way he himself stands behind Samson's unworthy motives, not to promote evil but to punish the Philistines; for without the ensuing exploits Israel could easily have succumbed to Philistine influence.

2 Samuel 24 (cf. 1 Chronicles 21.1-7)

Most commentators connect 2 Samuel 24.1 with 1 Chronicles 21.1-14, where a first punishment from Yahweh is meted out. The reason why Yahweh's anger is again burning against Israel is not made clear, although some think it is connected with the Bathsheba incident.[7] Nor is it very clear in what way David here sins. There is no doubt at all, however, that his action in commanding the census makes him morally culpable (cf. 24.10, 17). Divine sovereignty does not function to reduce human responsibility; David is not less guilty because Yahweh himself[8] incites him to number Israel. 'The language leaves no doubt ... that God incites men to do that for which he afterwards punishes them.'[9] We may perhaps assume, after the pattern of 2 Samuel 21.1-14, that Yahweh's action in 24.1 is judicial; at any rate, no moral blame attaches to Yahweh himself. But the point to note is the manner in which divine sovereignty and human responsibility are here interrelated. Contrary to views which see divine sovereignty and human responsibility as mutually limiting, the former does not in fact alleviate the latter, while the latter in no way curtails the former.

Appeal to 1 Chronicles 21.1 does not help. That Satan, not

Yahweh, here stands up and incites David to number the people has caused not a few scholars to see a theological development: the Chronicler 'could no longer endure this great theological tension.'[10] That there is both development and a different theological perspective is undeniable; but the claim that the change from Yahweh to Satan is part of that development is more doubtful. By itself, of course, 1 Chronicles 21.1 manifests no tension; but early readers, taking 2 Samuel 24.1 and 1 Chronicles 21.1 together, would find in the change from Yahweh to Satan no more and no less trouble than in the first two chapters of Job.[11]

Some think that the difference in perspective is clear as soon as we remember that only 2 Samuel 24 gives the background to the building of the Temple. This fact alone would be enough to trace the genesis of the action back to Yahweh himself: the secret overruling of God behind the stage of phenomenal history makes it clear that Yahweh, not David, is the one who selects the Temple site. The final result of the matter is a major redemptive appointment, and no human offence could be the ultimate trigger to release so grand a gift.

1 Kings 8.57-60

Solomon's prayer at the dedication of the temple (8.22ff.) lays repeated stress on the responsibility of the people to repent and turn from their wicked ways. Especially from 8.31 on, the plea to the God whom the heaven of heavens cannot contain (8.27) is that he might respond favourably to the people's repentance. Such language clearly places the responsibility to repent squarely on the shoulders of the people.

Nevertheless, the concluding verses sound a different note. In 8.57-60 the request is rather that God will work in the hearts of his people so that they will follow his ways. Of course, that Yahweh inclines the hearts of the people to him is not a potential excuse for personal indolence, but functions as an incentive to thorough devotion and obedience (1 Kgs. 8.61).

1 Kings 11.11-13, 29-39; 12.1ff (cf. 2 Chronicles 10.15; 11.4)

That the behaviour of Rehoboam was foolish, immature, harsh and unsympathetic cannot be doubted. Nevertheless, the entire event—including Rehoboam's folly—is attributed to a 'turn of affairs' (1 Kgs. 12.15; 2 Chr. 10.15) from Yahweh.[12] At least part of the reason for Yahweh's action is given to us: he was fulfilling his word through Ahijah the prophet (11.29-39). This in turn arose out of Solomon's idolatry (11.11-13; cf. Exod. 20.5b=Deut. 5.9b), and therefore Yahweh's action was in part judicial. It functions further to explain why Rehoboam did not fight. But the crucial point to observe is the tension between God's sovereignty over the event, and Rehoboam's reprehensible conduct within that framework. The sovereignty-responsibility tension is certainly not eased by the later developments of Jeroboam's evil (14.6ff.).

Isaiah 10.5ff.

This passage throbs with tension. On the one hand, Yahweh's sovereignty over the nations is highlighted in the most absolute terms. He it is who sends Assyria against his people to punish them for their wickedness. He manipulates nations the way men manipulate tools (10.15); and hence it is the most pompous arrogance to suppose one may act independently of him. Can lifeless wood lift 'not-wood'? Shall finite, human Assyria move God?

But that brings us to the other side of the question. It is possible that the prophet believes Assyria to have overstepped her commission (10.7), but this is at best a secondary point.[13] The really heinous crime of Assyria, for which there is to be a most rigorous accounting, is her attitude of self-congratulating independence. The king's arrant boasting fails to acknowledge the real source of Assyria's strength: Yahweh himself (10.13ff.).

The problem of how to construe the parts played by Yahweh and by Assyria is acute. Clearly, Yahweh's use of Assyria entails no honour for Assyria; yet it is inadequate to say, with Rowley, that God chose a nation like Assyria for its punitive task simply because he saw that 'the very iniquity of their heart would lead them to the course that He could use.'[14] The expressions used do not make God so secondary and contingent. On the other hand, Calvin's warning is well-advised: 'We must not suppose that there is a violent compulsion, as if God dragged them against their will; but in a wonderful and inconceivable manner he regulates all the movements of men, so that they still have the exercise of their will.'[15] Indeed, it is for the self-aggrandisement at the core of the Assyrian will that she will be condemned. From the passage, one might almost conclude that Assyria would have borne no chastening at all if only she had adopted a humble servant spirit toward Yahweh. At the same time, the comfort afforded the Israelites by the assurance of Yahweh's sovereignty over their oppressors helps to keep their own punishment in perspective.

In the one event, Isaiah is able in this way to divide up the roles of Yahweh and Assyria. This division does not so much make the total event the summation of the component roles of the two actors, as affirm both the transcendent and unyielding sovereignty of God over history, and the responsibility of all his creatures, including foreign kings, to acknowledge him as sovereign: all this without benefit of convenient harmonising explanation. The historical actions and motives of Assyria are understood to be significant, the basis upon which she will be punished; yet this significance does not reside in some action which escapes the sphere of divine sovereignty.

Such an approach to the sovereignty-responsibility tension is not unique: cf. 2 Kings 19.25; Isaiah 30.28; 37.22ff.; 44.24-45.13; Jeremiah 25.12ff.; 50-51.

Jeremiah 29.10-14

Yahweh promises to visit the exiles in Babylon at the end of seventy years, fulfil his word, and bring them back to the land. All this arises out of his plans for their well-being, not for calamity (29.10f.). He will be found by his people, and he will restore their fortunes (29.14).

But vv. 12f. put the onus of responsibility on the calling, coming, praying, and seeking of the people. It is true that some commentators take these verses as an encouragement to the exiled Israelites to seek God throughout the exilic period in a spiritual, non-cultic fashion now that they are removed from the Temple. But the flow of the argument better suits the interpretation given here: the 'seeking' and 'finding' of 29.13 are most naturally related to the 'being found' in 29.14. In the latter verse, Yahweh's self-disclosure, his gracious decision to 'be found' by his people, is clearly related to the close of the exile. Once again, then, the divine activity calls for response, not fatalism; while human calling and seeking do not make the divine activity contingent. (Cf. on Lev. 20.7f.; 22.31f.; 1 Kgs. 8.57ff., *supra*.)

Jeremiah 52.3 (cf. 2 Kings 24.19f.)

Some scholars insist that this text cannot mean that the anger of Yahweh was the cause of Zedekiah's evil. It is much better to admit that, however awkward the phraseology may appear, the MT conveys 'the impression that the divine anger was the cause of the iniquity rampant in Judah rather than being the result of it.'[16] The thought is no more difficult than 2 Samuel 24.1ff. (*supra*); and, as in that case, the divine action is most likely judicial, presupposing a long list of earlier breaches.

The crucial point for this study is the tension between the divine and human aspects of Zedekiah's rebellion. The writer regards that rebellion as inevitable: Yahweh stands behind it. But Yahweh's character remains unsullied; his action is just and judicial. Meanwhile, Zedekiah's action is not the knee-jerk movement of a puppet, but is characterised as 'evil in the sight of the LORD' (52.2). The reason for Zedekiah's disastrous defeat lies in his own guilt; the reason he persists in that guilt even in the face of impending disaster lies in Yahweh's anger, judicially understood. Divine sovereignty thus gives an ultimate dimension to the agony of the exile, while serving as the supreme warning to future generations.

Joel 2.32 (MT 3.5)

At the beginning of the verse the initiative of the 'whoever' (NASB) receives emphasis; at the end, it is Yahweh who is doing the calling. The 'and' of the last line is a *waw* explicative: the same group is defined differently. Ironically, this difference is a major factor in causing some commentators to misconstrue the tension by insisting that the last line is a later addition. The preposition *b* in *ûḇaśśᵉrîdîm* ('and among the survivors'; lit. 'and in the remnant') does not imply that Yahweh calls only some from among the remnant. Rather, it has the same significance as in the parallel expressions *bᵉhar-siyyôn ûḇîrûšālayim* ('in Mount Zion and in Jerusalem'): the sphere of God's operation is in view. Thus, all who call on the name of Yahweh will be saved—i.e. all whom Yahweh calls.

Haggai 1.12-14

On the one hand, the people respond to the preaching of Haggai and obey Yahweh (1.12); and on the other, Yahweh himself stirs up the spirit of leaders and people alike. The expression 'stir up the spirit of' suggests that the spirit of a man is aroused in such a way that he becomes willing to perform some task (cf. Isa. 42.1; Jer. 50.9; Ezr. 1.1, 5; 1 Chr. 5.26; 2 Chr. 21.16). 'Though the impact of Haggai's sermon was such that a unanimous decision was taken to resume work on the Temple, he took none of the credit. It was the Lord's doing. ... Behind the willing response of both leaders and people was the silent working of the Lord, creating a willing attitude by His Spirit.'[17] Thus, whereas on the one hand the obedience of the people is the condition for Yahweh's blessing, nevertheless the people can scarcely boast of their obedience because it is Yahweh who has stirred up the spirit of the people. This fact, that Yahweh is working among them, serves to encourage the people (cf. 2.4ff.).

Psalm 105.24f.

It is typical of the praises of Israel that Yahweh is seen as the ultimate cause behind everything. In this passage, the psalmist declares that Yahweh[18] not only made Israel stronger than their adversaries (105.24), but that he turned the heart of those very adversaries to hate his people. It is possible to take hāp̄ak ('he turned') intransitively ('Thus their heart turned ...'); but in view of the context, in which Yahweh is a most active subject for an impressive list of verbs, it is more reasonable to accept the active mood of the Masoretic pointing. It is often suggested that God's only part in causing that hatred was his multiplication of Israel;[19] the Egyptians responded with hate born of jealousy and fear. But the language of the psalm makes such a view simplistic (cf. also Exod. 4.21). The psalmist is at pains to stress the unconditioned sovereignty of Yahweh in the entire event. He would certainly be horrified to attach any wickedness to Yahweh; but he insists nevertheless that Yahweh not only stood behind the drama of the plagues and the exodus, but set the stage for that drama. This limitless sovereignty forms part of the psalmist's expansive praise.

CONCLUDING REMARKS

So far, our attention has been focused on a few select passages which embrace a remarkable tension between divine sovereignty and human responsibility. I have also indicated that the same sort of tension can again be found when a single event is dealt with in two or more different places. Many more instances could be enumerated. One example is the destruction of Sihon, brought about by divine hardening so that the king might be destroyed (Deut. 2.30f.), and yet, phenomenologically, brought about by the king's own distrust of Israel (Judg. 11.19f.). Another example is the foundation of the monarchy as discussed in Deuteronomy 17.14-17; 1 Samuel 8.4ff.; 10.24ff.; Hosea 13.9-11.

Since the rise of modern criticism, many scholars have contented themselves with identifying sources, and establishing their theology, while ignoring whatever structure and theology lay in the mind of the compiler of 1 Samuel, for instance. In this particular case, over the years a steady minority of scholars has approached the text of 1 Samuel with the question of the compiler's theology in mind, and some have come to the conclusion that there are not two different accounts of Saul's accession to the throne after all.[20]

In all events, as the Hebrew canon now stands it is clear that at least some of the alleged difficulties may be absorbed into the larger tension between divine sovereignty and human responsibility. The perspective which on the one hand sees Yahweh's absolute sovereignty behind everything, and on the other sees Yahweh standing sufficiently aloof to be able to hold his people responsible and judge them accordingly, might well fail to see any insuperable contradiction in the narratives.

CHAPTER THREE

BROAD MOTIFS IN THE OLD TESTAMENT

Having demonstrated that the tension under study erupts in specific passages, it is now necessary to turn to the Hebrew canon at large and observe how both human responsibility and divine sovereignty are worked into the very fabric of these writings. The result, as we shall see, is a tension of varied forms, a tension very frequently assumed and never far from the surface, even if it is seldom made explicit.

MEN AS RESPONSIBLE

1. Men face a plethora of exhortations and commands

The point is so obvious that it scarcely requires making. From the first prohibition in Eden (Gen. 2.16f.), through commands to individuals like Noah and Abraham—whether commands to build an ark or to walk blamelessly (Gen. 6.13ff.; 17.1-6)—to the prescriptions laid on the covenant people, human responsibility is presupposed. Such prescriptions include the details of tabernacle construction and acceptable cultic worship, as well as the broad 'moral' commandments, specific civil legislation, and sweeping commands to be holy. The requirements of God touch all of life, not merely worship abstracted from life, with the result that his people are to be different from the surrounding nations. (Cf. Exod. 20.3ff.; Lev. 11.44f.; 20.7f.; 22.31-3; Deut. 10.12f.; 12.29-31; 14.1f.; Isa. 56.1; Jonah 1.2; Mic. 6.8; Mal. 3.10; Ps. 119.1-3; etc.)

In addition, men are exhorted to seek the Lord: this theme is particularly reiterated by the prophets (e.g. Isa. 55.6f.; Amos 5.6-9; Zeph. 2.3). The Tabernacle itself was established as a place where men might seek Yahweh (Exod. 33.7). Deuteronomy encourages the people to believe that after they have rebelled and God has turned away from them, they will find him again when they seek for him (Deut. 4.26-32; 30.1-3). God has only good purposes for those who seek him (Ezra 8.22f.). Asa is bluntly told, 'The LORD is with you, while you are with him. If you seek him, he will be found by you, but if you forsake him, he will forsake you' (2 Chr. 15.2). The Psalms frequently spell out the same message (e.g. 105.4; 145.18).

2. Men are said to obey, believe, choose

God may choose Abraham and promise him great blessing; but it is Abraham who believes the promise (Gen. 15.4-6) and obeys God's voice (Gen. 22.16-18). In Exodus the Israelites agree to be obedient (Exod. 19.8; 24.3-7). Frequently they do 'just as God commanded' (e.g. Exod. 16.34; 38-40; Num. 8.20; 9.8, 23; 31.31); indeed, even with a willing heart (Exod. 35.5, 21). The Israelites are told to choose Yahweh (Deut. 30.15-19; Josh. 24.14-25; 1 Kgs. 18.22), and indeed do so (Josh. 24:22); and when instead they serve the gods of pagan neighbours, it is because they have chosen them (Judg. 10.14). They make solemn vows (e.g. Num. 21.2; Judg. 11.30f.). Two ways are set before the people (cf. Lev. 26.1-45; Deut. 28; 30.15-20; Ps. 1), and the way that brings blessing turns on human repentance and obedience. Similarly in human relationships, there is a certain freedom of choice (e.g. Num. 36.6). All such categories presuppose human responsibility.

3. Men sin and rebel

From the first disobedience onward, the pages of the Old Testament are blotched with every conceivable form of transgression. The imagination of men turns constantly toward evil; and this description (Gen. 6.5) could rightly be applied to more than antediluvian people. The resources of language are exhausted as the loathsomeness of particularly vile men or periods is ruthlessly exposed (e.g. Gen. 18.20f; Exod. 32.7-14; Num. 16.3-35; Judg. 19f.; Deut. 1.26ff.; 9.22-4; 2 Kgs. 17.34-41; Isa. 1.2ff.; 30.9ff.; Jer. 2.13ff.; 5.3; 6.16f.; 42.10ff.; Ezek. 8; 22; Hos. 2.7; 4.2, 7, 13). The people 'corrupt themselves' (Exod. 32.7), or do what is right in their own eyes (Judg. 17.6; 21.25). Such language is incongruous if men are not rightly held accountable for what they are and do.

4. Men's sins are judged by God

Men are not held to be responsible in some merely abstract fashion; they are responsible *to someone.* God is the judge of all the earth, of all nations; men are ultimately answerable to him.

Drumming through the Old Testament is the motif of judgment. Yahweh reacts against sin with terrible punishments. Even those parts of the Old Testament which wrestle with the fact that God's judgments are not always immediate and temporal do not diminish this theme, but prepare the way for a heavier accent on the certainty of eschatological judgment. (Cf. Gen. 6-8; 18.25; Exod. 23.7; 32.7-12, 26-35; Lev. 10.1ff.; Num. 11.1ff.; 16.3-35; Deut. 32.19-22; Josh. 7; Judg. 2.11ff.; 3.5ff.; 4.1ff.; 1 Sam. 25.38f.; 2 Sam. 21.1; 2 Kgs. 17.18ff.; 22.15ff.; 23.26ff.; Isa. 14.26f.; 66.4; Jer. 7.13f.; Ezek. 5.8ff.; 25-28; Nahum 3.1ff.; Hag. 1.9-11; Zech. 7.12-14; Ps. 75.6f.; 82.8; 96.10; Eccles. 11.9; 12.14.) Human accountability is all the more deeply stressed when the writers insist God is longsuffering and slow to anger (Exod. 34.6; Num. 14.18; Joel 2.13; Jonah 4.2; Ps. 86.15; 103.8; Neh. 9.17). In short: divine judgment presupposes human responsibility.

5. Men are tested by God

The testing of men is often couched in the anthropomorphic language by which Yahweh declares he wishes to know what is in men's hearts (e.g. Gen. 22.12; Exod. 16.4; Deut. 13.1-4; Judg. 2.20-3.4; 2 Chr. 32.31); but this is not invariably so (e.g. Ps. 11.5; 105.19). From the examples cited in these references it is clear that God's tests can be directed either toward individuals or toward his entire people. Such tests entail no guaranteed result: Abraham passes his test, Hezekiah does not. Some tests spring out of God's judicial discipline of sin previously committed by the people (e.g. Judg. 2.20-3.4). In any case the testing inevitably concerns the obedience and faithfulness of those tested, and presupposes their accountability for such virtues.

6. Men receive divine rewards

This point overlaps the last two. Judgment, after all, may be viewed as negative reward; and the tests of the Old Testament entail positive reward for those who pass them. These positive rewards now concern us. The blessing of Abraham is related to his obedience (Gen. 22.18). The midwives of the captive Israelites are blessed because they feared God (Exod. 1.20f.). The people are assured that if they will obey they will see Yahweh's glory (Lev. 9.6); if they keep the law they will live

(18.3-6). Caleb receives special treatment because he follows Yahweh fully (Num. 11.32; Josh. 14.9, 14). God will thrust out the rest of the Canaanites, but the people must be obedient (Josh. 23.4-9). If the people will return to Yahweh, acknowledging their sin, he will bless them (Jer. 3.12-22; 7.3-7, 23-28). God will stuff the storehouses of the people if they will be faithful in the matter of tithes and offerings (Mal. 3.10f.). Much of the prophetic preaching looks forward to great blessing, contingent upon the obedience of the people (e.g. Isa. 58.10-14; Jer. 7.23; Zech. 6.15). Such promises appear utterly ridiculous if human responsibility is not presupposed.

7. Human responsibility may arise out of God's initiative

Whatever the implications of election in the Old Testament (*infra*), it is clear that although election brought high privilege to Israel, 'it also laid heavy responsibility on her, and was charged with constraint, which she could only disclaim to her hurt.'[1] Here is responsibility arising out of Yahweh's choice. The prophets especially make it clear that the privilege of election by Yahweh brings with it extensive demands on his people. Judge of all the nations Yahweh may be; but Amos insists that Yahweh's 'knowing' of Israel in particular is in fact the basis of special and imminent judgment (Amos 3.2). The responsibility which Israel faces stems not so much from God's naked choice of the nation, as from that allegiance to him which is entailed by election. Once the law is given, allegiance to Yahweh and obedience to the law can scarcely be distinguished. Hence, responsibility to obey all that Yahweh has commanded is based on, and arises out of, the election of Israel. (Cf. Exod. 19.4-6; Deut. 4.5-8; 6.6ff.; 10.15ff.; 11.7-9; Hos. 13.4; Mic. 3.2.)

The Wisdom literature never descends to the level of secular common sense, partly because the demands of Yahweh lie inextricably interwoven with others in which no explicit reference to Yahweh is made, but even more because, in the latter cases, it is presupposed that the fear of Yahweh is fundamental to wisdom (cf. Prov. 9.10; 16.7-12)—this Yahweh who, it is understood from Deuteronomy on, always commands what is for the good of *his people* (Deut. 6.24).[2] Privilege stemming from divine grace enhances responsibility, and never reduces it.

8. The prayers of men are not mere show-pieces

That God has spoken propositionally was a fundamental conviction of the Old Testament writers. But the intercourse between God and man involved man speaking to God as well.[3] Man's voice in addressing God is never the pre-programmed recording of the robot; it is the adoration of worship, the cry of desperation, the relief of gratitude, the petition of the needy. The personal, accountable character of man is nowhere more clearly seen than in his prayers of intercession and petition.

Some such prayers are well-planned, even if intense (e.g. 1 Kgs. 8.46ff.; 2 Chr. 7.12-22). Others are the cries of desperation (e.g. Exod. 32.7-13, 31f.; Josh. 10.11-14). Some are answered positively (e.g. Gen. 25.21; Judg. 6.36-40; 1 Kgs. 3.6-9; 2 Kgs. 20.1-6; Isa. 38); and others are categorically turned down (e.g. Jer. 14.11; 15.1f.; 1 Sam. 15.35-16.1). Some prayers magnify the wretchedness of sin (e.g. Exod. 32; Deut. 9.25ff.), others the greatness of Yahweh and his love for Israel (e.g. Josh. 10.12-14). In any case, the idea that men may prevail in prayer with God again presupposes human responsibility, and a significant measure of human freedom; for such language depicts the interplay of personalities, not the determinism of machines.

9. God utters pleas for repentance

The pre-exilic prophets unite in presenting Yahweh as the one who finds no pleasure in the death of the wicked, who pleads with men to return to him and avoid the otherwise inevitable and horrible consequences of their own rebellion. When he does afflict his people, it is unwillingly. (Cf. Isa. 30.18; 65.2; Lam. 3.31-6; Ezek. 18.30-32; 33.11; Hos. 11.7ff.) Even when all due allowance is made for anthropomorphisms, the necessary conclusion is that men are viewed as responsible creatures whose rebellion Yahweh is enduring with merciful if painful forbearance, and punishing with reluctant wrath.

10. Concluding remarks

Qoheleth reminds us that God made men upright, but they have sought out many 'devices' (Eccl. 7.29). God is customarily in some way removed from man when he sins. This pattern of preserving a distance between God and sin comes to the fore in

God's rejection of sinners, a rejection which, far from asserting God's contingency, underlines rather the certainty of his holy judgment (especially when divine omniscience is in view: e.g. Isa. 29.15f.; Jer. 16.17f.) or the real guilt of the transgressor (e.g. 1 Sam. 15.23b). When instead God is implicated as the cause (in some sense) of a particular sin, there are invariably other factors involved, notably a display of his judicial hardening or of his sovereign hand behind a major event of salvation history.

It is instructive to observe how the various motifs discussed above function in the Old Testament writings. Injunctions to choose Yahweh, and the tests which God administers to men and nations, are not given to evoke metaphysical definitions concerning the nature and limitations of human freedom, but to command committed assent and obedience. When a right choice is made (e.g. Josh. 24.22), it tends to become an incentive for continued faithfulness and the fresh abandonment of encroaching idolatry. Similarly the positive rewards which follow faith and obedience (e.g. Gen. 22.18; Exod. 1.20f.; Num. 11.32; Josh. 23.4-9) become motivation for increased and continuing obedience, not grounds for boasting once they have been attained. At most, conduct pleasing to God may function in some petitions as the ground for vindication and divine approval (as in some psalms—e.g. 34, 69, 79, 109, 137; cf. also Neh. 5.19; 13.14, 22, 31), but even in these cases there is no self-confident boasting. When contingency language is used of God, it does not function as a basis on which conclusions may be drawn concerning his ontological limitations: for example, statements about his longsuffering function to underscore the enormity of sin (Num. 14.18), as a foil for human littleness (Jer. 15.15; Ps. 86.15), and as an attribute to be praised (Exod. 34.6). Similarly, God's pleas for men to repent heighten human wickedness and justify divine wrath (e.g. Jer. 3.22; Ezek. 18.30f.; 33.11; Hos. 14.1), and may even be taken as a measure of his love and hence the evidence that he will act unilaterally on behalf of his people (e.g. Isa. 30.18f.; Hos. 11.7-9).

GOD AS SOVEREIGN

If the Old Testament writers everywhere presuppose human responsibility, they not only presuppose divine sovereignty but insistently underscore it, even when the devastations of observable phenomena appear to fly in the face of such belief.

1. God the Creator, Possessor, and Ruler of all

Not only did God make everything (Gen. 1f.; Isa. 42.5; Ps. 102.25; Neh. 9.6; etc.), he made it all good (Gen. 1.31). When Israel sang Yahweh's praise, the remembrance of the fact that he was Maker of heaven and earth afforded great comfort to the people (Ps. 121.2; 124.8). It is not surprising therefore to learn that God is the possessor of heaven and earth (Gen. 14.19,22 (NASB); Ps. 89.11; 1 Chr. 29.11f.), or to hear Yahweh insist that all is his (Exod. 19.5; Deut. 10.14; Job 41.3). Hand in hand with such a conception goes the omnipotence of Yahweh. If Yahweh made the heaven and earth, he is the 'God of all flesh', and nothing is too hard for him (Jer. 32.17,27; Job 42.2). Since all things are his, no one can give him anything (Job 41.11). All history and nature are at his disposal.

It follows that, if God is sovereign over all the earth, he reigns over all nations (Ps. 47.8f.; 60.6-8; 83.17f.; etc.). This is reasonable enough: all nations belong to him (Ps. 82.8). Indeed, it is when Israel's fortunes plummet to the darkest depths that her prophets most clearly see Yahweh's sovereignty over all foreign powers, and take comfort in this truth. The substance of Dan. 2, 4,7f., 10, 11f. is that the Most High rules the kingdom of men (4.25.). To Yahweh, the nations are a mere drop in the bucket, the fine dust of the balance, less than nothing (Isa. 40.15ff.). The pre-exilic prophets in particular teach that Yahweh 'raises or calls up on the stage of history foreign peoples, Assyrians, Egyptians, Syrians, Philistines, to use them as His instruments ... (and) that the foreign peoples, who menaced Israel, were raised up by Yahweh to carry out His plans for the elect people.'[4] (Cf. Isa. 7.18; 9.10f.; 10.5f., 26; Jer. 2.6f.; 27.4-8; 31.32; Hos. 2.17; 11.1; 13.4; Amos 2.9f.; 3.1; 9.7; Mic. 6.3ff.; etc.) Examples might easily be multiplied. Yahweh appoints Jehu and Hazael to their tasks; raises Rezin and Pekah against Israel; calls up the king of Assyria; sends the

Medes against Babylon, and the Philistines and the Arabians against Judah (1 Kings 19.15-17; 2 Kings 15.37 and Isa. 9.10f.; Isa. 7.17ff. and 10.5; 13.17-19; 2 Chr. 21.16f.). Nor are these foreign powers used only for destruction: Cyrus and the Persians are raised up to restore Israel to the land of her fathers (Isa. 45.1ff.; Ezra 1.1).

Yahweh can well judge all men and nations (Ps. 67.5), for not only is he all-powerful, he is all-knowing. His omniscience is not infrequently associated with the certainty and exhaustive nature of his impending judgment (e.g. Isa. 29.15f.; Jer. 16.16-18; Ezek. 11.2,5; Ps. 139.1ff.; Prov. 5.21; 24.2). When Yahweh has decreed judgment on all nations, who can turn back his hand (Isa. 14.26f.)?

There is no god like the God of Israel (Deut. 32.36-43; 33.26f.; Isa. 40.10ff.). Yahweh has prepared his throne in the heavens, and his kingdom rules over all (Ps. 103.19). All life is dependent on him; should he take away their breath, they would perish (Ps. 104.27-30). The idols of men are impotent; but the God of Israel, whose abode is in the heavens, does whatever he pleases in every sphere of the created universe (Ps. 115.3; 135.5f.). It is not surprising to learn therefore that all of a man's days are ordained by God (Ps. 139.16; Prov. 20.24). Certainly no wisdom or counsel can frustrate him (Prov. 21.30). Yahweh is absolutely sovereign (Isa. 43.13; 44.24-7; Eccles. 3.14; 7.13f.; Dan. 2.19-22; 4.31f., 34). Wind, calamity, prosperity—all are under his control (e.g. Exod. 15.10; Isa. 54.16; Jer. 47.7; Amos 3.5f; Lam. 3.37-9). It is rare to hear that 'it rains' (Amos 4.7 is close): men prefer to say that God sends rain (Ps. 65.10; Job 36.27; 38.26). Job enlarges upon God's detailed control of men and nature (Job 14.5; 28.24-7 38.8-11,33; cf. Isa. 40.12,26; Jer. 5.22; 31.35f.; Jonah 1.17; 4.6ff.; Ps. 104.9f.; 148.3ff.; Prov. 8.27). 'Israel, too, knows of conception and birth, of streams that go to the sea, and of the cycle of nature. But this knowledge does not stifle her "Thou, Lord". In her knowledge, she still looks to the living God, the Unchangeable.'[5] Chance is excluded; and if here and there we read of something that might be considered a chance event, it is not really thought of apart from God's direction (1 Sam. 6.9; 20.26; 1 Kgs. 22.34; Ruth 2.3; 2 Chr. 18.33). Hence the lot is used to discover Yahweh's will, 'and is didactically recognised as under His control' (Prov. 16.33; cf. Josh. 7.16; 14.2; 18.6;

1 Sam. 10.19-21; Jonah 1.7).[6]

With such sweeping sovereignty at his disposal, Yahweh's predictions concerning what will take place in the future, and his control over that future, cannot always be decisively distinguished (cf. Gen. 15.13-16; 25.22f.; 41.16, 25, 32; Josh. 6.26 and 1 Kgs. 16.34; Isa. 46.8-10; 48.5f.). What he decrees must come to pass.

The ways in which the divine activity are presented are very diverse, and cannot be set under a single common denominator. Yahweh may break into history dramatically and send ten plagues (Exod. 5ff), flash fire from heaven (1 Kgs. 18.38). or force Sennacherib and his hordes into premature retreat (Isa. 37); but 'it is striking to observe how often the purpose of God is reached without radical intervention.'[7] He uses Saul and his army to fulfil his vow against the Amalekites (1 Sam. 15.2-6); or, more subtly, he so rules in the conflict between the Shechemites and Abimelech, without their knowledge, that both parties are destroyed. This is Yahweh's fitting retribution for the sin of Abimelech towards his brothers and for the shameful assistance of the Shechemites.

The rule of Yahweh over history entails a teleological perspective, for such an almighty and all-knowing Person cannot be supposed to govern unconsciously or capriciously. Lindblom lays heavy stress on this point in his discussion of the pre-exilic prophets:

> What distinguishes the prophetic view of history from that of other oriental peoples is not the thought that Yahweh works in historical events, but rather that the prophets regarded the history of Israel as a *coherent* history directed by *moral principles* and in accordance with a *fixed plan.* At the beginning of the history stood the fact of election ... The events which followed were the consequences of this historical fact; and the final goal of this historical sequence was the full realisation of the idea of election. Other ancient peoples had nothing corresponding to this view of history.[8]

As Proverbs puts it, 'The Lord has made everything for its (or his) purpose, even the wicked for the day of trouble' (Prov. 16.4). Whether *yôm rā'āh* ('day of trouble' or 'day of evil') refers to what the wicked suffer as retribution, or to the evil they perform (cf. Isa. 54.16), the 'general meaning is that there are ultimately no loose ends in God's world.'[9] 'He determined for which purpose everything that exists was made. There is nothing aimless in the world. ...'[10]

It is difficult to conceive how Yahweh could thus control even the details of history unless he controls the minds and emotions of men. And in fact, the Old Testament writers do not hesitate to describe events in precisely those terms. Yahweh controls whole peoples by sending terror among them (e.g. Gen. 35.5; Exod. 23.27; Deut. 2.25; 1 Sam. 11.6f.). Alternatively, he gives his people favour in the eyes of the Egyptians (Exod. 12.36; cf. Dan. 1.9). Again, he destroys an invading army by setting the soldiers' weapons against each other (Judg. 7.22). If a few men attach themselves to Saul, it is because God has touched their hearts (1 Sam. 10.26). Human thoughts and decisions are often attributed directly to God's determining (e.g. 2 Sam. 24.1; Isa. 19.13f.; 37.7; Prov. 21.1; Ezra 1.1; 7.6, 27f.; Neh. 2.11f.). In other words, we may consider:

2. God as the ultimate personal cause

The people of the Old Testament constantly discern the hand of God behind the merely phenomenological perception of events. 'The Bible does not exercise itself to deny chains of causation, but equally it is not accustomed to clog up its reasoning by giving them undue prominence. It leaps back directly to the divine Agent from whom come all things and by whose will they happen.'[11] Human procreation, for instance, is the Lord's doing (e.g. Gen. 4.1, 25; 18.13f.; 25.21; 30.1f.; Deut. 10.22; Ruth 4.13). When Joseph's brothers are stunned by the discovery of the returned money in their sacks, they understand this to be God's doing (Gen. 42.28). It was Yahweh who took off the wheels of the Egyptian chariots (Exod. 14.25); and to him is attributed the ultimate cause of Shimei's curse (2 Sam. 16.10f.) and Naomi's sorrow (Ruth 1.20). Even the book of Esther, for all its failure to mention God explicitly, is of the same stamp. Whatever other purposes were in the writer's mind (such as the presentation of the historical background to the institution of a feast not prescribed in Torah), 'the literary skill of the author leaves the reader in little doubt that he is observing the operation of divine providence as the narrative proceeds, and that the indestructible nature of the Covenant People will ultimately be made evident'.[12]

It is difficult to find an adequate word or phrase to express this 'ultimacy' in God. The crucial point is that his activity is so sovereign and detailed that nothing can take place in the world of men without at least his permission; and conversely, if he sets himself against some course, then that course cannot develop. Unless Yahweh builds the house and keeps the city, the house will not be built and the watchmen may just as well go to sleep (Ps. 127.1). If Yahweh fights with them, whole armies need not fear (Deut. 3.22); but if Yahweh refuses to go with them they lose (Josh. 7.11f.).

A great deal of biblical phraseology presupposes this ultimacy in Yahweh. Yahweh insists, '*I* gave you a land on which you had not laboured' (Josh. 24.13); and to David, he says, '*I* took you from the pasture ... that you should be over my people' (2 Sam. 7.8). When wars cease, it is Yahweh who has given his people rest (2 Sam. 7.1; cf. Ps. 147.12ff.); and if Ezra and his party arrive in Jerusalem with speed and safety, it is because the good hand of Yahweh is upon them (Ezra 7.9; cf. Neh. 2.8; Ps. 121.2). Yahweh gives the power to get wealth (Deut. 8.18); indeed, the varieties of agricultural possibilities and the farmer's knowledge of them are alike from him (Isa. 28.23ff.). Especially in judgment is the ultimacy of Yahweh made plain (Isa. 10.21-3; Jer. 16.16; 20.5; 21.3-7; Ezek. 7.9; 11.7ff.; Mic. 2.3; Nahum 2.13; Zeph. 1.2ff.; etc.). But the ultimacy of Yahweh is nowhere more clearly seen than in the nature psalms (19, 33, 89, 104, 148). In one sense, therefore, miracles do not attest divine intervention into the sphere of normally-operating laws. A miracle means only that God at a given moment wills something to occur in a manner differing from that by which he normally wills it to occur. Old Testament believers do not so much see miracles in terms of 'breakthrough' as in terms of a new and surprising mode of divine activity (e.g. Exod. 34.10; Num. 16.30; Isa. 48.6ff.).

So thorough is the ascription of reality to God, that Moses in Deuteronomy 29.4 does not hesitate to describe Israel's slowness in terms of what Yahweh has not given them. The writer does not mean to suggest that Yahweh's gifts are niggardly, much less to ascribe sin to him; yet the Old Testament writers do not shy away from making Yahweh himself in some mysterious way (the mysteriousness of which safeguards him from being himself charged with evil) the 'ultimate' cause of many evils.

Examples are so numerous that only a few instances may be cited. Micaiah's description of the heavenly courts and the selection of a lying spirit whose success is guaranteed (1 Kgs. 22.19-22; 2 Chr. 18.18-22), the inciting of David to evil purpose (2 Sam. 24.1), the selling of Joseph into slavery (Gen. 50.20), the sending forth of evil spirits to their appointed tasks (e.g. Judg. 9.23ff.; 1 Sam. 16.14; 18.10), the prologue of Job, not to mention the specific remarks of the prophets (e.g. 'Does evil (*rā'āh*) befall a city, unless the LORD has done it?' Amos 3.6; cf. Isa. 14.24-7; 45.7), all clamour for attention. Although most of these cases are related to the judgment of God (cf. also Jer. 6.21; Ezek. 3.20), this cannot be said of the Joseph narrative. There are in any case too many instances in which it is inadequate to think of divine sovereignty as an admirable capacity for snatching an eleventh hour victory out of the jaws of defeat. 'A necessary thought is not only that God redeems a situation but that the situation is itself precipitated by his d(etermination). Not only the remedy, but the situation to be remedied, is run back to the d. of his will.'[13] This sort of world-view, where it occurs, does not suggest henotheism, but a very pure and consistent form of monotheism.

At the same time, of course, God is also said to control the minds of his people for good. Sometimes he is petitioned to do so. Such expressions are particularly common in the prophets who look forward to the new covenant (cf. Jer. 31.31-4; 32.40; Ezek. 11.19f.; 36.22ff.; Zeph. 3.9-13; etc.), but are certainly not restricted to such a framework (e.g. 1 Chr. 29.17-19).

Mention of the new covenant invites comment on Old Testament eschatology. We have already noted that history is often seen teleologically in the Old Testament. Inherent in this perspective, both among pre- and post-exilic prophets, is an expectation of Yahweh's intervention in so climactic a fashion that a new order will be introduced (e.g. Jer. 31; Hos. 2; and more difficult passages like Isa. 2; 7.19ff.; 11). This hope does not mean that God is not acting redemptively in the present, but that the greatest display of his redemptive activity (including judgment) must await the future. Beyond this point, the relationship between the exercise of divine sovereignty *now* and *then* is not probed; and the silence of the Old Testament on these points gives rise to considerable speculation later, as we shall see.

Yahweh is holy, sovereign, full of special regard for his elect, and personally ruling in the affairs of men. This view of God makes the perplexity of his people understandable when, from the human perspective, it appears that Yahweh has dealt harshly (Ruth 1.20f.), unfairly (Job 3ff.), or without due consideration of the wickedness of other men (Habbakuk; Ps. 73). It prompts a cry like that in Isaiah 63.17: 'O LORD, why dost thou make us err from thy ways, and harden our heart, so that we fear thee not? Return for the sake of thy servants, for the tribes of thy heritage.' (Cf. also Isa. 64.7f.).

3. God and election

Some attention must be devoted to the peculiar manifestation of divine providence witnessed in election. The Old Testament Israelite faith was established on the belief that Israel was Yahweh's chosen people, based on two complementary acts: the choosing of Abraham (Gen. 12.1ff.; 17.1ff.; 18.17-19), and the exodus together with the gift of the promised land as their national home (Exod. 3.6-10; Deut. 6.21-3; Ezek. 20.5; Ps. 105; cf. Isa. 43.1).[14] As Yahweh chose the people, he likewise chose the land as a place of special concern to him (Deut. 11.12), his own land (Lev. 25.23); and in particular he chose Mt. Zion, Jerusalem, as his peculiar dwelling-place (Zech. 2.11f.; 3.2; Ps. 78.68ff.).

Though Abraham is chosen, not all of his offspring enjoy the same privilege: Isaac is chosen, not Ishmael (Gen. 17.18-21); and Jacob is preferred, before his birth, to Esau (Gen. 25.23; 28.14; Mal. 1.2; Isa. 41.8ff.; Ps. 135.3f.). Even within Israel, it is God who chooses the outstanding leaders: e.g. Moses (Exod. 3; Num. 16.5, 7, 28); Aaron as priest (Num. 16.40; 17.18ff.); the Levites (Deut. 18.5; 2 Chr. 21.11ff.); the skilled workers Bezalel and Oholiab (Exod. 31.2, 6; 35.31-4); Joshua (Num. 27.16-21); the men who are to apportion the land (Num. 34.16ff.); David (1 Sam. 13.13f.; 2 Sam. 6.21; Ps. 78.68, 70; 89.19f.; 25; 1 Chr. 28.4-10); the prophets—e.g. Jeremiah, 'known'[15] by God before conception (Jer. 1.5).

The election of Israel means not only that Israel must be different, peculiarly holy, reserved for Yahweh, as compared with all other peoples (Exod. 11.7; 19.4-6; Lev. 20.23-6; Deut. 10.14f.; 14.2; Isa. 43.21; Ps. 33.12; 135.4; etc.), but more: Yahweh uses other nations to bring about his good purposes for

Israel, sets their boundaries by the number of his own people, sacrificing other men for her, and punishing them the more severely because their cruelty has been directed toward her (e.g. Deut. 32.8f.; Isa. 43.4; Jer. 51.5-10; Zech. 1.14-17). Even when Yahweh takes his servant Cyrus by the hand (as opposed to whistling him up, as he did with the Assyrians, Isa. 5.26), his purposes in so doing centre on his people Israel (Isa. 45.1-5).

There is thus a centrality about Israel that is in one sense exclusivistic. This is relieved by a universalistic note (e.g. Isa. 19.23; 66.23; Ps. 86.9; 96.10), directly related to election itself: all the nations will be blessed because of God's choice of Abraham.[16] 'The election of Abraham ... was meant as a particularistic means towards a universalistic end.'[17]

The election of Israel does not lapse with the apostasy of the nation, nor with the resulting exile, for the concept of the 'remnant' people of God is clearly well-established. Especially noteworthy are the passages in which the concept is a fixed theological term in prophetic eschatology (e.g. Mic. 4.7 uses $\check{s}^{e}$'*erît* ('remnant') absolutely; cf. 2.12; 5.7; Isa. 8.16-18).

It is incorrect to deduce from the covenant-breaking of the people, that election itself is contingent upon the people. Since Mendenhall wrote his crucial transitional essys on the subject of covenant, some twenty years ago, most Old Testament scholars have understood that the covenant at Sinai, patterned after contemporary suzerainty treaties, pictures Yahweh imposing this covenant upon his willing but responsible vassals.[18] Breach of covenant, envisaged as possible on the side of the vassal only, necessarily brings down the wrath of the sovereign. Similarly the prophets insist that election and covenant do not necessarily entail protection; rather, where there is rebellion, they necessarily entail punishment. Because this covenant was established with Yahweh's elected people, election and covenant overlap: but they are not to be strictly identified, either in nature or extent, for the remnant is seen as the real continuance of Israel (Isa. 41.8ff.; 43.4ff.; Jer. 51.5; etc.), that which constitutes the genuine elect of God (Isa. 65.8-10; Amos 9.8-15). The 'elect' (the returning remnant) thus become a smaller group than all of the 'covenant people' taken together; and it is only the former who enjoy the new covenant (Jer. 31.33; 32.37-40; 50.5; cf. Isa. 55.3). Only this smaller group of faithful, righteous people are the elected ones (Isa. 1.21-6; 4.20; 10.20ff.).[19]

This remnant group is grounded not in its own piety but in God's action. It is Yahweh who forges a new covenant; and it is also he who will give to the heirs of that covenant a heart to fear him (Jer. 32.40). He it is who will give men fleshy hearts, pour our his Spirit, gathering his own to himself (Jer. 31.31-4; Ezek. 11.16-21; 36.22-32; etc.). He may sift Israel and remove the sinners of his people; but he will restore the remnant (Amos 9.8-15). The constant emphasis is on what Yahweh will do. The restoration is nothing less than God-given life to dead bones (Ezek. 37). The covenant is indeed broken; but Yahweh is acting not so much for the sake either of the people or the remnant, as for the sake of his own name: it is because *he* does not change that the sons of Jacob are not consumed (Mal. 3.6; cf. Ezek. 20.9f., 14; 36.22-32). This suggests that God's elective purposes are sure because divine.

There is thus a shift in the significance of election, an individualising which only in its summation answers to the fulfilment of God's promises for Israel. 'The elective principle, abolished as to nationality, continues in force as to individuals.'[20]

Thus, the tension found, for example, in the pre-exilic prophets, between Yahweh's love and Yahweh's wrath for his people, finds its genesis in the matrix of concepts surrounding election and covenant.[21] The reader never fails to perceive that Israel alone was responsible for her apostasy and unfaithfulness; but never does he receive the impression that God is frustrated and his purposes thwarted, even when God manifests his wrath and pleads for repentance. Two distinctions have thus been introduced: between the present and the future people of God (the motif of covenantal renewal), and between the false and the true people of God (the motif of the remnant). Yet despite these distinctions, God's elective purposes are preserved intact. Indeed, one might almost conclude that God's elective purposes contribute not a little to the formulation of these distinctions.

When Old Testament writers trace out any particular reason for the divine election, they ultimately wind up retreating to the free, unconditioned, matchless love of God. W. Eichrodt rightly remarks, concerning election in the Old Testament: 'For there can be no escaping the fact that in the Old Testament *divine love is absolutely free and unconditioned in its choices*; it is directed to one man out of thousands and lays hold on him with jealous exclusiveness despite all his deficiencies.'[22] Abraham is the archetypal example. So strong is the election motif that when Abraham sins against Abimelech, it is nevertheless Abimelech who must ask for prayer from the chosen Abraham (Gen. 20). Deuteronomy lays special emphasis on the fact that Yahweh did not choose Israel as a people because she was intrinsically superior to other peoples (Deut. 7.6-11), nor because she was righteous (Deut. 9.4-6), but rather in defiance of her rebellion, and out of nothing other than his own free, sovereign, electing love (Deut. 4.32-40; 7.6-11; 10.14f.; 23.5; cf. Ezek. 16.6).[23] Precisely the same phenomenon is evident when we consider the remnant. The remnant has its origin 'not in the quality of those saved, but in the saving action of God' (Gen. 7.23b; 45.7; 1 Kgs. 19.18; Amos 5.15).[24] This is most clearly seen in passages in which there is reference to the sins of the remnant (cf. Isa. 4.4; Jer. 50.20; Ezek. 9.8; 11.13; Mic. 7.18; Zeph. 3.12f.; Zech. 13.8f). The remnant escapes judgment only through God's grace.

The inverse side of election is reprobation. In the Old Testament this commonly takes the form of some sort of hardening.[25] The best known case is that of Pharaoh. Eight times God is said to harden Pharaoh's heart (Exod. 7.3; 9.12; 10.1f.; 10.20; 10.27; 11.9f.; 14.14f., 17) but we also read that his heart was hardened (Exod. 7.13f.; 8.15), and that he hardened his own heart (Exod. 8.32; 9.34). It is, of course, arbitrary to interpret the former in terms of the latter (or vice versa), especially because some of the texts inject a teleological element into the divine hardening: Yahweh hardens Pharaoh in order to destroy him, while displaying his own might (Exod. 7.3; 10.1f.; 14.14f.,17).

But Pharaoh is certainly not the only instance. Yahweh not infrequently hardens the hearts of men in order to set them up for destruction (e.g. Deut. 2.30f.; 1 Sam. 2.24f.; Ezek. 38.10,16f., 21; Hos. 5.6; 2 Chr. 25.20). Indeed, Yahweh gives the *command* to make the hearts of the people insensitive, their ears dull and their eyes dim (Isa. 6.9f.). But the Old Testament writers in such cases seem to presuppose that this is nothing other than due judgment; while elsewhere *self*-hardening is pictured as reprehensible action for which the person is morally accountable (Zech. 7.11; Prov. 28.14). Impersonal determinism might well harden arbitrarily; but behind the hardening of the Old

Testament is the God who cries, 'Harden not your hearts' (Ps. 95.8).

The significance of election is sometimes obscured by false deductions drawn from the fact that God has servants outside the covenant people (e.g. Cyrus, Ezra 1.1; Isa. 44.24-8; Nebuchadnezzar, Jer. 25.7-9, 13f.; 27.4-8; Nebuchadnezzar and his army paid by being given Egypt, Ezek. 29.19-20; etc.). Rowley calls this phenomenon 'election without covenant'.[26] But the phrase is improper, not only because, as we have seen, such outside servants function solely for the development of the divine purposes for the Israelites, but also because the vocabulary of election is invariably reserved for the covenant people and for 'covenant functionaries drawn from Israel's own ranks.'[27] What is highlighted by the existence of such non-Israelite servants is the extent of divine sovereignty. It is a particularisation of passages which affirm Yahweh's sovereignty over the nations.

4. God unacknowledged

One of the most peculiar features connected with divine sovereignty in the Old Testament is the manner in which individuals and peoples are brought by Yahweh to perform some deed, and then held accountable for failing to acknowledge God's hand in that deed. The message to Pharaoh is that, because Yahweh made him great but Pharaoh thought he had done it himself, Yahweh will bring him low (Ezek. 31.7-10; cf. Ezek. 29). Nebuchadnezzar learned that the failure to acknowledge the sovereignty of God, and the correlative pride, are punishable offences before Yahweh (Dan. 4), while Belshazzar was destroyed for failing to learn the same lesson (Dan. 5.21-3). If Yahweh is sovereign, human self-sufficiency fails to acknowledge God as it ought. Therefore men must learn that Yahweh lives only with the contrite in heart (Isa. 66.1f.).

The reprehensibility of 'God unacknowledged' is thrown into relief when the praises of Israel are remembered. Nowhere is the 'ultimacy' of God's action (in election as in other things) more consistently displayed than in Israel's praises. To fail to acknowledge Yahweh's ultimacy—to fail to praise—is not real independence from divine dominion, but overt rebellion, a misguided declaration of self-dependence, for which men are responsible. Thus the absoluteness of divine sovereignty and the reality of human responsibility meet in the human obligation to acknowledge divine sovereignty with grateful humility.

5. Concluding remarks

The idea that God really is the sovereign disposer of all is consistently woven into the fabric of the Old Testament, even if there is relatively infrequent explicit reflection on the sovereignty-responsibility tension. Taken as a whole, the all-embracing activity of the sovereign God in the Old Testament must be distinguished from deism, which cuts the world off from him; from cosmic dualism, which divides the control of the world between God and other(s); from determinism, which posits such a direct and rigid control, or such an impersonal one, that human responsibility is destroyed; from indeterminism and chance, which deny either the existence or the rationality of a sovereign God; and from pantheism, which virtually identifies God with the world.[28]

Yet the sovereignty of God in the Old Testament is not permitted to devour human responsibility. Some limitations, or at least qualifications, are imposed by alternative descriptions of God within the same literature. Perhaps the most telling of these are the passages which speak of God 'repenting'. Of the many, perhaps Genesis 6.6; 1 Samuel 15.10, 35 (but see 15.29!); Amos 7.3,6 stand out. It has been shown that such language, applied so regularly to Deity, stands without close parallel in the literature of the ancient near east.[29] How much of this is anthropomorphic language is difficult to decide (and will be discussed in Part Four). What is clear is that, just as the Old Testament writers can speak of the God of love and the God of wrath, so they can speak of the God of sovereign purpose and power, and the God of 'repenting'. Perhaps, then, in the Amos passages referred to (Amos 7.3, 6), we are not to think of the prayers of Amos as if they coerced God into changing his mind. Rather, as J. A. Motyer puts it:

> The wrath of God is perpetual: the automatic reaction of a holy nature faced with rebellion and unholiness. But equally eternal is His determination to take, save and keep a people for Himself ... It is because we cannot unify these two revealed strands of the divine nature that the Lord graciously accommodates the truth to our powers of expression and speaks of Himself as 'repenting'.[30]

In any case, whether this sort of attempt at synthesis is acceptable or not, it is important to remember that there is more to the God of the Old Testament than mere sovereignty, however grand the contemplation of his sovereignty may be.

Moreover, when the Old Testament writers say that God does something, they do not necessarily mean that the human beings involved are merely acted upon like lifeless tools. God gives children; but couples copulate. Yahweh clears the land of the Canaanites (Deut. 7.22-4), but the people must fight. The problems of 'secondary causality' formulations are still to be probed; but it is essential to recognise that, however successful such formulations may be, real responsibility is ascribed to Old Testament man for what he is and does. This fact must compel interpreters to grapple with the relationship between God and man in other than rigid machine-like categories.

Although it is true that one can find examples of Yahweh behind just about every kind of action, important distinctions must be observed. God does not stand behind evil action in precisely the same way that he stands behind good action. The Old Testament writers understand God to be holy, just, righteous, good, longsuffering (Gen. 18.25; Lev. 11.44; Isa. 6.3; 61.8; Zeph. 3.5; Ps. 5.4; 11.5; 145.17; Job 34.10-15; etc.). Everything God made was 'very good' (Gen. 1.31). A certain distance is preserved between God and his people when they sin. Atoning sacrifice is required; and he may so far disassociate himself from them as to refuse to call them his people (e.g. Exod. 32.7-14). Frequently the divine ultimacy in some human sin is seen to be part of divine retribution, or at least a necessary step toward it (e.g. Jer. 52.3). It can also form part of a long-term divine plan connected with salvation history— whether punishing the Philistines (Judg. 14.40) or selecting a site for the Temple (2 Sam. 24.1ff.). But at other times the Old Testament writers are careful to distinguish between what God does and what men do (e.g. Ezek. 11.16,21; Ps. 78; Eccles. 7.29). P. Volz, *Das Dämonische in Jahwe*,[31] fails to come to grips with such considerations when he likens Yahweh's action to the malicious hatred and envy which mar not a few ancient near eastern deities. There is always, in the Old Testament, an implicit or explicit recognition of God's higher justice (e.g. Jer. 12.1). In short, although we may lack the categories needed for full exposition of the problem, *nevertheless we must insist that divine ultimacy stands behind good and evil asymmetrically.*

The theme of God's sovereignty is put to various uses in the Old Testament; i.e. it functions in various ways. These provide further qualifications for the manner in which the theme should be handled by theologians. For example, election is not only to privilege, but to the observance of far-reaching ethical and covenantal obligations (Exod. 11.7; 19.4-6; Lev. 20.23-6; Deut. 10.14f., 26-40; 14.2; Ps. 33.12; 105 culminating in 105.43; etc.), the ignoring of which entails strict judgment (Lev. 26.13ff.; Deut. 28.15ff.; Amos 3.2) not preferential treatment (Jer. 5.12; Mic. 3.11f.). In other words, election functions as motivation for keeping God's covenant and law (Deut. 14.1f.; Ezek. 20.5-7; cf. Lev. 18.2-5). Especially do the pre-exilic prophets use the election traditions to remind Israelites of the grace in which they stand and of the heinousness of disloyalty. Furthermore, because of election, not only can history be interpreted around the centrality of God's purposes for his people, but the leaders of the people can successfully intercede for them by referring to the immutability of Yahweh's elective decisions and the disparagement which would befall his Name should he rescind those purposes. Thus, even after sin and retribution, there can be a pulsating hope among the people, a hope engendered by a particular use of the election traditions (e.g. Isa. 41.8-14; 44.1f.; Hag. 2.23; Ps. 106.4f.).

More broadly, divine sovereignty is never used as a peg either for pride or for resignation, but as a call to humility, obedience, patience and trust (2 Sam. 7.8ff.; Isa. 66.1f.; Hag. 1.14; Ps. 37; Prov. 16.4; cf. Job 38ff.; etc.).[32] This is seen even in that most predestinarian of models, the potter and the clay. Isaiah 45.9 uses the model to castigate the rebellion of the clay, the people. Jeremiah 18.2ff. uses it, not to reduce the people to puppet status, but to drive home the principle that Yahweh is free to take whatever sovereign steps he chooses to ensure that the pot turns out all right in the end: the lesson to be learned is the urgency of immediate repentance, before Yahweh's drastic measures get under way. Even in Isaiah 64.8 the model is really used as no more than a plea for mercy from Yahweh on the ground of human inability apart from God's sovereign power (cf. Jer. 10.23). Many passages which deal with Yahweh's

greatness or goodness or transcendence are quite openly designed to instil awe, reverence, and submission (Exod. 33.18-20;
Deut. 10.10-22; Ps. 8.3f.; 62; 105; etc.). Indeed, the greatness
and power of God function as sufficient motive for seeking him
(Amos 5.6-9), or for repentance and fear before him
(Joel 2.11-14; Amos 4.9-12; Eccles. 3.14). And divine omniscience, far from being used in protracted discussions about the
natures of time, eternity, foreknowledge, and decree, commonly
functions as the guarantor of the certainty and justice of God's
impending judgment (e.g. Isa. 29.15f.; Jer. 16.16-18;
Ezek. 11.2,5; Ps. 139.1ff.; Prov. 5.21; 24.2; 2 Chr. 16.9).

That brings up the final point which emerges from this
survey of the Old Testament approaches to the sovereignty-
responsibility tension. The Old Testament writers are not
interested in struggling with this tension as a metaphysical
problem.[33] In so far as they do wrestle with it (as in Job,
Ecclesiastes, Habakkuk, and many shorter passages), their
interest is focused on a practical area, viz. how to reconcile
God's goodness and power and elective purposes with the
vicissitudes they actually experience. Their concern, in short, is
the practical side of the problem of theodicy. And the ultimate
answers they are granted assure them that God is greater than
their questions.

PART TWO

THE SOVEREIGNTY-
RESPONSIBILITY TENSION
IN INTERTESTAMENTAL
JEWISH LITERATURE

CHAPTER FOUR

THE SEPTUAGINT
TRANSLATION

It is very difficult to discern any unambiguous shift in the understanding of the sovereignty-responsibility tension when one moves from the Hebrew Bible to its translation in the LXX. This is clear from at least two considerations.

THE TRANSLATION OF THE TWELVE OLD TESTAMENT
PASSAGES PREVIOUSLY EXAMINED

Most of the twelve evince no significant change in meaning. Two betray a marked looseness of translation, but not such as affects the tension (Isa. 10.5ff.; Joel 2.32). One (Judg. 14.4a) presents us with a minor textual variation: A has *antapodoma* and B the harsher *ekdikēsis;* but again, the sovereignty-responsibility tension is unaffected. The two Jeremiah passages are most disturbed. Jeremiah 52.3 is not found in the LXX. Jeremiah 29.10-14 (LXX 36.10-14) is so truncated in translation that it is no longer clear that the prophet is talking about the restoration throughout the five verses, and as a result there is a blurring of the tension between Yahweh's unconditional promise to restore the people and the required prayer of the people to that end. But the problems related to difference between MT and LXX, especially in Jeremiah, are so intricate that any observation purporting to uncover a relevant theological bias in the translator would be highly presumptuous.

The only passage requiring more substantial comment is Genesis 50.19f. Genesis 50.20 is pretty much the same in LXX and MT, the verb *bouleuesthai* translating *ḥšb.* But there is a clear difference between MT and LXX in 50.19. In MT, Joseph tells the brothers not to fear, and then asks the question ('for am I in the place of God?'). The LXX, however, provides a statement: *tou gar theou eimi ego* ('for I am God's'). It would be wrong to suggest that the translator is straining to avoid any suggestion of a man standing in God's place, for in 30.2, in a

virtually identical construction, he translates accurately, *Mē anti theou egō eimi* ... ('Am I in the place of God. ...?').
Whence, then, this strange 'translation' in 50.19?

Assuming an MT-type text behind the LXX at this point, the context suggests that the translator is attempting to smooth the flow. In the LXX, the brothers say they are Joseph's servants (50.18), and Joseph replies with one unified thought in 50.19f.; because he belongs to God[1] (50.19) and God's intentions in the event were good (50.20), therefore Joseph will follow God's example, and the brothers need not fear. In the MT, however, Joseph's attempt to dissolve his brothers' fears comes in two separate points: (1) Joseph will not thrust himself into God's role as judge (50.19); and (2) in any case he will follow the divine pattern of behaviour, remembering that God's intentions in the evil event were for good (50.20). The latter point, however, is left somewhat hanging in MT: it is really only an implication of 50.20. The LXX sacrifices the first point (MT 50.19) to spell out the second (MT 50.20), by linking its 'translation' of 50.19 with 50.20. But again it would be precarious to claim there is a shift in theological perspective.

RELEVANT THEOLOGICAL TENDENCIES IN THE LXX

This area of Septuagintal studies is still in its infancy; very little can be concluded with any marked degree of probability. However, studies which purport to prove that the LXX translators sought to avoid anthropomorphism and anthropopathy impinge on this inquiry, because within the sovereignty-responsibility tension the personal categories of God are bound up with such phenomena. A. W. Argyle suggests the LXX shies away from God's 'repenting'.[2] D. H. Gard examines a host of theological tendencies in the book of Job, including an avoidance of human arrogance before God, an array of anti-anthropomorphisms, and a shunning or transformation of any description of God which appears to cast some aspersion on his character.[3] C. T. Fritsch has carried out a similar study in the Pentateuch.[4]

Yet these results are received with notable reserve by most scholars. Manson, Katz, Jellicoe and Wittstruck agree, with various degrees of insistence, that Fritsch's conclusions must be received with some caution.[5] Orlinsky goes farther, not only calling in question Fritsch's thesis, which relates only to the Pentateuch, but refusing likewise to concede that anti-anthropomorphisms are a mark of the LXX translators of Job, his most recent area of study.[6] His conclusions may be something of an over-reaction. Some anti-anthropomorphisms must be admitted. It is difficult to see what else other than a growing aversion to anthropomorphism could call forth the LXX rendering of Exodus 24.10, for example: the LXX offers 'and they saw the place where the God of Israel had stood' for MT's 'and they saw the God of Israel'. Orlinsky's principal objection is that the 'anti-anthropomorphists' (his term) too frequently indulge in a 'heads I win, tails you lose' argument: if the LXX translator preserves an anthropomorphism it is to be interpreted symbolically, and if not, its displacement is taken as evidence of anti-anthropomorphism. That criticism is just; but in itself it surely says no more than that the analyses of the 'anti-anthropomorphists' are too black-and-white. If we speak more cautiously of 'tendencies' and 'trends', the evidence for the rise of anti-anthropomorphisms remains weakened, but not eliminated.

A few other trends are noteworthy. Both Gard and Gerleman[7] agree that the LXX of Job tries to avoid or soften the idea that God is the agent of human destruction; and this removal of God from some spheres of activity in his universe tends to *diminish* his sovereignty. In another connection, D. W. Gooding has drawn attention to the tendency of 3 Reigns to whitewash David.[8] This is the beginning of a tendency to make heroes out of certain biblical characters; but it has the effect of minimising their sin, and, in principle, their accountability. God's 'frustration' (for that is how the Hebrew noun should be translated) is frustrated by the LXX in Numbers 14.34; but the LXX is only one of many translations and paraphrases which adopt similar manoeuvres.[9] Again, there is a demonstrable predilection for *eklegesthai* and cognates. Note, for example, the gratuitous addition of the term in Haggai 2.22A. In Psalm 88.4 (LXX), the reference to the people is imported. In some cases synagogue exegesis has apparently established that a particular reference is to the chosen people (e.g. Isa. 5.2 (*v.1.*); Ezek. 19.12,14; Zech. 11.16; S. of S. 6.9f. Mistakes likewise confirm the growing liking for the term: Num. 11.28; 2 Reigns 21.6; Amos 5.11; Job 37.11; Prov. 12.24). Such diversity in the kinds of passages affected, however, suggests that it would be pressing the evidence much too far were we to infer that a self-conscious theological bent in favour of divine election lay behind every such example.

Perhaps the increasing inclination to emphasise the election of Israel was a measure of the extent to which election-consciousness was generating pride. If so it was part of the broader movement which, as we shall see, *tended* to view human merit and worth as the rationale for the divine choice, instead of understanding that choice to be in defiance of human demerit and unworthiness. Indeed, whenever election becomes the basis of religious conceit, the functions it exercises in the Old Testament are being left far behind. But such a development cannot be demonstrated conclusively in the LXX, largely because the translators were hampered by the very nature of their work: theirs was to translate (however loosely), not to create.

CHAPTER FIVE

NON-APOCALYPTIC APOCRYPHA AND PSEUDEPIGRAPHA

In dividing up the intertestamental literature in the way I have, I would not want to give the impression that fixed chasms exist between each type. That is manifestly not the case. Nevertheless, for convenience of treatment some distinctions must be introduced, even if they entail simplifications.

As far as the division between apocalyptic and non-apocalyptic literature is concerned, this discussion adopts the classification of D. S. Russell, and accepts the preliminary definition of 'apocalyptic' offered by K. Koch.[1] Some of the books on Russell's list are only 'predominantly' apocalyptic, but these are treated in the next chapter along with those whose apocalyptic nature is undisputed. This seems to be methodologically superior to an arbitrary narrowing of the apocalyptic category, stemming from a debatable thesis. The outstanding example is the approach of Schmithals, who not only compares apocalyptic with gnosis but who tends to eliminate what does not fit his overlap of these two categories.[2]

These chapters cannot hope to be exhaustive. I have purposely avoided mentioning Pseudo-Philo. 1 Esdras is cited rarely because most of the relevant passages are free translations of Ezra and 1 Chronicles, and because the unambiguous theological tendencies of the book are in any case irrelevant to this study. Fragments of a Zadokite work will be considered with the Qumran literature.

NON-APOCALYPTIC LITERATURE

Most of the Old Testament features relating to divine sovereignty continue in the non-apocalyptic intertestamental literature. God is the creator of all (Rest of Esther 13.10;

2 Macc. 1.27; Pr. of Man. 1.1-3; Bel & Dr. 5; Ep. Arist. §§15f.,201; 4 Macc. 5.25), and rules over everything (e.g. Ecclus. 10.4f.; 17.17; Bel & Dr. 5; Ep. Arist. §§16f.,201,210). In prayer these beliefs are extravagantly phrased by a wealth of epithets which describe the limitless reaches of divine sovereignty (e.g. 2 Macc. 1.24f.; 3 Macc. 2.2f.: 'O Lord, Lord, King of the heavens, and Ruler of the whole creation, Holy among the holy, sole Governor, Almighty. ...' Cf. also Pr. of Man. 1-4). Numerous passages spell out the direct control of God over complex sequences of events. Tobias's marriage really was made in heaven (Tobit 6.18). Mordecai's dream shows that the entire Esther episode was pre-determined (Rest of Esther 13.1ff.; 10.4f.). Judith acknowledges divine sovereignty in her crisis (Judith 9.5ff.). In these instances, the sovereignty-responsibility tension inheres; for Judith's acknowledgement forms part and parcel of her petition for divine assistance to make her deceit successful, while Mordecai prays for divine deliverance (Rest of Esther 13.8ff.). In other words, belief in the proposition that God sovereignly predetermines these unpleasant events engenders not fatalism but prayerful intercession: the tension of the Old Testament persists.

The writer of the Wisdom of Solomon displays the same sort of tension in his re-interpretation of the exodus. The Egyptians forgot what God had already done and pursued the Israelites to the Red Sea, because they were being drawn on to their appointed destiny of torments. The same writer, within the space of a few verses, also speaks of the Egyptians deserving this end, and of God foreknowing what they would do. Again, Judas Maccabeus recognises both the divine ruling over his hour of death, and his own responsibility to fight manfully (1 Macc. 9.10; cf. 3.60). 'Judaism, indeed, managed to combine a very strict notion of predestination with the conviction that each individual is at the same time fully accountable for his choices.'[3] That judgment is sound for at least some elements of Judaism.

Ecclesiasticus presents God's sovereignty in a slightly different manner. Ben Sira says that God made men as the potter makes his vessels: according to his own pleasure. Some he exalted and blessed; others he cursed and abased (33.10-15; Gr. 36.10-15). Pfeiffer and others consider this to be polemic against a group contending for the essential equality of different races of men.[4] Whether that interpretation is sound or not, the passage certainly affirms the creatorship and authority of God over the *whole* of reality—even that which seems evil. God himself, of course, is good (39.16); but the paired opposites of good and evil, godly and sinner, death and life, are all under his rule. As far as Ben Sira is concerned, they argue for a system in which no person is qualified to make adequate judgments (39.16), since God is good and yet has set up the opposites to provide appropriate contrasts.[5] No man can assess one thing as worse than another, for everything is marvellous in its time (39.33f.).

To see God in some way standing behind all of reality forms the essence of recognising his ultimacy as the personal cause: and indeed, in many respects this theme emerges in the intertestamental non-apocalyptic literature unchanged from earlier Old Testament parallels. Occasionally God is portrayed regulating and controlling nature (e.g. Ecclus. 42.15ff.; Ep. Jer. 1.60-63). Kings enjoy their power by his decree (Wisd. 6.1ff.; Ep. Arist. §224; 4 Macc. 12.11). Health and food are simply his benefits, his gifts; even medicines of themselves can do nothing (Wisd. 16.12f.; Ep. Arist. §190). This does not mean the medical profession is rejected; rather, God made both the physician and his herbs, and so these God-provided benefits are to be used (Ecclus. 38.1f., 4, 9f., 12, 15). God gives wealth (Ep. Arist. §196); and even human popularity is considered one of his best gifts (Ep. Arist. §225). The source of all wisdom, knowledge and skill is God, and this fact is recognised both abstractly (e.g. 1 Esdr. 4.59f.; Wisd. 7.15-21) and in the concrete crisis (e.g. Sus. 45). The Epistle of Aristeas especially emphasises that God is the source of all human virtues (e.g. §§216, 231, 236, 238, 248).

But it is perhaps in the recognition of the immediate hand of God in personal and national victories that this corpus of literature most stresses divine ultimacy. It is God who smites Holofernes by the hand of a woman (Judith 13.15; 14.10; 15.8). Indeed, in Judith 9.1ff., the Genesis 36 story is re-interpreted to make God the moving force behind the massacre by Simeon and Levi. But note that such a belief even *before* her success (8.15ff.) does not prevent Judith from taking some remarkable initiative. Again, the reason Tobit becomes Enemessar's purveyor is because the Most High gives him grace and favour before the king (Tobit 1.13). The multiple reprieves in 3 Maccabees, ostensibly due to such mundane circumstances as a paper shortage, oversleeping, and a faulty memory, are in reality the work of God (4.20f.; 5.12ff., 28,30). There is, of course, considerable variation from book to book as to how much stress is laid on divine ultimacy. But even so sober an historical recital as 1 Maccabees never permits this ultimacy to be far from the surface (e.g. 3.18f., 21f., 53, 60; 4.55; 9.46), even if it is missing at junctures where one might expect it (e.g. 13.41). 2 Maccabees, which is much more interested in the religious struggle than the political one, underscores the divine ultimacy not only with pious phrases (e.g. 1.20; 10.1) holy-war cries (8.23; 13.15), and a statement about the divine control of Antiochus' mind (13.4; cf. Ep. Arist. §§17, 20f., 227, 256, 266), but also with a theological appraisal of historical observations: e.g. pious Onias is slain by Andronicus, who is in turn killed by Antiochus: thus the Lord rewarded Andronicus with the punishment he deserved (4.38). Very occasionally God is seen to stand behind both good and evil (Ecclus. 33.7-15; Ep. Arist. §197).

With such themes not hard to isolate, it is only to be expected that the concept of election should be given some prominence as well. God chose individuals: Moses (Ecclus. 45.16), David (Ecclus. 47.2), Solomon as king (Wisd. 9.1ff.), the prophet Jeremiah (Par. Jer. 1.5, 8; 3.5, 7; 7.9; etc.). God's righteous ones are in his hand; they are his elect (Wisd. 3.1ff.,7-10; 4.15). As for the nation, God not only chose the fathers (2 Macc. 1.25), he chose the people *as opposed* to the giants (Baruch 3.26-8), he favoured Israel *instead of* the Gentiles (Rest of Esther 10.10-12; Ecclus. 17.17; 36.11ff.). None protects Israel but God alone (Judith 9.14; 1 Macc. 4.10; 3 Macc. 6.15). Further, while there is nothing of a catholic hope in several of the books[6] (e.g. Tobit, 2 Maccabees), 3 Maccabees narrows down God's people to those who remain faithful under persecution (chap. 7). As a rule, however, election pertains to the Jews as a whole, rather than to the individual.[7] As in the Old Testament, the city of Jerusalem and its temple are frequently said to be chosen by God (e.g. Tobit 1.4 (*v. 1.*);[8] 1 Macc. 4.10; 7.37f.; 2 Macc. 1.30; 3 Macc. 2.9; Ecclus. 36.13; 49.6; Par. Jer. 1.6), although now for the first time we are told that the place was chosen for the sake of the people, and not vice versa (2 Macc. 5.19f.).

In numerous cases a particular doctrine or concept functions in this literature as in the Old Testament. Ecclesiasticus 5.2f., 6 forbids using God's mercy as a cloak for sin, while 15.9-12 prohibits using God's sovereignty to excuse man's sin. The ancient covenant with the fathers is brought up before God as a ground for contemporary rescue (1 Macc. 4.10; Dan. 3.34-6 (LXX)). With the same end in view, appeal is made to God's choice of Jerusalem and his love for Israel (3 Macc. 2.2ff.). Divine sovereignty over the hour of death, far from evoking fatalism, functions as sufficient ground for responsible behaviour as long as there is life (1 Macc. 9.10), while Judith uses God's infinite knowledge to plead for religious faithfulness. Indeed, the strongest predestinarian language on Judith's lips functions as part of the plea for divine intervention against the invading Assyrians (sic; 9.5; cf. the battle-cries, 2 Macc. 8.23; 13.15). Wisdom 6.1ff. reasons from God's authority over kings to their responsibility (cf. 4 Macc. 12.11). Divine omniscience becomes a reason for being good (Ep. Arist. §189) as well as for fearing judgment (Rest of Esther 16.4; Ecclus. 15.18f.; Ep. Arist. §§131f.).

There is in this literature an equivalent stress on human responsibility. Men are said to choose: e.g. the people choose Jonathan (1 Macc. 9.30), who in turn chooses other men (12.1); Solomon chooses Wisdom (Wisd. 7.7-10); and the mother of the martyrs chooses, instead of her sons, that religion which leads to eternal life (4 Macc. 15.2f.). Indeed, Ben Sira didactically affirms the freedom of man to choose (Ecclus. 15.11-20); but this has no clear parallel in the Old Testament. Men face the demands of the law; they are said to be good or wicked, to obey and repent: they seek the Lord or sin and rebel, receive rewards or endure judgment (e.g. Judith 5.17; 8.28; Tobit 13.6; 2 Macc. 4.38; 5.9f.; 6.12-17; 15.32f.; Pr. of Man. 1.13; Ep. Jer. 1.2). The sin of failing to recognise God's ultimacy is exemplified in Antiochus (2 Macc. 5.17; cf. Isa. 10.5ff.). The converse formulation, by which the recognition of divine ultimacy is nothing less than the summum bonum, is explicitly enunciated in Ep. Arist. §195.

And yet, despite the admitted parallels with the Old Testament, there are some readily identifiable differences between the way in which the sovereignty-responsibility tension is handled in some of these writings and the way it appears there. It is not just that human freedom is propositionally formulated (as we noted, supra; cf. Ecclus. 15.11-20. Compare

4 Macc. 3.3f.), there is something more: an unmistakable accent on human merit in all divine-human relationships. That the guilt of the people is sufficient cause for disaster is a commonplace both in this literature (2 Macc. 7.18f., 36; Ep. Jer. 1.2; etc.) and in the Old Testament. But it is much more difficult to find Old Testament parallels for the way in which good actions are treated as meritorious in this literature. Nicanor, for example, is humbled and forced to admit that the Jews have God to fight for them and therefore remain unbeatable—because they follow his laws (2 Macc. 8.34-6; cf. 15.21, where the recipients of divine support are said to be worthy). Men are dear to God because they have trained their minds to contemplate the noblest themes (Ep. Arist. §287; cf. §199). Mattathias's dying speech pulsates with the same idea, ascribing success to leaders from Abraham onward on the basis of their obedience, fervency, faithfulness, and so forth (1 Macc. 2.49ff.; cf. Ecclus. 44ff.; only the example of Caleb has specific Old Testament warrant).

Enslin understands the main theme of Judith to be 'that righteousness will ultimately triumph and that the children of Israel will be victorious over their enemies as long as they obey the laws of God.'[9] Indeed, this idea is made explicit: while they did not sin before their God they prospered, because the God who hates iniquity was with them (Judith 5.17). But Enslin is surely mistaken, or at least oversimplifying, when he repeatedly says[10] that this agrees with the Deuteronomic special stress: *Do this and prosper.* In the first place, despite passages like Deuteronomy 27f., it is also Deuteronomy which insists that God chose the people in defiance of their demerits and insignificance (especially Deut. 4,7; although some for this theological reason see evidence of an independent source). Second, there are other passages in Deuteronomy which make retribution less than mechanical. See especially 8.1-9.6 in which God tests Israel, allows her to hunger, reminds her that it is God and not man who is the ultimate power in the accumulation of wealth, and that Israel dispossessed the nations because of God's promise to the fathers, not because of her own righteousness. In the third place, Deuteronomy 27f. and related passages are framed in terms of promised blessing and threat of curse, while the intertestamental literature tends to concretise and historicise both. This is not done in the fashion of the

'Deuteronomic historians' who use Israel's history to deduce urgent lessons. Rather, it goes a step farther and claims God's blessing *because* of the people's obedience (so Judith 8.18-20).[11] By contrast, the Old Testament prophets frequently urge that God will hear and bless if the people *repent*; but when do they say he will hear and bless because the people are *good*?

Tobit reflects the same trend toward a view of earned merits, with his heavy emphasis on the so-called 'three pillars of Judaism', prayer, almsgiving and fasting. Despite the fact that righteousness and almsgiving are already becoming confused, the book is spared the hypocrisy and externalism of extreme legalism by virtue of its heart-felt prayers and warm devotion bordering on mysticism. But what is truly symptomatic of this growing theological conception is the pride which repeatedly surfaces (e.g. Tobit 1.3, 5ff., 16, 22ff.), only barely relieved by the occasional admission of sin (3.2-6). Other examples of the same sort of pride emerge again and again in this literature (e.g. Wisd. 8.19-21; 12.1-7; Ep. Arist. §§3-8, 37-9, 226; 4 Macc. 9.18), few examples of which can be paralleled in the Old Testament.

Another indication that 'merit theology'[12] is in the ascendancy comes from the vanity of the theodicies which surface in this literature. Although there is some recognition of the limits of human knowledge (e.g. Judith 8.11f.; Wisd. 9.13; Ecclus. 3.21-4; 11.4; 42.15ff.), other approaches gain dominance. The pressure of merit theology does not easily allow for a non-solution shrouded in divine 'unknownness'; it demands the answer that sin and rebellion never pay except in the coinage of judgment, while obedience earns blessing and reward (e.g. Tobit 4.6; 2 Macc. 7.18f.; 12.40-42; Ecclus. 51.30 (Gr.); Baruch 1.13; 2.10, 22ff.; 3.10-13; 4.6-8; Ep. Arist. §§232, 255; Par. Jer. 4.7f.). Ecclesiasticus appears to argue that justice is done by the manner of one's death (11.26-8); but it also insists that God is sovereign over the paired opposites formed at creation by divine decree. These demand the choice of men, even though all the divine decrees are themselves good and right in their own time.[13] 2 Maccabees 6.12-17 draws comfort by viewing divine punishment as loving chastening for God's people, as opposed to the experience of all other nations which are simply ignored until the day of reckoning (cf. 9.5-29). In the first part of Wisdom (1.1-6.8), suffering tests the righteous and

proves them worthy of immortality (3.1-6); while farther on
(11.21ff.), punishment seems to be deserved but remedial.
Although the facts of experience often harshly contradict such
theories, nevertheless theodicies based on a final accounting
after death become popular only in apocalyptic literature dealt
with in the next chapter.

Merit theology is also suggested by the prayers in these
writings. There is very little pure praise[14] (Ecclus. 42.15-43.33
is a notable exception); the overwhelming majority of the
prayers are requests (e.g. Rest of Esther 13.8ff.; Judith 4.9ff.;
6.18ff.; 9, 1-14; 13.7; Tobit 3.2-6, 11ff.; 1 Macc. 4.10, 30-33;
7.37f.; 9.46; 11.71ff.; 2 Macc. 1.8,24,30; 2.22ff.; 8.1ff.; 11.6-13;
12.6, 11,15f., 28; 13.9-17; 14.34ff.; 3 Macc. 1.16f.; 2.2f.; 5.7f.,
22, 50f.; 6.2ff.; Pr. of Man.; Wisd. 8.21; Ecclus. 48.20;
51.6ff.,13; Sus. 42.44; Ep. Arist. §17; Par. Jer. 1.2), the incor-
porated praise serving as part of the plea, a sort of precursor of
the request (e.g. especially Rest of Esther 13.8ff.; Judith 9.5ff.;
Tobit 6.18; 3 Macc. 2.2ff.). In itself this use of praise does not
differ from the Old Testament (e.g. Ps. 80.1ff.; 94.1ff.), except
in degree; but the praise of this literature becomes more and
more specialised, uttered with the particular request in view.
For example, God is praised for previous mercy and asked to
show more mercy (Tobit 8.17). 'In all these prayers ... the aim
dictates the phrasing of the act of adoration by which the
petitioner hopes to influence God to grant the request.'[15] Rarely
is there any reference to God's will in the matter (although cf.
Ecclus. 39.5f.): more commonly there is something of a knee-
jerk reflex view of prayer and blessing, dependent only on
human obedience, or even on the fervency with which the
prayer is offered (Judith 4.9ff.).

There are a few other indications that merit theology is on
the rise. The doctrine of creation is used not only to formulate a
proposition about divine ultimacy in areas like power and
beauty and speech (Ep. Arist. §201), but to establish the
freedom of human choice (4 Macc. 2.21) or the finality of the
law (since the Creator himself gave it: 4 Macc. 5.25). Divine
omniscience is now used, not only to threaten judgment, but to
justify Mordecai (Rest of Esther 13.12). We have already
observed how often human faithfulness becomes the ground of
petition: the divine sense of fair play, rather than the divine
mercy, is thus being appealed to. Hence, in not a few instances

human merit provides the explanation for some notable success (2 Macc. 8.34-6; 15.2ff.; Ecclus. 44.16ff.). True, Ecclesiasticus 47.16-22 uses the election promises to build confidence in God's faithfulness to provide a remnant, despite human sin; but it is more common to show the human heroes in a less injurious light, possibly even without sin (Pr. of Man. 8). No longer are there any overwhelming statements about being born in sin, about human acts of righteousness being the equivalent of menstruous cloths, about hearts set to do evil (the hearts of the persecutors excepted, of course!). And where is the heart-rending wrestling of Job and Qoheleth? The theodicies have become too glib, too rigid, too rationalistic. We have seen that election in the Old Testament is not only to privilege but to far-reaching ethical and covenantal obligations: where in this later literature is election used to underline such national responsibilities? There are a few instances where individual (as opposed to national) election entails service (e.g. Ecclus. 45.16). However, such individual election is rare in this literature, being squeezed out by the rewards and punishments *schema*. And where are the passages which portray God as *in some sense* behind *specific* evil actions—passages like Genesis 50.19f.; Judges 14.4a; 2 Samuel 24.1? Although there is diversity in this literature, the Epistle of Aristeas, perhaps the most anaemic book when it comes to sin, goes to the extreme, so emphasising God's benignity and forbearance that he is described as the One who 'rules the whole world in the spirit of kindness *and without wrath at all*' (§254).

Thus, ultimately it is the view of God which has changed. True, God is in one sense increasingly sovereign: the potter-and-clay model for the first time is used to spell out a deterministic view of man (Ecclus. 33.10-15 (Gr. 36.10-15); cf. Ep. Arist. §197); but this is mild metaphysical speculation in the wisdom tradition, not agonising wrestling. God is increasingly transcendent, sovereign in an abtract sort of way; but this progressive exaltation of God is at the expense of meaningful divine personality. Yahweh is now God or the Lord; he is the God of heaven, the Lord of heaven (e.g. Tobit 10.11; 13.7), and, most popularly, the Most High God. 1 Maccabees repeatedly uses 'Heaven' as the divine surrogate (e.g. 3.18f.; 4.40). The tendency to substitute some attribute, or the divine dwelling-place, for the name of deity, is part of the process which is stripping God-language of its anthropomorphisms and anthropopothisms. Because anthropomorphisms and anthropopothisms bring home God's personality, the sacrifice of the former *tends* to obliterate the latter. Hence there is no longer any place, for example, for the God of this literature to plead with men to turn from their wicked ways. Of course, it would be tendentious to read too much into these developments, not only because their distribution is uneven in the literature, but also because it is extremely difficult to assess conceptual changes by the *lack* of certain descriptive epithets. Nevertheless it is wishful thinking which sees no significant theological change whatever.

What W. O. E. Oesterley perceptively writes about 1 Maccabees is true of more books than the one with which he is concerned:

> Just as there was a disinclination, on account of its transcendent holiness, to utter the name of God, and instead, to substitute paraphrases for it, so there arose also a disinclination to ascribe actions among men directly to God, because of his inexpressible majesty. One result of this was the further tendency to emphasise and extend the scope of human free-will. These tendencies were only beginning to exert their influence, but they largely explain the religious characteristics of the book.[16]

The tension persists, but the historical situation in which Israel now finds herself has changed its focus. Before the exile idolatry was the problem; but now, almost as an over-reaction, divine transcendence is being stressed at the expense of divine personality. With this development, and with merit theology on the increase, statements about divine sovereignty *tend* to become all-embracing only in the abstract, while in fact specific human decisions are being fenced off from divine control. In this sense the sovereignty-responsibility tension is polarising. More ontological descriptions are being introduced, and more speculation about the origin of sin. The relationship between God and man turns less and less on spontaneous, sovereign grace and more and more on human merits and demerits, while the Jews as a people look more and more like wonderful heroes and less and less like the cherished objects of God's elective love.

CHAPTER SIX

INTERTESTAMENTAL APOCALYPTIC

Because it is so extraordinarily difficult to treat apocalyptic literature precisely, a few prefatory remarks are required to mention difficulties and call attention to the procedure followed here.

The difficulties begin with scholarly disagreement about the extent (not to mention the essential characteristics!) of apocalyptic literature. Some works usually labelled 'apocalyptic' contain relatively small apocalyptic sections (e.g. Life of Adam and Eve). Not a few works are rejected *in toto* by some investigators. Thus, although A. Nissen marshals five reasons for accepting Jubilees as an example of genuine apocalyptic,[1] K. Koch assesses those reasons as inconclusive.[2] D. S. Russell presents the mediating view adopted here: 'Jubilees is not, strictly speaking, an apocalyptic book; but it belongs to the same milieu.'[3] Similarly, G. E. Ladd says that the Psalms of Solomon and the Sibylline Oracles are not really apocalyptic, 'although they include elements of apocalyptic eschatology'.[4] Again, however, I shall for convenience include them in that category.

The second problem relates to large numbers of conflicting opinions about the date, provenance, and *Sitz im Leben* of many of the books. The complexity of the discussion threatens to mire the student in a bog of speculation before he can say anything certain. By and large, the present section follows majority opinion on these matters. Therefore it does not, for example, follow M. R. James who thinks that the Testament of Abraham is a christian work.[5] More difficult is 2 Enoch. Although some have thought it to be a christian document dependent on the Apocalypse of Peter, it seems best to follow Russell in giving 'the benefit of the doubt to the earlier dating',[6] even while recognising that the book as we have it is by no means free from christian influence. There is also a wide diversity of scholarly opinion on the date and provenance of the Testament of Moses (=Assumption of Moses≠Apocalypse of Moses), and of the

Testaments of the Twelve Patriarchs, which M. de Jonge[7] thinks to be not so much interpolated by Christians as compiled by them from Jewish sources. Such opinions, though in the minority, encourage restraint in drawing major conclusions from disputed and unsupported passages. With some hesitation, I have excluded from this chapter both canonical apocalyptic and apocalyptically-oriented books among the Dead Sea Scrolls, as they are being treated elsewhere.

The adjective 'intertestamental' also bears explanation. It is used to designate a general period, but it does not suggest that no Jewish apocalyptic which post-dates a New Testament work has been included. The major Jewish apocalypses from about 200 BC to approximately AD 100 are covered by the rubric. For various reasons I have not included references to little known or barely accessible works.

One final preliminary point concerns the problem of ascertaining the nature and degree of extra-Jewish influences on Jewish apocalyptic. A number of scholars minimise the Jewish content in favour of overwhelming Iranian[8] or Hellenistic[9] influence. F. M. Cross thinks the taproot goes back through a Hebrew milieu to Canaanite myth and epic poetry;[10] G. von Rad looks to Wisdom literature;[11] and P. D. Hanson says that apocalyptic not only reaches back for its earliest beginnings to the second and third millennia BC, but was long naturalised within Israel but suppressed by the prophets.[12] It would certainly be wrong to deny significant foreign influence on Jewish apocalyptic, and indeed it is not difficult to find elements, say, of Iranian astrology or Zoroastrian schematisation of history. But sweeping statements are too easily made; judicious documentation and nuanced statements about a plurality of contributing backgrounds are needed.[13] The conclusion of L. Morris, although it could do with qualification, is surely correct, and is basic to this chapter: 'Nobody seems to have disposed of the stubborn fact that apocalyptic is a Jewish and Christian phenomenon. It is hard to see this literature as derived from a source which does not know it. Granted that there have been borrowings from many sources, the main idea is surely Jewish.'[14]

THE APOCALYPTIC LITERATURE

The freedom of man is expressed more strongly in apocalyptic than in anything so far mentioned. Men are told to make their hearts good and their ways straight (T. Sim. 5.2), to choose between light and darkness, between the law of the Lord and the works of Beliar (T. Levi 19.1). The Life of Adam 4.3 gives new overtones to the story of the fall by a formidable emphasis on Adam's voluntary repentance; the Testament of Simeon 2.13; 3.4f. does a similar thing for Simeon. The doctrine of two spirits (T. Jud. 20.1-3), two 'inclinations' (T. Ash. 1.3-9; 5.1ff.; etc.), two ways (2 En. 30.15) comes up in various forms, and in each case there is emphasis on the responsibility of man to choose between the two. When God made man, he showed him two ways and told him which was good and which was bad, so as to learn who in the human race bear love toward God, and who bear him hatred (2 En. 30.15). According to 2 Enoch, man still has freedom of will, even if the incorporation of the soul into the body, with its limitations, biases its preferences towards evil.

Of course, there is some variation from book to book as to the extent of moral freedom since the fall. In 2 Esdras 3.20-22, man has a *cor malignum.* This is denied by 2 Baruch, which, although it sees man as a danger both to himself and to angels (56.10), nevertheless repeatedly emphasises the unfettered freedom of man's will (e.g. 19.1, 3; 54.15, 19; 85.7). In 2 Enoch 31.6-8, we learn that the Satan, conceiving thought against Adam, seduced Eve, but did not touch Adam. As a result, God cursed ignorance and man's evil fruit, his works; but he did not curse *man,* nor the earth, nor other creatures. Indeed, in the same book, Jeremiah is pure from sin (9.1).

Needful knowledge was not withheld even from the Gentiles (2 Bar. 51.16; 59.2), and so their rebellion is entirely their own fault (2 En. 7.3). The Psalms of Solomon 9.7 agrees that our works are subject to our own choice and power;[15] while in the concrete case, we learn that Terah refused to listen to God's voice because he chose not to, even though Abraham chose positively (Apoc. Ab. II, 26). There is, then, 'the greatest stress upon man's unfettered choice between good and evil, upon his unrestricted capacity to obey the law and to transgress it. Man's will (is) free.'[16]

Although the apocalyptists give more space to eschatology

than to ethics, it is incorrect to pit these two motifs against each other and conclude that the writers are escapists with little sense of responsibility. Apocalyptic, says W. D. Davies, is 'no less concerned with the observance of Torah than was Pharisaism.'[17] There is a sense in which such a sweeping statement is correct, and indeed the necessary antidote to L. Morris's judgment of the apocalyptists: 'But when all this is said the ethical imperative is not characteristic of them as it is of the prophets. In the last resort their interest is in eschatology, not ethics.'[18] Davies is correct inasmuch as the pervasive merit theology (see below) *presupposes* the centrality of Torah and Torah's ethics; there is no participation in the felicity of the life to come without personal meritorious righteousness. Morris is correct inasmuch as the apocalyptists are not interested in setting forth detailed ethical teaching (Tests. 12 Pats. and Jub. 20.1ff. excepted); but it would be wrong to draw from this the conclusion that the apocalyptic eschatological perspective encouraged moral indolence. The constant emphasis on judgment, and on God as the sovereign, righteous Judge, confirms the reasonableness of this conclusion (cf. Jub. 5.1ff. with 7.25; Sib. Or. III. 71,97; IV, 40-44; Ps. Sol. 9.4; 17.4; etc.).

With these observations in mind, it is not surprising to discover many instances of God responding to man's initiative, and few the other way around. Some such passages merely echo the Old Testament: e.g. God blesses Abraham because of his faithfulness (Jub. 18.15), and men are told to turn and offer many sacrifices in the hope that God will listen (Sib. Or. III, 624-9). But the nature and number of such passages suggest a drift to a situation where the iniative in God-and-man relationships has passed from God to men (the introduction of the eschaton excepted). Men first turn and repent, and then God hears (Jub. 1.15ff.,23; T. Jud. 23.5; T. Dan. 5.9; 6.4). Hence, at the time of the exodus it was the 'sheep' in Egypt who first sought the Lord (1 En. 89.16). Abraham chooses God (Jub. 12.19ff.); and it appears that although God created Abraham according to his good pleasure, that good pleasure was established by his advance knowledge of what a righteous fellow Abraham would be (Jub. 16.26). Indeed, everyone who performs God's law will be loved by him (T. Jos. 11.2; cf. 18.1). This is demonstrated by the fact that God responds to men who seek him by making their way smooth and preserving the works of their hands (Ps. Sol. 6.1-3). A concrete example lies in God's determination to lay the ages to come before Abraham *because* Abraham has loved to search him out (Apoc. Ab. ii, 9).

Few of the above examples in themselves would be conclusive to establish this shift in initiative. Moreover, it would be inaccurate to suggest that human freedom is *completely* unbounded. In the language of prayer and testimony, the apocalyptists still speak of God creating a right spirit in his people, strengthening them to do his will, not permitting them to wander and keeping them back from sin (Jub. 1.19ff.; 21.25; 22.7-10; Ps. Sol. 16.1ff., 7,9f.; cf. T. Benj. 6.1). Following the exile, at the end of days God will stir up for himself a faithful people whom he shall save for eternity, while the impious, those who have refused to love the law, shall be punished by God their king (Vita Ad. 29.7ff.). The human will needs God's strengthening (Jub. 21.25; 22.10). This moral dynamic has a negative counterpart in Martyrdom of Isaiah 2.4, where Manasseh is made strong in his sin by the angel of lawlessness. One book, 2 Esdras, is especially aware of the need for an inner dynamic in a man. Although it explicitly teaches human freedom (7.127-130; 8.59f.), it contains such 'an agonised confession of moral impotence'[19] as to become tantamount to a denial of freedom, indeed an 'unconscious and unexpected cry ... for a moral dynamic, which legalism could not supply'.[20] (Cf. 2 Esd. 3.20) From this discussion, then, it is clear that at least some apocalyptic writers who saw the human will as free did not understand such freedom to mean that God did not influence or strengthen the will.

Yet for all that there is nevertheless a shift in initiative from God to man. This is best seen in the manner in which the apocalyptists handle election (on which see below); but it is also attested by the extraordinary extravagance of the praise accorded to special men. Jacob, for example, appears marvellously strong and merciful in his wars with Esau (Jub. 37f.). After Jacob's death, the surviving brothers get along famously (Jub. 46.1f.). Jubilees is particularly excessive, but it is by no means unique. Abraham, above all other Old Testament figures, is singled out for an abundance of praise (e.g. Jub. 17.15; Test. Ab. §1(A)). He is nothing less than sinless (Test. Ab. §10(A)). The archangel Michael loves to listen to his conversation (Test. Ab. §2(B)), and even Death becomes

60 SOVEREIGNTY AND RESPONSIBILITY

beautiful because of Abraham's worthiness (Test. Ab. §17(A)). He seems to have figured out the folly of idolatry all by himself (Apoc. Ab. I,1-8). In the matter of Sarah, Pharaoh is said to have seized her and then been punished by the Lord: i.e. Abraham is whitewashed (Jub. 13.13). And the insolent petulance he exhibits toward God in refusing to die (Apoc. Ab. (A)) is simply colossal. Small wonder he can afford to brag a little just before his death (Jub. 21.2ff.).

These two phenomena, whitewashing and bragging, are fairly extensively distributed throughout the historical surveys found in apocalyptic literature. Sometimes whitewashing is accomplished by mere suppression: e.g. Isaac's deceit in the matter of Abimelech (Gen. 26) is not recorded at the appropriate place in Jubilees 24. At other times whitewashing is explicit. It was the Lord who ordained that Levi and Simeon destroy the Shechemites (Jub. 30.5f.; T. Levi 5.1ff.). Isaac comes round to love Jacob more than Esau (Jub. 35.13); and Jacob is cleared of any ungracious behaviour toward Leah by making up to her after Rachel's death, and discovering what a wonderful woman she really is (Jub. 36.23f.). Adam is often whitewashed at the expense of Eve (e.g. Vita Ad. 13.1ff.); and once there is the bald assertion that the fathers and forefathers did not tempt God so as to transgress (Test. Mos. 9.3f.).

Boasting occurs not less frequently. Even Jacob manages to brag that he has not sinned (Jub. 25.4ff.). The book with the greatest concentration of such pretensions, ironically, is the one with the greatest number of ethical maxims, viz. The Testaments of the Twelve Patriarchs (e.g. T. Iss. 3.1-8; 7.1; T. Naph. 1.6ff.; T. Jos. 10.1ff.) Perhaps it is not so ironical after all; for if free will and ethical sensitivity are joined, it is difficult to see why conceit of accomplishment should not become a mark of virtue. Zebulun's only sin was a sin of ignorance (!) in the matter of selling his brother Joseph (T. Zeb. 1.4f.); and so he was rewarded by God (5.2; cf. 6.4-8.3 (v.l.)). Even 2 Esdras, which is far and away the most pessimistic of the apocalyptic books when it comes to assessing human nature, states that the Most High revealed many things to Ezra because of his righteous conduct (10.38f.; 13.53b-6). We have again penetrated near the heart of merit theology.

Turning now from man and his freedom to God and his sovereignty, we come upon numerous references to the creatorship of God (Jub. 2.1ff.; 12.19; 1 En. 9.1ff.; Sib. Or. III, 35; Test. Mos. 12.3; 2 En. 24.2; 2 Esd. 3.4; 6.1-6; 7.70; 9.2; Apoc. Ab. 1,8; etc.). Belief in this truth is shared by all the apocalyptists, whether they understand God to have made the world *ex nihilo*, or no (cf. 2 En. 24.2 and 25.1). Since God is the creator of all, all belongs to him, and he is the ultimate ruler (Slav. Vit. Ad. 33.1; 34.4; Jub. 12.4,17f.). His sovereignty extends to the whole creation (1 En. 84.2f.), and he gives good things to all men (T. Gad 7.2), for he rules the world with compassion and righteousness (Test. Mos. 12.17). The unlimited extent of God's sovereignty is frequently underscored by the force of multiplied epithets and descriptive clauses (e.g. Test. Mos. 4.1ff.; 2 Bar. 21.1ff.; 54.13; Ps. Sol. 2.34f.). The Sibylline Oracles have as chief concern the unity and sovereignty of God (e.g. III,11f.).

Some elements of the Old Testament presentation of divine 'ultimacy' crop up. Abraham praises God who caused him to see day (Jub. 22.7). Rebecca blesses God for giving her Jacob as a pure son and a holy seed (25.12ff.). Similarly, it was the Lord who opened Rachel's womb (28.24). The Lord stands as the ultimate cause of Joseph's prosperity (40; 43.19). Valour is given by the Most High (T. Sim. 2.5), who is also credited with preventing murder by not permitting Dan to find Joseph alone (T. Dan. 1.9; cf. 6.5, where the angel of peace will keep Israel from an extremity of sin). And when Israel does indeed sin, God not only does not restrain Pompey from attacking her (Ps. Sol. 2.1—a 'passive' undertaking), he actually brings nations against his people (2.24). Pompey ought to recognise God's sovereignty (Ps. Sol. 2.32f.).

Morris rightly insists that the dualism between good and evil is never absolute: God remains objectively sovereign.[21] God, and only God, is sufficient to bind evil spirits; and even the chief of such spirits, Mastema, is helpless without the divine permission (Jub. 10.2ff.). Ultimately, God is sovereign over evil, which cannot occur without his indulgence (1 En. 9.1-11). God created all forces; there is none who resists him, none who does not subject himself to God or labour for his sole rule (2 En. 33.7A).

God's rule in apocalyptic is conceived in distinctly deterministic categories. History can in principle be systematically arranged and schematised, even if there is little agreement as to the scheme (compare, for example, the Apocalypse of Weeks in

1 Enoch, and the two different schemes of jubilees in Jubilees and the Assumption of Moses). But schematisation of history entails history's predetermination. 'There was therefore an inevitability about history; through travail and persecution it would move unerringly to its predetermined goal—the defeat of evil and the establishment of God's kingdom in the time of the End. The past was fixed; the future was fixed also.'[22] (Cf. Jub. 1.26ff.; 6.29-38; Vit. Ad. 29.1ff.; 1 En. 89f.; Sib. Or. IV, 47ff.; Test. Mos. 2.3ff.; 6.1ff.; 12.3ff.; 2 En. 65.3f.; 2 Bar. 27-30; 2 Esd. 4.28-32; etc.) None of God's words and thoughts lack fulfilment (Sib. Or. III, 698-701). The destinies of not only Levi and Judah are ordained by God (Jub. 31.31; 52.21), but those of all the tribes (52.21). Whatever is, is determined by God, including people for destruction (Apoc. Ab. II,22). The number of the elect is likewise determined, and until that number is filled up, salvation cannot come (2 Esd. 4.36; cf. Rev. 6.11). The 'times' are so rigidly determined as to appear to take on an almost ontological status (cf. especially 2 Esd. 4.36f.; 7.74).

It should not be thought that only abstract 'times' and 'destinies' are controlled by God: specific events likewise fall within his purview. The murder of Abel by Cain appears to have been fixed in advance (Vit. Ad. 22.4; Apoc. Mos. 3.2). Isaiah tells Hezekiah how monstrous his son will be, insisting that the future events he describes are determined, even though they are the counsel of Sammael (Mar. Isa. 1.7-13).[23] Enoch foretells the flood to Noah (1 En. 65.1ff.). The Testaments of the Twelve Patriarchs include many specific 'predictions' (e.g. T. Levi 10.5; 14.1ff.; 15.6; T. Zeb. 9.7; etc.), and the day of Abraham's death is destined (Test. Ab. §15(A)).

A number of beliefs about divine sovereignty serve purposes quite like those in the Old Testament. For example, the fact that God is creator and ruler calls men to worship him only (Jub. 12.4,19f.). Again, because God made all things in order, men are exhorted not to corrupt their ways (T. Naph. 2.9ff.). Divine omniscience entails perfect judgment (1 En. 9.11). God's election of his people functions in one place as the basis for a plea for mercy (2 Bar. 48.20); yet in a book which so consistently underscores the value and efficacy of good works (e.g. 2.2; 14.7, 12f.; 51.7; 63.3, 5; 67.6; 85.2, 10; cf. infra), it is less than clear that God chose the people out of grace. It is in any case more common to discover that beliefs about divine sovereignty serve purposes rather unlike their functions in the Old Testament, providing some indication of the new form the sovereignty-responsibility tension is assuming. In a confused passage (T. Naph. 2.2-5), the potter and clay model is used to bolster thorough-going determinism, yet suddenly stops short of ascribing evil to God. In the Sibylline Oracles, which are apparently addressed to pagans, belief in God's sovereignty is the basis for arguing against idol worship and wicked behaviour, but it is never used to support a doctrine of gracious election.

Completely determined are the nature and time of arrival of the messianic kingdom, the new age, the day of judgment, the restoration of all things, the end of time—however the eschaton is variously conceived. Fully developed eschatological dualism does not appear until 2 Esdras (e.g. 7.50, 113; 8.1). Yet, as H. Ringgren insists, 'The thought is not explicitly formulated in the oldest apocalypses, but the conception stands out clearly in the background.'[24]

Why, then, do some scholars maximise God's distance from history in apocalyptic thought? H. D. Betz says the apocalyptists have 'dispensed with historical thinking'.[25] W. R. Murdock insists that in Jewish apocalyptic God does not act in history, except to reveal secrets to certain choice men.[26] A. Nissen,[27] followed by G. E. Ladd,[28] enunciates the fairly common view that for the apocalyptists God does not rule from the beginning of the exile on (some would add: until 165 BC). Nissen depends heavily on 1 En. 89 and Dan. 11.36 (Ladd, solely on the former); but K. Koch, commenting on Nissen's essay, correctly remarks that the very opposite can be deduced from the passages cited.[29]

On the other hand, some scholars make much of apocalyptic's deterministic view of history. J. Bright, for example, says that '[Apocalypticism] represented a legitimate, if bazarre, expression of [Israel's] faith in the God who is sovereign Lord of History.'[30] T. W. Manson writes, 'Apocalyptic is really an attempt to rationalise and systematise the predictive side of Prophecy as one side of the whole providential ordering of the Universe.'[31] R. H. Charles goes so far as to argue that the unity of history is first grasped by the apocalyptists;[32] while D. S. Russell, more moderately, thinks apocalyptic carried prophecy to its logical conclusion, seeing all history *sub specie aeternitatis*, tying together the temporal and the eternal by the divine purpose.[33]

The chasm between the two viewpoints could not be wider. The first—that God had relinquished control of history with all of the divine activity reserved for a supernatural inbreaking at some imminent juncture—although it cannot be sustained in the light of all this evidence, is not completely mistaken. As expressed, it is surely erroneous; but what has led its supporters to their conclusion? The consciousness that there is a problem is seen by H. H. Rowley's argument that for the apocalyptist God *is* in control *despite appearances*. In the prophets the tension between God's role and man's role takes place *in history*; while in apocalyptic, the focus of attention is on man's role *in history*, with all his sin exposed, and on God's act (which can only be God's) *at the end of history*.[34] Rowley is thus trying to have his cake and eat it too: God is in control of history even if God really acts only at the end of history.

A more helpful distinction comes from G. E. Ladd. He differentiates between prophetic-apocalyptic and non-prophetic apocalyptic. The latter is devoid of the sense of God's acts in history and looks to the end, while the former retains the consciousness of God's acts in history even while retaining the two-age structure. Non-prophetic apocalyptic is completely pessimistic about history; prophetic-apocalyptic allows a much more positive picture.[35] Ladd is thus able to draw attention to some notable differences between New Testament apocalyptic and much of the apocalyptic that comes earlier. But the distinction fails to answer the pressing question of God's relation to history in intertestamental apocalyptic, most of which Ladd classifies as non-prophetic apocalyptic—even though, as we have shown, God is reigning in some sense, and the times are determined.

The solution to the problem lies in a more sweeping understanding of what is meant by such phrases as 'God acting in history'. What Ladd really means by 'prophetic apocalyptic' is not so much an apocalyptic eschatological perspective which still retains the consciousness of God's *acts* in history, but an apocalyptic eschatological perspective which still retains the consciousness of God's *saving acts* in history. In apocalyptic, God is still acting in history; but he is acting in such a way that evil is having its day, the grapes of wrath are being stored, and the suffering people of God hang on grimly while they anticipate the new age. During the new age, God's judgment is executed against sinners, and his people enjoy felicity: i.e. God takes positive saving action on behalf of his people. It is understandable, therefore, why his people view the present age pessimistically.

Two small caveats must be entered. (1) God's saving activity in intertestamental apocalyptic is not *quite* reserved for the age to come. 2 Esdras 4.36 informs us that the number of the elect is determined. The same thought is implicit elsewhere. Since the end comes only when their number is complete, the process of making up the number of the elect might well be thought of as a saving action of God within the present evil age. But this, it must be noted, has to do with the designation of the status of individuals, not the emancipation of the people of God individually or as a whole, nor with the introduction of a new heaven and earth. (2) Related to this is the meaning placed upon the phrase 'God's saving activity'. It means the observable good which comes about as the concrete result of divine action. This limitation is necessary in order to exclude those divine acts which guarantee the special place and designation of God's people in history, i.e. in this evil age (e.g. God created the world for the salvation of his people, Test. Mos. 1.12-14; 2 Esd. 6.55; the law was a special gift to Israel, 2 Esd. 3.19f.; 9.31f.; God chastens his people now—indeed, not as much as they deserve, 2 Bar. 78.5; 84.11), but which do not at the present time bring material and pleasurable blessings to them.

Those scholars then who maximise God's distance from history are interested in God's positive, saving activity. Those on the other hand who see God in control of history, focus on his non-saving activity. This simple observation takes us once again to the heart of the sovereignty-responsibility tension: the nature of God. The apocalyptic literature judges quite erroneous two opposing views of God: (1) that view which so stresses God's good actions that his otherwise limitless sovereignty is tacitly circumscribed; or (2) that view which describes God's sovereignty in such a way that his positive, salvific activity cannot be adequately distinguished from his general providence, his 'ultimacy'. The latter error flattens the varieties of God's activity, makes all reality his immediate responsibility, forbids distinctions between good and evil and reduces human beings to manipulated robots. Monotheism, and Jewish apocalyptic monotheism in particular, requires notions *both* of God's total sovereignty *and* of his special activity on behalf of his people. Such a two-fold conception of God is already found in the Old Testament. In apocalyptic, however, the solution to the tension takes on eschatological overtones. The emphasis on the eschatological dimension is making the two aspects oscillate in an unexpected fashion. God's ultimacy is presupposed during the present age; but his saving activity is by and large reserved for the age to come. This distinction must in no way weaken the fact that the two ages are related by the divine purpose, the evil age moving in a predetermined way towards the eschaton.

This conclusion is confirmed by comparing the dominant theodicy of intertestamental apocalyptic literature with that of intertestamental non-apocalyptic literature, in which the eschatological dualism fades to a shadow. In the non-apocalyptic literature, as we have seen, the most important theodicy is based on merit theology. In bald terms, human goodness eventually pays. Harsh experience forces the 'eventually' to take on the occasional eschatological overtone. But in apocalyptic, in which the structure of eschatological dualism is becoming fully assembled, and behind which in all likelihood experience is even harsher, the heart of theodicy lies in the hope of the new age. 'Apocalyptic was a Judeo-Christian world-view which located the believer in a minority community and gave his life meaning by relating it to the end, soon to come, which would reverse his present status.'[36] Indeed, when J. J. Collins argues that the chief factor distinguishing prophecy from apocalyptic is the transcendence of death in the latter,[37] the concluding paragraphs of his essay reveal he is really talking about post-death theodicy. The whole structure of intertestamental apocalyptic thought, in which God's saving action is reserved for the eschaton, requires that the final vindication of God await the advent of that eschaton.

Three further caveats are required in order to secure a balanced presentation of this area of apocalyptic thought.

(i) As noted earlier, a significant proportion of the individual apocalyptic books are not really apocalyptic in nature. Further, many of the apocalyptic visions summarise history under the guise of prophecy (as opposed to the eschatological dimensions of the visions). Whenever one or the other of these two conditions occurs, theodicies more typical of the non-apocalyptic intertestamental literature appear. In the life summaries of the Testaments of the Twelve Patriarchs, for example, or in the descriptions of Abraham or Enoch, the merits of the revered saint in question, and his corresponding attractiveness to God and earned blessings from him, become highly prominent.

(ii) The predominance of the underlying eschatological theodicy in apocalyptic literature does not preclude other types, even within thoroughly apocalyptic sections. God is vindicated of any possible charge of wrongdoing in the trial of Abraham concerning the sacrifice of his son, inasmuch as Mastema is said to be behind the temptation (Jub. 17.15—much as in the case of Job). Concerning the fall, not only do we learn that God made everything good in the first place (T. Naph. 2.8), but that nothing was wrong with the fruit until the Satan poisoned it (Apoc. Mos. 19.3). The adversary tempted Eve when her two protecting angels were away worshipping (Vit. Ad. 33.1-3; i.e. God had afforded Eve adequate protection in principle?). Answers, of course, may differ from book to book. For example, 2 Baruch and 2 Enoch trace sin back to the first pair, while 1 Enoch and Jubilees go back to wicked angels behind them.

(iii) The tensions inherent in the apocalyptic *Weltanschauung*, and the painful historical circumstances which have given rise to them, not surprisingly call forth two works whose primary themes include theodicy. (1) The first of these is 2 Baruch.[38] A great part of the answer of this book to the problem of evil turns on the freedom of the will (e.g. 19.1-3; cf. Apoc. Ab. ΙΙ, 23-6). Even the Gentiles originally enjoyed all needful knowledge; but pride kept them from the knowledge of the law, for the choice of evil on man's part is deliberate (59.2; 51.16). The conclusion must be that Gentiles have always worked impiety and wickedness (62.7). (2) The second, and even more important, is the Salathiel Apocalypse of 2 Esdras. Like Habakkuk, the author asks why God's people suffer at the hands of the Gentiles whose sins are even worse than those of the chosen people. But he learns that God's ways are inscrutable and man's intelligence limited (4.1-32; 5.35f.). Both the course and duration of the present world are predetermined (4.33-50). In any case, despite appearances God's love for Israel never falters (5.31-40; cf. 8.47). But in any event, the coming age will resolve all problems for the few who are precious and worth saving (7.49-61). The crucial theodicy, then, is the eschatological one. When the seer remains unsatisfied by these answers (7.62-9), appeal is made to God's compassion (7.132-40).[39]

Before the relationship in this literature between man's freedom and God's sovereignty can be examined, the apocalyptic viewpoint on election must be outlined. This viewpoint bears superficial similarity to election in previously considered literature (even, for example, in so small a detail as God's choice of the land, 2 En. 40.2); but in two respects it is really quite different. (1) The first, though well-known, is relatively incidental to the present study: the Messiah is presented as God's Elect One, notably but not exclusively in 1 Enoch (e.g. 1 En. 39.6; 40.4f.; 45.3f.; 46.3; 61.8; cf. Apoc. Ab. II, 31). The title apparently goes back to Isaiah 42.1. (2) The second, however, is crucial: merit theology transforms election into a divine choice which is neither lost in divine 'unknownness' nor based on sovereign love bestowed in defiance of demerit, but which is explicitly grounded on human righteousness and worth. God chose the people to whom he could find no equal (2 Bar. 48.20). Israel alone is God's elect people (2 Esd. 5.23-30; 6.58; 8.16; etc.), those for whom the world was made (6.55; 7.11). Although the law was a special gift to Israel (3.19f.; 9.31f.) it was sinfully refused by the other nations (7.23f., 72): by implication, Israel alone made the right choice. God chose Jacob's seed from all that he saw (Jub. 2.20). Those whom the Elect One chooses are the righteous and holy (1 En. 51.2), prompting P. Volz to remark, 'They are the elect, because God has chosen them for participation in salvation, on the basis of their piety.'[40] Clearly, the very term 'elect' undergoes a shift in semantic value, and as an adjective it becomes a synonym for 'righteous': the righteous perform elect works (1 En. 38.2), and men must choose an elect life (1 En. 94.4). In 1 Enoch, God's people are often designated 'elect and righteous' or the like (e.g. 1.1; 5.7; 41.2; 50.1). This semantic shift in 'election' necessarily provokes concomitant shifts in the meanings of 'grace' and 'mercy'. A major part of E. P. Sanders's argument, to be considered in detail a little further on, is that in intertestamental Judaism the prevailing 'covenantal nomism' continues to hold that salvation is according to grace or mercy, and condemnation is according to works. But this repeated assertion fails to come to grips with the diluted value of 'grace' and 'mercy'. God may be 'gracious' to his people, but it is no longer grace in defiance of demerit and rooted in the sovereign goodness of God. Rather, it is a kind response to merit.

A few passages are admittedly ambiguous, but in most of these cases the idea of human merit is not too far away, and in none of them does election ever spring from grace. In the Testament of Levi 2.4; 4.4, for example, it is God who 'chooses' Levi; but it seems to be in response to Levi's prayer. Although God's people are called beloved for his name's sake (2 Bar. 21.21), in context it is clear that they are somewhat superior to the surrounding types. God chose Abraham (2 Esd. 3.13ff.) and raised up David (3.23); but perhaps the contextual description of the sinfulness of the people at that time is meant to establish a black-versus-white contrast. Enoch was chosen of all men to be the writer of all creation (2 En. 64.5; cf. 65.11f.); but there can be no doubt that the total representation of the man suggests he deserved the honour. The same holds true for God's choice of Abraham (Apoc. Ab. ii,10). In a few instances the mention of election functions as the basis of a plea to God to remember his covenant promises to the fathers (e.g. Ass. Mos. 4.1ff.; Ps. Sol. 9.16-19; 17.5-28; cf. 7.8), and here the worth of the fathers is not brought up; but neither is God's grace. The overwhelming evidence is accurately summarised by G. Schrenk, who points out that election is now 'in terms of merit, namely, that the people is chosen because none is more worthy.'[41]

A few passages restrict the number of the elect so as to exclude some Israelites. In the Psalms of Solomon the pious are a smaller group than the whole nation. In 2 Baruch 40.2, the Messiah protects only a remnant of the people, viz. those left alive. (Among the passages with this narrowing tendency, cf. Jub. 1.29; 1 En. 51.1f.; Sib. Or. iii,69; Test. Mos. 1.12f.; 5.1ff.) The sinners of Israel are progressively being excluded, the more so since, conceptually speaking, the difference between being righteous and being elect is scarcely discernible. The fact that different parties tend to define who is and who is not righteous in different ways leads to certain sectarian limitations on election found at Qumran (infra).

On the other hand, some apocalyptic thought tends toward

universalism. Unfortunately, discussion of 'universalism' is semantically problematic.

> Universalism in religion may mean either that the dominion and power of the deity are world-wide, or that his favour and self-revelation are world-wide. The first meaning involves the essence and nature of the deity; the second involves his manifestation among men. Since monotheism asserts that there is but one creator and ruler of the universe, it is perforce universalistic in the first sense. But there is no inner necessity that compels it to distribute the favour of the one God equally among all men. That the God creates and governs all does not of itself imply that all are equal in his sight. Nothing prohibits his choosing a particular group among men as his elect. Indeed the monotheistic religions have always assumed that he does just that. This idea circumscribes the realm in which God's favour is manifested without, however, affecting the universality of his dominion.[42]

There are other ambiguities. In apocalyptic, the more liberal emphasis is generally the older (e.g. 1 En. 10.21; cf. Sib. Or. III, 757-61); but the Testaments of the Twelve Patriarchs seems to be an exception (T. Levi 4.4; T. Zeb. 9.8 (v.1.); T. Naph. 8.4; T. Ash. 7.3). Other questions must be asked. Do the references to 'all the Gentiles' and 'all nations' mean 'all Gentiles without exception' or 'all Gentiles without distinction'? How is universalism (however understood) related to eschatology? What part, if any, does a 'mission' outlook play in early apocalyptic thinking?[43]

Above all, the wide diversity of views within the literature must be given full weight. As D. S. Russell points out, the perspective ranges from the almost gleeful assignation of all but the elite of Israel to hell fire, to liberal universalism.[44] Jubilees, 2 Enoch, 2 Esdras and many isolated texts in other books (e.g. 1 En. 91.9; 2 Bar. 82.3-9; Test. Mos. 10.7-10), offer no hope for the Gentiles. In 1 Enoch 90.20-36, some nations submit to Israel and partake of the final blessings; while in 2 Baruch 72.2ff., nations are spared selectively on the basis of their attitude toward Israel. Further, even when a more liberal attitude is upheld, Israel remains in centre stage. In the Sibylline Oracles, for example, salvation is extended beyond Israel, 'without thereby the superiority of God's people being violated'.[45] Apocalyptic becomes harsher with time; but M.-J. Lagrange catches the spirit of much of it: 'Far from renouncing the passionate nationalism of Israel, it [apocalyptic] pushed it to the point of exasperation, even while simultaneously remaining under higher aspirations. The righteous will be well rewarded as righteous, and the sinners punished for their evil: but it goes without saying that the righteous are the true Israel.'[46]

Perhaps the most important observation about apocalyptic universalism, from the point of view of this study, concerns the basis of Gentile salvation whenever such salvation is envisaged. However many Gentiles are saved, not only are they not called 'elect', they are accepted solely on the basis of their own goodness—sometimes measured in terms of their attitude toward Israel. This is consistent with merit theology; and it is on this theme that a little more attention must now be focused.

Glorification of the law is a dominant motif of Jewish apocalyptic (e.g. 2 Bar. 15.5; 48.2; 77.16; 2 Esdr. 9.29-37). The law is eternally valid, manifest in time (Jub. 2.18ff., 31ff.). People perish for ignoring the law (Jub. 1.10ff.). Levi is given the 'sovereignty' among his brethren because he is to know the law of God (T. Reub. 15.4). This stress on law constitutes the necessary backdrop to the explicit merit theology. Salvation and blessing are specifically and repeatedly attributed to accumulated merits (e.g. Jub. 30.19ff.; 1 En. 1.8; 38.4; Frag. Bk. Noah 108.7ff.; T. Naph. 8.5; T. Gad 5.9-11; Ps. Sol. 9.8). The righteous are saved by their works (2 Bar. 51.7; 67.6), and prayers are answered on the same ground (2 Bar. 63.3,5; 85.2). The righteous constantly examine themselves; and as for sins of ignorance, atonement may be secured by such procedures as fasting (Ps. Sol. 3.8f.). Chastening also blots out sin (Ps. Sol. 13.8f.). Even Adam will be raised up to life again if subsequent to the fall he keeps himself from all sin (Apoc. Mos. 28.3f.). Now it is no more a question of Jacob's having been chosen before his birth; rather, Abraham, still alive, witnesses the deeds of both Jacob and Esau and perceives that God will choose Jacob (Jub. 19.12ff.; cf. 22.10).

More sophisticated characteristics of merit theology also appear. The Jews receive mercy on account of the patriarchs, Abraham and Isaac and Jacob (T. Levi 15.4). The sinlessness of the fathers functions elsewhere as an encouragement to endure suffering and death rather than succumb to sin

(Test. Mos. 9.3f.). The works of evil and the works of righteousness are balanced against each other in the judgment of Zion (2 Bar. 14.7). The good works of the righteous not only give confidence at death (2 Bar. 14.12f.), but serve as a tower of strength to the people (2.2), and remain a lasting ground of merit (14.7; 84.10). Indeed, 3 Baruch 11.9 (later than our period) pictures the vessel where the merits of the righteous are stored. Inevitably, a case arises where a soul comes to judgment freighted down with equal merits and demerits (Test. Ab. §§12-14(A)). The only hope for that soul, which must await decision, is the merit (prayers) of others.

There are, it is true, some voices within the Jewish apocalyptic tradition which do not quite fit into this pattern, even if those who point this out overstate the differences. For example, R. H. Charles says that the Testament of Moses (cf. especially 12.3-13) in its concepts of righteousness and grace is closer to the Old Testament than to the rabbis. God's call 'alike of the individual as of the nation was a matter of grace, and the covenant relation between God and Israel was based on divine grace and not on human merit.'[47] It is necessary to cite the entire relevant passage:

(12.3) Joshua, do not despise thyself, but set thy mind at ease, and hearken to my words. (4) All the nations which are in the earth hath God created and us, He hath foreseen them and us from the beginning of the creation of the earth unto the end of the age, and nothing has been neglected by him even to the least thing, but all things He hath foreseen and caused all to come forth [*textual uncertainty*]. (5) [Yea] all things which are to be in this earth the Lord hath foreseen and lo! they are brought forward [into the light. ... (6) The Lord] hath on their behalf appointed me to [pray] for their sins and [make intercession] for them. (7) For not for any virtue or strength of mine, but of His good pleasure have His compassion and longsuffering fallen to my lot. (8) For I say unto you, Joshua: it is not on account of the godliness of this people that thou shalt root out the nations. (9) The lights of the heaven, the foundations of the earth have been made and approved by God and are under the signet ring of His right hand. (10) Those, therefore, who do and fulfill the commandments of God shall increase and be prospered: (11) But those who sin and set at nought the commandments shall be without the blessings before mentioned, and they shall be punished with many torments by the nations. (12) But wholly to root out and destroy them is not permitted. (13) For God will go forth who has foreseen all things for ever, and His covenant has been established and by the oath which ... [text ends].[48]

Granted that Charles' translation is accurate,[49] his conclusion that God's call is 'a matter of grace' appears extravagant. There are several mitigating factors: (1) The Testament of Moses purports to retell the events of Deuteronomy 31-4, and so it is not surprising if some of the attitudes of Deuteronomy are reflected in this book. More surprising is the discovery of how blurred the detail of the reflection really is. (2) The grace of God is nowhere explicitly spelled out in these verses. (3) It is true that neither the election of Moses (v.7) nor the promise of victory to the nations (v.8) are attributable to the godliness and worth of Moses and the people respectively, and indeed this is atypical of Jewish apocalyptic; but the root cause in both cases has more to do with God's sweeping determination of events (vv.4f. and 9 respectively) than with sovereign, electing *grace*. (4) The same sort of determination offers a whitewashing rationale for Israel's failure to defeat all the pagan nations (v.12). (5) The way God has structured the world, merit theology still determines who is blessed and who is punished (vv.9-11). (6) Elsewhere in the book, there is the explicit statement that the forefathers did not tempt God so as to transgress his commands (9.3f.). (7) The election of Moses may possibly be disconnected from his worth in this passage in order to agree with the doctrine of Moses' pre-existence (1.14). (8) In v. 8 it is not so much the election of Israel that is in view as Israel's appointment to the task of annihilating the Canaanites.

In a similar fashion, G. Schrenk goes much too far when he affirms that the function of the merciful righteousness of God in 2 Esdras 8.36 'approximates closely to the usage of Paul.'[50] 2 Esdras 8.36 is placed on the praying lips of pessimistic Ezra. The divine reply (8.37-40), however, sets aside this part of Ezra's prayer. God will not concern himself with the creation of those who have sinned, nor with their death, judgment, and perdition. He will rejoice rather over the creation of the righteous. This is consistent with the idea found elsewhere, to the effect that if many have sinned, many others have been righteous (2 Bar. 21.11).

There is one kind of genuine exception which cannot be gainsaid. Unlike the bulk of Jewish apocalyptic literature, 2 Enoch 53.1 and 2 Esdras 7.102-15 come out *against* the belief that others can effectively pray for us when we sin.[51] There is no helper for us when we sin, and no repentance after death (62.2). But this exception remains within the borders of a full-blown merit theology. There are other inconsistencies. A few texts suggest that man's status in the after-life, or in the eschaton, is pre-determined (e.g. 1 En. 41.8; Ps. Sol. 5.6; 2 En. 49.2). Most, however, insist it depends on man's own righteousness (e.g. 1 En. 41.1, 5; 43.2; 61.8; 2 Bar. 54.15, 19; cf. 3 Bar. 11.9; 12.4f.; 15.2f.).

To sum up: freedom of the human will is taught in the most unequivocal fashion; but so also is the divine determining. This study has therefore validated the conclusions of several scholars who have stressed the co-existence of both themes in apocalyptic. Yet these twin poles of the Old Testament tension are being forced apart. History is more determined than ever; but at the same time the freedom of the human will is becoming so absolute it is difficult to conceive how logical contradiction can be avoided. Moreover, perhaps because of the eschatological dualism, there is a reduction in the sense of the immediate presence of God.

But however great the tension between divine sovereignty and human responsibility in Jewish apocalyptic literature, there is one aspect of that tension which has been virtually eliminated, viz. election. The combined forces of the drumming merit theology and the apocalyptic brand of eschatological dualism have snuffed out the tension in this area. The former makes man earn his own salvation; the latter makes the present evil world less the sphere of God's saving activity than a platform for probationary examination.

CHAPTER SEVEN

THE DEAD SEA SCROLLS

Having become accustomed to the emphasis on free will in Jewish apocalyptic, it is natural to try to determine the attitude of the covenanters to such a doctrine; and here there are some surprises. At first glance the Dead Sea Scrolls seem to repeat the apocalyptic pattern. They hold that the patriarchs were blessed because of their choices. Abraham did not choose his own will (lit. he did not choose the will of his own spirit, CD 4.2), and, having kept God's commandments, he handed them on to Isaac and Jacob, who also kept them and were recorded as friends of God (CD 4.3). Although God chooses the sons of Zadok (1QSb 3.23), they are credited with walking in the way God chose (3.24f.). Members of the community are exhorted to choose what God approves, shunning the evil 'inclination' (CD 3.1f.; cf. 1QS 1.3f.). The explicit purpose for the writing of 1QS is that the saints may seek God (1.1). Indeed, at the time of the affliction, the prince of the congregation will establish God's holy law with those who seek him (1QSb 5.23). There is need for perseverance: only the ones who hold fast to God are (heading) for the life of eternity (CD 5.6; cf. 1QH 2.21f.; 14.25f.; 15.10). Conversely, the reason for the fall of the mighty men of old was that they did their own will and did not keep the commandments of their Maker (CD 3.7; 4.5, 7, 9f.; 4QF1 1.17). Each chose the stubbornness of his heart (CD 9.18), for sinners act high-handedly against revealed things (1QS 5.11f.).

Men within the community are chosen by other community members (often priests) for certain posts (1QSa 1.16, 20). In the eschatological war, the fighting men will be chosen (1QM 2.7); but on the other hand, only those who are freely willing of heart to fight are considered eligible (1QM 10.5f.). Indeed, this 'willingness of heart' is required of all who wish to join the community[1] (e.g. 1QS 1.8, 11; 5.1, 6, 8; 6.13).[2] To belong to the covenant community, the candidate 'must not only be a member of the chosen people; a free act of choice is also necessary'.[3]

Provisions for the excommunication of backsliding members entail similar responsibilities (1QS 7.22-5).

But a closer inspection reveals that the DSS lay no stress on free will in any formulated sense. Within that context, it is difficult to see how any of the above expressions differ very greatly from Old Testament parallels. Before too hastily assuming that merit theology is operating here, broader aspects of the sovereignty-responsibility tension must be examined.

Some of the community's rigid code of law is a reiteration of Mosaic law; but some of it is more strict (especially in CD), and not a little flows from the fact that the community is, after all, a religious hermitage where asceticism and a rigid ranking system prevail (cf. 1QS 5-9). Perhaps the stringency of Qumran rules and the inherent difficulty in keeping them all enhance the theme of God's judgment. God is seen to act as the sovereign Judge not only in history (CD 1.9-17; 2.4; 4QDibHam 5.3ff.) but especially in the eschatological judgment to come (e.g. CD 9.2f. (A & B); 1QS 2.4ff.; 1QH 4.18-21; and the very essence of 1QM). Indeed, divine judgment in the past is the paradigm of the final judgment (1QM 11.9f.) when the living God will render to each man his reward (1QS 10.18) and destroy from the earth all idolatrous and wicked men (1QpHab 12.2-4 (on 2.19f.)).

Yet, surprisingly, this rigid legal code produces little legalistic self-righteousness. Especially in *Hodayoth* there is constant emphasis on the fact that men are but creatures of clay (1QH 4.29ff.; 10.4-7; 11.3ff.; etc.). Sometimes this is explicitly related to the inability of such creatures to understand God's ways (7.32f.; 15.21), sometimes as a starting point for sheer praise (11.3ff.; 12.27ff.), and not infrequently as a formula summing up human sinfulness (1QH 1.22f.; 3.23f.; 12.27-32). This acknowledgement of profound guilt is not restricted to the 'creature of clay' sayings. Within *Hodayoth,*'[it]is a view that is consistently maintained and that is more pessimistic than one usually encounters in Hebrew-Jewish writings'.[4] Indeed, it may be argued that this perspective permeates all of the Qumran scrolls. The goodness of God and the sinfulness of man are contrasted more than once (1QS 10.23f.; 1QH 1.6, 26f.; 17.18ff.). Frequently the sinfulness of man, both generally and personally, is bemoaned, often in the richest language (e.g. CD 1.6; 1QS 11.9-11; 1QH 1.25f.; 4.33-6; 5.5f.; 12.19;

4QDibHam 2.15; 5.3ff.). Praise erupts from a Qumran psalmist because he has not been judged according to his guilt, nor been abandoned despite the intentions of his *yṣr*; rather, he has been saved from the pit (1QH 5.5f.). Those who enter the Qumran community begin by confessing their sins (1QS 1.24f.). Their God is the One wealthy in forgiveness to pardon those who repent (CD 1.6f.; 2.3; 9.50-54(в); 1QS 11.12ff.; 1QH 14.24). Generally, then, the exclusiveness of the sect and its belief in election (on which see *infra*) do not lead to pride, because 'an acute sense of sinfulness'[5] contributes an important part to its total theological make-up.

Concomitant with this consciousness of sin is a remarkable awareness of the need for and sufficiency of the grace of God (e.g. 1QS 11.12; 1QH 4.30-32, 37-40; 7.16ff.; 12.11f.; 18.19f.; 1QM 11.4): the covenanters have not been treated according to their works but according to the divine mercies. Elsewhere God is praised for opening his servant's heart to knowledge (1QS 11.15f.), for engraving the law on the heart (1QH 4.10). The Most High is addressed by the writer of 1QS 10.12 as 'Author of my goodness' as well as 'Fountain of knowledge' and 'Source of holiness'. God remembered his covenant and raised up from Aaron men of understanding and made them hearken (CD 8.3f.). Holy things are known only because God desires it (1QH 1.8, 21; 7.26; 11.9f.); and even then the covenanters have listened only by the spirit which God has given them (1QH 12.11f.). It is God who is the source of wisdom, righteousness, justification (1QS 11.7f.; 1QH 4; 16.11), enabling the Qumran psalmist, like his canonical counterpart, to acknowledge that God set his feet on a rock (1QH 4.3f.). The unknown psalmist praises God for not casting his 'lot' in the congregation of vanity, but instead giving him grace and forgiveness (1QH 7.34f.). After thus sparing his elect, it is still God who delivers them from sinning against him (4QDibHam 2.16). The same positive divine ultimacy is recognised in the testimonies of privilege (1QH 2.9, 13; 8.16) as in the invocations (1QS 2.2-4; 1QSb 4.27); and the war standards (1QM 3f.) show that the eschatological conflict is the Lord's (1QM 11.1, 5) who teaches the hands of his people to war (1QM 14.6).

Qumran's heavy stress on election simply completes this pattern. The covenanters are God's elect, God's chosen ones

(1QS 11.7f.; 1QpHab 9.9-12 (on 2.8b)). In one place the Qumran exegetes manage to invest the Scriptures with the precise opposite of their original import in order to find a reference to the elect (4QpPs 37.3:4f. (on 37.20)). The purifying of the covenanters God has undertaken for himself (4QDibHam 6.2-4). Just as God chose the covenanters (1QSb 1.3), placing their lives in the bundle of life (1QS 2.20f.), in the branches of the holy community (1QH 7.10),[6] so also he chose the priests, the sons of Zadok (CD 6.2; 1QSb 3.23). Like Jeremiah (1.4) the elect are known from conception (1QH 9.29f.); indeed they were created to hearken to God's covenant. Who is like God, and who is like the people Israel whom he has chosen (1QM 10.8f.)?

Yet not all of racial Israel has really been elected. History has shown that in every period of apostasy God has left himself a remnant, raised up men to know his Holy Spirit (CD 2.9f.); and he will certainly do this again in the future, raising up survivors and establishing them in his community, made up of all who share this common 'lot' (1QH 6.8-13). As G. Schrenk points out, especially in the War Scroll is election specifically narrowed to the remnant (e.g. 1QM 12.1; 13.7-10; 14.8-10).[7] There is thus both a clear individualising of election (out of Israel) and an integrating of it (into the community). The former phenomenon occurs in the Old Testament; the latter, only in an incipient way. Perhaps the Qumran view of election emerged in part out of historical necessity: the Qumran covenanters grew numerically, not by the birth of members into the community, but by personal commitment; and so election could not be restricted to a divine choice of the race, but necessarily became individualised. In any case, *Hodayoth* goes on to insist in personal terms that God's elect are divinely preserved (1QH 2.31, 35f.; 5.5; 7.6f.; 9.32; cf. 1QM 14.8-11).[8]

It appears, then, that despite some exceptions which do indeed betray merit theology (notably 1QS 3.6ff.; 9.3ff.; 1QpHab 5.4-6; 8.1-3; 4QDibHam 6.4-13), the trend in the DSS is toward a firm belief in sovereign, gracious election, even if such belief brings the sovereignty-responsibility tension back into the soteriological arena.[9]

Positive ultimacy and gracious election are not the only elements of predestinarian thought in the DSS. Reprobation is likewise taught. Passively, God did not choose certain men from the beginning of the world (CD 2.6f.). Actively, just as God created Belial for the pit (1QM 13.11), so he created the wicked for wrath, to be a sign and a wonder for all eternity (1QH 15.17f.) It is within this framework that men choose wickedness and are responsible creatures (1QH 15.18f.). These wicked men were not only created for the [end-times of] God's [wr]ath, but are sanctified for the day of slaughter (1QM 15.14-19). Small wonder that the Teacher is not even to instruct the men of the pit (1QS 9.14-17). If after the eschatological struggle any remnant of the nations remains, it is only to do homage to Israel and to Israel's God (1QM 11.15). In fact, the War Scroll assures us that no remnant will be left to the Kittim (1QM 1.6), which comes as no surprise when God's people wave standards on which are the words, 'Annihilation by God of all nations of vanity' (1QM 4.12). In the Temple, no *gr* (proselyte?) will enter, but only God's holy ones (4QF1 1.4). The Qumran covenanters are not open to universalism.[10]

Implicit in such teaching is the recognition that God's ultimacy is not merely positive, it embraces the negative as well. Just as God's goodness is the source of his forgiveness, so his wrath stands behind all chastisement (1QH 11.8f.). Righteousness does not come from man; but more, *every yṣr* is in God's hand (1QH 15.12-14). The Most High, the Great God, the King of all worlds and Ruler of the sons of heaven, is not only God of Israel, but Governor of the creation, the Lord of history, the incomparably Wise and Powerful (1QapGen 2.4f.; 1QM 10.8-15; 11.1-4; 1QS 11.17-19; 1QH 10.8ff.). Without God's will, nothing exists (1QH 10.2), and he has done all for himself (1QH 18.21f.). God knows all things (CD 2.8), and therefore his prophets predict accurately (e.g. CD 6.9ff.— whether or not we think Isaiah's words are well served by the Zadokite interpretation; and in 1QM, the progress of the eschatological war is completely determined). God is eternal and so his ways are determined (1QH 7.31f.). There is repeated emphasis on the fact that the times and cycles of years are numbered, fixed, appointed by the sovereign God (1QH 1.24f.; 1QM 1.10; 14.4f.; 17.5; 1QpHab 7.13). An apparently astrological fragment from Cave 4 confirms the conclusion that predestination/determinism was profoundly believed by the Qumran covenanters.[11] Yet, lest God's activity behind good and evil be thought symmetrical, 1QH 4.12f. makes it clear the fixedness of his ways enables him to despise Belial's schemes.

As in the case of apocalyptic, Qumran eschatology is significantly related to the way divine sovereignty is understood. Whatever other features make up the eschatology of the scrolls, the most unavoidable theme is the conviction that the end is near and the covenanters are living in the last days. The covenanters are still living under the dominion of Belial during the period of the mysteries of malevolence (1QM 14.8-10),— even if there are some elements of realised eschatology in the DSS[12]—but God has preserved his elect and not permitted them to stray from his covenant. In other words, as in apocalyptic, God's sovereignty, conceived as his 'ultimacy', is preserved so that the one true God always remains in control; but his sovereignty, conceived as the consummation of his saving activity on behalf of his people (cf. 1QS 4.25), is still to come.

It is within the context of a study like the preceding that the 'Two Spirits' doctrine of Qumran is best understood. Although echoes of this doctrine are scattered here and there in the scrolls (e.g. 1QS 9.14f.(?); 1QH 14.11f.; 4Q 'Amram), the crucial passage is 1QS 3.13-4.26, and it remains very difficult to interpret. There are two not-uncommon interpretations which do justice neither to the passage itself, nor to the corpus of the DSS:

(i) It is possible to oversimplify and render rigid the accent on predestination. This is accomplished by pointing out, correctly, that God is represented in 1QS 3.13-4.26 as the Creator of both sides of the dualistic structure, and then arguing that the two sides, light and darkness, are virtually mutually exclusive. Every man is either a son of light or a son of darkness. In this debate 1QS 3.19 is crucial. Vermes translates: 'Those born of truth spring from a fountain of light, but those born of falsehood spring from a source of darkness.'[13] Burrows: 'In the abode of light are the origins of truth, and from the source of darkness are the origins of error.'[14] Leaney: 'In a dwelling of light are the generations of truth and from a well of darkness come the generations of perversity.'[15] The problematical term is twldwt. If the translation offered by Vermes is correct, the cleavage between the sons of light and the sons of darkness is absolute, so much so as to allow no struggle within the individual (although Vermes does allow it). But if the operative word means something like family/class/division/ generation, then there is no necessary contextual contradiction. (Burrows's effort to make the meaning impersonal is not convincing.) The context informs us that even the sons of light suffer from some admixture of error to be purged out at the renewal (4.25; cf. 3.21f., where the angel of darkness leads even the children of *righteousness* astray). Although each man's inheritance (*sc.* of the spirit) governs the way he walks, the two spirits struggle within him. That God should thus stand behind both good and evil entails some mystery (3.23; 4.18); but this representation of Deity does not make him aloof and transcendent, for, on the positive side, he actively takes the part of the angel of truth in succouring the sons of light, and negatively, he loathes evil ways (3.24-4.1; cf. 1QH 6.20f.; 7.3f., where God commands the evil men to turn from their ways). This pattern is much closer to Old Testament thought than is other contemporary Jewish literature. It appears, then, that 1QS 3.13-4.26 divides mankind into two lots by an eternal divine decree, and 'the whole conception is a corollary of God's absolute sovereignty and man's complete dependence upon him.'[16] However, there is no oversimplified division.[17] The elect still struggle; and God is portrayed *both* as transcendent Creator over all *and* as the Sovereign who sides with his angels of truth and loathes evil. This twofold conception of God is very strong, and the final synthesis awaits the new creation (4.25).

(ii) Some scholars continue to argue that Qumran texts in general, and 1QS 3.13-4.26 in particular, are virtually devoid of predestinatory thought. This remarkable conclusion is arrived at by one of two methods. The first begins by outlining all the elements in the DSS which support notions of human freedom and responsibility, and ends by concluding that no doctrine of predestination is really compatible with all this evidence—all without seriously wrestling with the passages which argue *for* predestination.[18] This is methodologically unacceptable. The second procedure is more subtle. It argues persuasively that the word 'spirit' is used in the psychological sense of 'impulse', rather than with cosmological meaning.[19] The two spirits of Qumran are then likened to the two 'inclinations' of the rabbis.[20] The dualism of 1QS 3.13ff. is then dismissed as merely ethical, with some such twentieth-century generalisation as: 'IQ *Serek* III, 15-17 refers to the immutability of the laws of nature.

and not to the predestination of the individual to sin, righteousness, damnation or salvation.'[21] But more recently, there have been two excellent defences of the majority position.[22] The dualism of Qumran *is* cosmological, but not absolutely so since God is the creator of all. It is also ethical and predestinarian, even though the cosmic dimensions of the struggle intrude into the heart of man (4.23). The passage 'presents a modified cosmic dualism, under which is a subordinate ethical dualism, and whose most conspicuous characteristic is the light-darkness paradigm, and most pervasive feature is the eschatological dimension.'[23] The dualism is a relative, ethico-cosmic dualism:[24] relative, because it is limited to history, while monism stands over all and is absolute before history and at the end; ethical, in the sense that it governs during the period of its regency.

Whether or not 1QS 3.13-4.26 'exerted a great influence' upon other Qumran passages, as A. R. C. Leaney suggests,[25] it is clear that this passage fits into the whole pattern of the sovereignty-responsibility tension which permeates this literature. G. Maier argues, with some plausibility, that 1QS 3.13ff. was an attempted theodicy to solve the problem of evil; but, as he rightly observes, 'the introduction of the teaching about two opposed spirits does not explain God's sovereignty *(Allwirksamkeit)*, but only confirms it.'[26]

The question of function is abused by A. Marx. He points out that the most predestinatory comments in the DSS emerge either in a context which seeks to explain why the covenanters differ from others—it is by God's sovereign grace—or in hymns of praise, where one is likely to find extravagant descriptions of God's activity. This observation by itself is correct; but on this basis he wants to write off the predestination of the DSS.[27] His argument will not stand up. The apocalyptists thought they were different, too, but attributed the difference largely to their own merit. And hymns must not be divorced from doctrine, because they are often the most innocent expression of it (cf. Phil. 2.6ff.).

There is no doubt that the various DSS reflect slightly different positions on the sovereignty-responsibility tension. CD, for example, attenuates both the predestination and the *sola gratia* of 1QS and 1QH. Yet when all is said and done, Qumran's view of the tension between divine sovereignty and human responsibility 'testifies to the virtual impossibility of being wholly deterministic or wholly voluntaristic in both theory and practice.'[28]

What is more important for the present study is the fact that the hitherto unbroken trend of development from the Old Testament to the Fourth Gospel has now been broken. It would have been very convenient to find in the Qumran covenanters the same pattern as in Jewish apocalyptic, the more so since the covenanters are often thought to be a more or less apocalyptic group. However, in this area they stand quite apart from contemporary theological developments in Jewish faith. With few exceptions among the Scrolls, merit theology is decisively rejected in favour of a restored emphasis on divine grace. This brings the sovereignty-responsibility tension back into the arena of soteriological predestination. At the same time the exclusiveness of the sect tends to squeeze out all possibility of hope for those who reject its theology: *extra ecclesiam nulla salus.*

Yet on second thought, this pattern at Qumran should not be unexpected. Theological development is seldom simply linear, and 'discoveries' of linear progression are too easily manufactured by a selective handling of the evidence. The covenanters constituted a disciplined, monastic sect, the sort of group that very easily sloughs off more recent traditions and seeks to return to the pristine source of inspiration. Hence they clung fast to the written law and would have none of the oral.[29] Even their asceticism might be considered a throwback to the prophetic spirit.[30] 'The Essenes' *(sic)* teaching on God, the world, and Man do not differ substantially from the Old Testament doctrine; they merely develop it.'[31] They are, perhaps, somewhat more predestinarian than much of the Old Testament, at least in so far as they have introduced quasi-ontological categories into their relative dualism; but if the result does not form an entirely consistent picture, it must be remembered that 'the people at Qumran were neither philosophers nor systematicians, but practitioners of a practical asceticism.'[32]

CHAPTER EIGHT

THE TARGUMS AND RABBINIC LITERATURE

The more I read the targums and rabbinic literature, not to mention the vast amount of secondary material they have called into being, the more bifurcated my desires become. On the one hand, I hesitate to write anything at all on the' subject, as it is not only vast, but a veritable minefield. On the other hand, I want to write at length, a book at least, and not a mere chapter on a subject which properly demands much more.

The problem is compounded by the lack of scholarly consensus. E. P. Sanders, in his recent magisterial work *Paul and Palestinian Judaism*,[1] has brought the debate into the open, and it is now almost impossible to write anything about rabbinic views on election, grace, merit, covenant, free will, and law, without interacting with him directly.

Bound as I am to the limitations of one short chapter, I propose to do three things. First, I intend to outline the work of Sanders, indicate something of its great strengths, and express a few important reservations. This section will make minimal use of the primary material. Second, I shall focus attention on the manner in which the twelve Old Testament texts, considered in the second chapter of this study, are handled in the targums and by some of the rabbis. Third, I shall sketch in my present understanding of the broad outlines of rabbinic thought in the relevant areas, making constant reference to the sources.

Before doing any of these things, something must be said about the sources themselves. The rabbinic material begins with the Mishnah, codified in written form about AD 200, but stretches into late *midrashim* and *haggadah* from the medieval period. Just how much of this is relevant to the first century? Rabbinic traditions about the Pharisees are extremely difficult in their own right, even though there are now several works of major importance dealing with this issue.[2] No doubt many traditions attributed to the Tannaim (roughly AD 70-220) and

Amoraim (roughly AD 220-350) spring from an earlier period. Nevertheless Judaism traversed two traumatic hurdles before such early traditions were written down; and it is difficult to believe that these hurdles had no effect on Judaism's inner character. The first hurdle was the destruction of AD 70, coupled with the devastations and Roman decrees associated with the crushing of the Bar-Kochba revolt (AD 132-135). The political, economic, and religious implications of these defeats must not be underestimated.[3] The second hurdle was scarcely less severe, viz. the rising influence of Christianity. Judaism responded with more than the *Birkat haMinim*: indeed, there is a sense in which rabbinic Judaism may be interpreted, at least in part, as a 'counter-reformation'. Just as it is anachronistic to read post-Tridentine Roman Catholicism back into pre-Luther Catholicism, so also it may be anachronistic to read post-Jabneh Judaism back into Pharisaism. Indeed, I would go so far as to say that if rabbinic Judaism and first century Pharisaism are pages. To grant the historical distinction between Pharisaism despite the many positive perspectives on Pharisaism within its pages. To grant the historical distinction between Pharisarism and rabbinic Judaism is to enable the student to read both the New Testament and the rabbis with greater sympathy and clearer understanding than is the case otherwise.

Two other factors must be borne in mind by those who wish to speak of 'rabbinic theology'. First of all, rabbinic Judaism is characterised by many discussions which are not resolved into an 'orthodox' position. There is a rich diversity of viewpoints which makes synthesis of the rabbinic material into one 'theology' not only impossible but forced and wrong-headed. Second, the rabbinic material, whether *halakah, haggadah,* expository *midrash*, or whatever, is primarily concerned with defining and applying the Hebrew Scriptures, especially Torah. There is little prayer, not much psalmic material, little that is overtly hortatory, no 'epistles', no apocalyptic monograph, no 'prophecy'. But to point this out is not necessarily to say that rabbinic Judaism was interested exclusively in the fine points of legal interpretation and application. Rather, it is to say that the rabbinic material must be accepted on its own terms, and that it is precarious to compare, without serious reflection, the material that emerges from this kind of literature with material arising from literature of quite another sort.

The dating and provenance of the targums is not less difficult. Targumic 'orthodoxy' as represented by the Kahle school holds that the Palestinian Targum (PT) is older than Onkelos, and probably pre-christian. Neofiti 1 is usually seen as the most ancient exemplar of the PT. Yet not only has the age of Neofiti 1 been questioned,[4] but the uniqueness and age of PT has been challenged.[5] G. J. Cowling goes so far as to suggest that it is a third century translation of a *Greek* document.[6] But with the discovery of targums at Qumran, such a reaction against the exuberances of Diez-Macho and McNamara seems somewhat excessive.

In the present chapter, then, I am not attempting to estimate how far the targumic and rabbinic traditions with which I deal may reflect first century belief. Nevertheless, in the rabbinic literature I have generally (but not exclusively) restricted myself to Tannaitic and Amoraic sources; for my aim is to sketch in a religious movement, at least in so far as it impinges on the sovereignty-responsibility tension. As this is done, some of the patterns of Jewish religion and worship in the period 200 BC to AD 200 become a little more complete.

THE WORK OF E. P. SANDERS

E. P. Sanders's book is a long, powerfully argued attack on one of the most deeply entrenched positions of much New Testament scholarship. To put his position briefly, he argues that Palestinian Judaism before AD 70 adopts a stance he designates as 'covenantal nomism'. Election of the Jews *qua* race is by grace. The works required do not secure salvation for any individual Jew, but are designed to keep him within the bounds of the elect covenant community. Even such works, however, are not measured on a simple commercial basis, good points versus bad points. Rather, God's mercy wins out, while talk of rewards and punishments guarantees that God's justice is preserved intact so his grace is not rendered arbitrary. On this reading of first century Judaism, there is no doctrine of supererogation; and even many of the rabbinic references to 'merits' or to 'the merits of the fathers' are better explained in a different way. Judaism was not a system of mere externals, a morose religion without inner religious experience and without joy. Rather, it was a religion of 'covenantal nomism', a religion which balanced grace and works, a religion whose covenant, granted and guaranteed by divine grace, provided for and prescribed a system of works and even a system for atonement when there was default.

To present his case, Sanders first of all outlines and criticises the writings of those whose position he is attacking, in particular Weber, Bousset, Thackeray, Billerbeck and Bultmann. His first major section (up to p. 238) focuses on the rabbinic literature, almost exclusively the Tannaitic sources. He then devotes about one hundred pages to the Dead Sea Scrolls, and another section to brief consideration of Ben Sirach, 1 Enoch, Jubilees, the Psalms of Solomon and 2 Esdras (=4 Ezra). He concludes his study of this literature by insisting that covenantal nomism was the common pattern of first century religion, 2 Esdras being the only notable exception to this pattern.

From p. 429 to p. 523, Sanders examines Paul and asks how it is that Paul seems to misunderstand first century Judaism. His reply is that Paul did not approach Judaism by working out an antithetical relationship between law and grace, and then proceed to the exclusive sufficiency of Christ; rather, he began with the exclusive sufficiency of Christ and worked back to the antithesis between law and grace. Sanders winds up the volume by including a summary of some recent German discussion, written by M. T. Brauch, and then by providing his own pointed conclusion.

This major work is the product of close study and wide reading. Besides the over-arching arguments, it is laced with valuable insights and provocative asides. With respect to the sovereignty-responsibility tension and rabbinic Judaism, its strong points include at least the following:

(i) Over against the extreme views of the Bousset/Bultmann line regarding merits, Sanders is basically correct. There is no unambiguous evidence to support a doctrine of supererogation in the Tannaitic period. When 'the merits of the fathers' are appealed to, the expression may mean no more than 'by virtue of the fathers', referring to the promises God himself made with them. Even where merits play a more prominent role in the sources, there is no simple weighing of merits and demerits in order to determine whether an individual is to be 'saved' or not; for most of the merit language refers to those already within the covenant, and in any case God's mercy regularly transcends whatever is achieved by merit. (See especially pp. 93, 128ff., 140ff., 185ff., 197.)

(ii) In this context, Sanders is right to point out that the absolute antithesis between grace and works is not found in rabbinic thought of the Tannaitic period, and it is anachronistic to read it into the material.

(iii) We need to be reminded that the rabbis found some sense of the presence of God and real joy in studying and applying Torah. They did not see their work as joyless, externalised, almost meaningless discipline, but as the proper response to the demands of their covenant relationship with God. (See especially pp. 83f., 212ff.)

(iv) The covenant provided the means for atonement. Before the fall of the Temple, the Torah stipulations concerning sacrifice could be minutely obeyed, and were regarded as efficacious because God had commanded that they be efficacious. After the fall of the Temple (which, after all, God had allowed), then other things were accepted as of atoning value: works, suffering, obedience, death. But these, too, were covenantal stipulations, and therefore within the covenant of grace. Very rarely is it clear that repentance was regarded as a meritorious work. (See especially pp. 147ff., 176ff.)

(v) Sanders repeatedly emphasises, in telling ways, the non-systematic nature of rabbinic literature. The Tannaitic rabbis are concerned to interpret and apply the biblical passages with which they deal; and within the framework of their own hermeneutical procedures they utilise relentless logic. Nevertheless they are not very often concerned with synthesising all of their own interpretations into a systematic theology. (See especially pp. 74, 76ff., 90, 141, 161.)

(vi) As an application of the last point, it is helpful to be reminded that, on the one hand the rabbis envisaged their emphasis on merits, rewards and punishments as a reflection of God's justice (i.e. his non-arbitrariness); and, on the other, that they perceived the total covenantal structure to be the result of divine grace. To focus on the former point and draw all sorts of conclusions which the rabbis themselves would have eschewed, is to do them serious disservice—the more so if the latter point is not taken into account. What is at stake is a sensitive evaluation of the way various components of rabbinic teaching *function* within their religious life and thought. (See, *inter alia*, pp. 104ff., 117ff., 122ff.)

(vii) Sanders rightly insists that the *kind* of literature which the rabbis produced necessarily limits the full range of religious *discussion*; and, unless this is taken into account, the limitations of *halakah* may be projected back on to the entire religious *life* of the rabbis. In *halakic* discussion, a particular rabbi may score points, and argue over pedantic detail, ruling that 'if one constructed a side-post for an alley and raised it three handbreadths from the ground, or removed it three handbreadths from the wall, his act is invalid' (B. Erub. 14*b*); yet elsewhere, in one of the few *prayers* preserved for us, the same rabbi may voice his felt unworthiness, pleading for the grace of God. Something of this distinction in genre must surely be taken into account.

Essentially, then, E. P. Sanders is correct in his basic contentions, and Bousset, Billerbeck, Bultmann *et al.* are basically incorrect when they deal with the same areas. Nevertheless, in my view Sanders has so strongly reacted against an admittedly false view that he has swung too far the other way. In a polemical work, this is almost inevitable. Again and again, in reading his book, when one arrives at disputed passages, one does not sense a dispassionate analysis of the evidence and a cool, reflective consideration of pros and cons (contrast, for example, the superb work of E. E. Urbach, *The Sages: Their Concepts and Beliefs*[7]), but a competently argued and polemically oriented thesis. That is not necessarily bad: it is the nature of the book Sanders has chosen to write. But perhaps in that case it will not appear too gauche if I express strong reservations at a number of points. I limit myself for the moment to Sanders's rabbinic section, as I hope to deal briefly with the rest of his non-Pauline material in chapter 10.

(i) Although, as Sanders says, the rabbis preserve a doctrine of election based on grace, nevertheless several serious caveats must be entered. This election has to do with the Jewish people as a whole, and stands as the divine commitment to uphold the covenant with the Jews *qua* people. Within this structure, every individual Jew is automatically 'saved' unless he consciously and wilfully opts out. Thus there is a harking back to Sinaitic and Abrahamic covenant traditions, but little emphasis on the prophetic warnings about breaking the covenant and about restoration of a (mere) remnant. Moreover, although majority rabbinic opinion held that a non-Jew could be 'saved' by becoming a proselyte, i.e. by voluntarily coming under the covenant (Sanders, pp. 206-8), in his case salvation does not involve election at all: he both enters the covenant and keeps himself in it by his voluntary adoption of 'covenantal nomism' and its implications. Even the election of Israel reflects some elements that are less than gracious. As Sanders himself notes (pp. 87-101), when the rabbis asked *why* Israel was chosen and granted the covenant, there are three kinds of answer given. The first is that God offered the covenant and its related commandments to all, but only Israel accepted it. The second is that God found some merit in the people, whether in the patriarchs, those of the Exodus generation, or those of some unseen future generation. The third is that God chose Israel for his own name's sake. The first two are very common, much more common than the contrary opinion that God chose Israel in defiance of demerit. It is not uncommon to read things like this, attributed to Tanna R. Judah: 'The Holy One, blessed be He, said, "If I am to scrutinise the deeds of Israel, they will never be redeemed (from Egypt); I will therefore fix my regard on their holy ancestors."' (Exod. R.15.4). Even the third answer (*supra*) might include a merit rationale; for if God redeems Israel for his own name's sake, this may only mean that he has pledged himself to do what he said he would do. This answer may therefore at times provide, not the grounds for election, but assurance as to its certainty. Even when all of Sanders's evidence regarding the semantic range of *z^ekut* ('merit') is admitted, his conclusion is much too generous: 'Despite the attempts to explain it,' he says, 'the cause of election finally goes unexplained, as it always must' (p. 101). The rabbis admit much more merit than that; and their perspective is a great distance removed from, say, Deuteronomy, where, as we have seen, election has no other ground than the free, unconditioned love of God. It does not help to say, with Sanders, that the rabbis were simply trying to *explain* that love (e.g. p. 87; p. 101, n. 72), precisely because it is the rabbinic *explanation* which tends to remove the mysterious, selectively loving sovereignty in favour of a divine choice based on the relative moral superiority of Israel.

(ii) Although Sanders rightly challenges the common belief

that the Tannaitic rabbis held to some doctrine of supererogation; and although he rightly shows that not every instance of $z^c kut$ 'abôt refers to 'merit of the fathers'; and although the merits of individuals are never utilised to counter-balance demerits at the judgment; yet Sanders consistently downplays the strength of the merit theology which the rabbis do accept. Even he is forced to admit, with respect to the merit of the fathers, that God performed certain deeds for Israel because of the good deeds of the fathers, and that in view of the merit of the fathers God does not punish the world as he otherwise would, and that the good deeds of the fathers benefit their descendants in given historical situations (p. 197); so even if there is no mention in the Tannaitic literature of a treasury of merits with transferable credits, it does not appear to be improper to speak of 'merit theology' among the Tannaim, even if such theology is extended considerably only in later generations. 'Merits,' Sanders says with considerable force, '*never* counterbalance demerits at the judgment'; but then he must add, 'although, in consideration of them, God may suspend punishment' (p. 197). There is no treasury of merits with transferable credits; yet, Sanders admits, 'At most we have here a view of *transfer of punishment* from the parents to the children' (p. 194). No doubt God's mercy forgives many transgressions; and no doubt there is no simple weighing of credits and debits; yet Sanders himself cites R. Hanina b. Gamaliel, 'If he that commits one transgression thereby forfeits his soul, how much more, if he performs one religious duty, shall his soul be restored to him!' (Makk. 3.15). No doubt the even-handedness of God's 'justice' is thereby being defended; but this is still a reflection of 'merit theology' which goes beyond anything in the Hebrew Bible. In fact, anyone who accepts even one single commandment with faith deserves to have the Holy Spirit rest upon him (*Mek. Beshallaḥ* 6) (Lauterbach, Vol. i, pp. 252ff.). Charity itself has a salvific effect (B.B.B. 10a). I shall discuss a few more examples a little further on; but, granted the limitations which Sanders himself rightly insists on, there should be no objection to speaking of the 'merit theology' of the Tannaim (not to mention the later sources!).

(iii) The rabbis introduce ideas not found in the Old Testament, ideas which necessarily impinge on the shape of the sovereignty-responsibility tension. Especially is this the case once the Temple has been destroyed, and the prescribed sacrificial system ended. The law had provided a system of atonement which, in the view of the rabbis, was both efficacious and also in accord with divine justice, as Sanders points out (p. 172). Following AD 70, however, other means of atonement are required and defended. A person can atone for his sins by obedience, by suffering (see especially pp. 168-173), and even by his own death. This forced change in the theology of atonement could not do other than contribute to merit theology. The sacrifice of animals was something people did; but it was the animal that died. In this light, the Old Testament sacrificial system provided a means of atonement which was one step removed from what the individual himself did; it encouraged the concept of atonement by a substituted death. But once atonement was judged to be something that could be secured entirely by personal deeds, even if it was insisted that such were efficacious because they were God-appointed means, then the primitive merit theology of the early rabbis was necessarily strengthened and set on the road to the full-blown merit theology of the later rabbis. Although Sanders discusses rabbinic teaching on atonement, yet these important distinctions he nowhere considers, even though they are crucial to one's understanding of the development of the rabbinic tradition. Similarly, he barely mentions the rabbinic treatment of the two 'inclinations', or the rabbinic tendency to formulate a free will position which overtly fences God off from certain moral decisions.

(iv) This brings up a related problem. Not only do the rabbis go beyond what the Old Testament says at certain points, they also contradict it. I am not referring to picayune details which, by our standards of exegesis, are contradicted because of rabbinic hermeneutical methods. I refer rather to broad issues and concepts. Sanders identifies one of these for us; it is a point to which I have already alluded. The prophets regularly picture the Israelites as delinquent with respect to the covenant, so much so that the continuation of the covenant (at least in that form) is called into question. By contrast, the rabbis are eager to fulfil their side of the covenant, and are never in doubt that God will fulfil his. As Sanders puts it (p. 106):

This last is a very important point, since it stands in contrast to a type of religious concern found in the prophets and in Job. It is a mark of the particular genius of prophetism that it was able to charge God with the responsibility of fulfilling the covenant and thus to imply that he might not have been doing so satisfactorily. But this note is never struck in the surviving Tannaitic literature. God's total faithfulness and reliability are always assumed and often stated. This is frequently indicated by comments on the biblical phrase 'I am the Lord your God'. The Rabbis often interpret this to mean: 'I am faithful to pay a reward; I am a faithful judge to punish.'

This, in my view, is a misinterpretation of the Old Testament prophetic stance. Note that Sanders says the prophets *charge* God with the responsibility of fulfilling the covenant and thereby *imply* that he might not have been doing so satisfactorily. It would be more accurate to say that, as compared with the rabbis, the prophets reflect a greater insight into divine ultimacy and a more pessimistic outlook about the nature of man. The prophets can cry to God about this catastrophe or that, precisely because they recognise that divine sovereignty is so extensive that God must indeed in some sense stand behind that catastrophe; yet they do this without impugning divine justice. They simply do not know how to fit God's justice, mercy and sovereignty together. Sanders is correct when he points out (*supra*) that the rabbinic perspective is quite different from this. The rabbis stress the fact that God is judge; but they are not as strong as the Old Testament writers in defence of his 'ultimacy' (in the sense developed in Part One). Moreover the prophets, as I earlier pointed out, were pessimistic about the ability of the people to repent; and in this they are not the only Old Testament witness. By contrast, as Sanders notes (p. 114), the rabbis believed there was no entailment from the fall. Men are free to obey or to disobey; and so the possibility exists that a person might not sin. This optimistic perspective is scarcely likely to call forth many divine promises to the effect that God himself would one day renew men's hearts and give them another spirit. Thus, the sovereignty-responsibility tension in the rabbinic material assumes a somewhat different shape because of the distance between the rabbis and the prophets in certain crucial themes

(v) This brings up a methodological question. Sanders is concerned to criticise part of the New Testament, and most of New Testament scholarship, for what he takes to be their misjudgments about rabbinic material. His criticism of New Testament scholarship is fundamentally justified. But as far as the relation between New Testament writers and the rabbis is concerned, perhaps it should be noted that *both* groups make appeal to the Old Testament: how then does each side stack up against this common standard? For clearly Paul (for example) believes that the Pharisees err in their understanding of the Old Testament; and equally clearly they share the same feelings about him. Now of course it would be unfair to expect Sanders to write a book he never intended to write; and I grant that he is first of all concerned to write a book which criticises a mistaken notion still rampant in New Testament scholarship, and he does this very well. But I cannot help wondering if, in this area of dispute, some thought should not be given to the standard to which both sides make appeal. I do not mean to raise the question of how the New Testament quotes the Old, nor to bring up the hermeneutics of rabbinism, nor to contrast rabbinic theories of oral tradition with the New Testament's insistence that the gospel assumes a revelatory stance of fulfilment *vis-à-vis* the Old Testament. I mean rather to suggest that the shape of the sovereignty-responsibility tension in the rabbinic literature, and in Paul or John needs to be compared with its shape in the Old Testament before they are compared with one another.

(vi) Although Sanders is convincing in his main argument, he seriously distorts the shape of the tension in the rabbinic literature, because he fails to comment on the *drift* of rabbinic thought. If the Tannaitic sources which impinge on the sovereignty-responsibility tension are compared both with Old Testament material *and also with later rabbinic material*, it becomes difficult not to see which way the wind is blowing. For example, Sanders correctly observes that God's justice is being defended in the reward/punishment/merit motifs, and that divine grace is defended in the election of Israel and in the forgiveness God grants (e.g. cf. pp. 119, 124, 127). These are important observations when confronting Bousset and correcting Billerbeck. But if the same themes are examined over the longer time span that I have suggested, it must be admitted that major shifts have taken place and are still taking place. Sin is more anthropocentric in its definition, and less theocentric, in first century Judaism than in the Hebrew canon. God's justice is stridently affirmed, but his 'ultimacy' is diluted. Man's freedom tends now to exclude God from certain areas. Merit theology has come a long way since the scrolls of the Old Testament were penned, even if it still has some distance to go. And although, as Sanders rightly observes, it is severely misleading to say that for the rabbis God was so transcendent and sovereign that there is among the rabbis less enjoyment of his presence or more need felt for mediators, nevertheless it is true to say that, with the decline of his 'ultimacy' and the rise of merit theology, God is more domesticated than he is in the Old Testament, despite the rabbinic emphasis on his transcendence. Consciously or not—and there is some of both—the rabbis are attempting to resolve the sovereignty-responsibility tension.

It remains to survey rapidly some of the most important evidence.

TARGUMIC AND RABBINIC TREATMENT OF THE TWELVE OLD TESTAMENT PASSAGES PREVIOUSLY EXAMINED

Genesis 45.5-8; 50.19f.

In 45.8 MT has: 'So it was not you who sent me here, but God.' Neofiti 1 has 'but Yahweh', although a marginal note offers 'the word of Yahweh'. But TJi puts the divine action into the passive voice, and prefers the periphrastic 'before Yahweh': 'So now it was not you that sent me hither, but the event was brought about before the Lord (*qdm h'*) ....' This eliminates the tension; but it may not be the tension which occasions the change, because the trend toward passive expression of divine action is quite strong in the targums.

In 50.19f., the evasive tactics are clearer. Joseph's rhetorical question, '... for am I in the place of God?', is quite displaced by TJi, TJii, and Neofiti 1. Further, in 50.20, TJi eliminates all trace of God's active participation in the selling of Joseph, while simultaneously introducing the glory of Joseph's father as the ground of Joseph's present position before God. TJii makes the brothers alone responsible, and stresses God's role as Judge: 'And Joseph said unto them, Fear not, for the evil which you did to me has ended; are not the reckonings of the sons of men

always before the Lord?' Neofiti 1 is closer to MT but, like TJɪ
on 45.8, makes God's role passive: 'And you planned evil
against me: before the Lord it was reckoned as good so as to
preserve alive this day a numerous people.'[8] The explicit tension
has again disappeared.

Joseph's willingness to forgive is often held up in rabbinic
literature as exemplary. Genesis Rabbah 90.9 (on 50.19f.) offers
a marvellous collection of the utterances Joseph used to comfort
his brothers, but fails to wrestle with the tension (cf. also
Est. R. 7.25). Strangely, it is *Pesikta Rabbati*, a late compilation
(fifth century?) and one that is full of merit theology, which at
12.5 cites Genesis 50.20 correctly. But it uses the Genesis
passage to show only how Joseph by being kind guarded
himself from committing murder.

Leviticus 20.7f.; 22.31f.

In Leviticus 20.8, the MT ends the verse with 'I am the Lord
who sanctifies you': *'ᵃnî yhwh mᶜqaddisᶜkem.* But Neofiti 1
offers an Aramaic perfect: *'ny yyy dqḏšt yṯḵwn:* hence
McNamara's correct translation, 'I am the Lord who sanctif*ied*
you.'[9] The same thing occurs at 22.32. This makes Yahweh's
sanctification of the people refer to an historic event (the
exodus?), and the tension disappears. What could have
prompted this change? It is difficult to imagine any other reason
than a desire to avoid the sovereignty-responsibility tension. At
both 20.8 and 22.32, TO preserves the tension: *'ny yyy
mqdšḵwn.* Pseudo-Jonathan (TJɪ) at both places likewise
preserves 'I am the Lord who sanctifies you'; but at 20.7 and
22.31 it inserts promises of reward: 'And sanctify yourselves
and be holy in your bodies, so that your prayers may be
favourably answered' (20.7); 'I am the Lord who gives a good
reward to those who keep my commandments and my laws'
(22.31).

Numbers Rabbah 9.7 (on 5.12) cites Leviticus 20.8
according to MT, but then destroys the tension by continuing,
'When does the Holy One, blessed be He, sanctify Israel?
When they observe His statutes.' When the relevant verses are
cited in the Talmuds, other interests than ours have evoked the
reference and so no help is offered to this study.[10]

Judges 14.4a

Targum Jonathan is similar to MT, except that the customary targumic anti-anthropomorphism[11] 'before Yahweh' *(qdm yyy)* displaces 'Yahweh' (as in TJi on Gen. 45.8, *supra*, and the PT on 2 Chr. 10.15; 11.4, *infra*). There are several rabbinic passages which cite Judges 14.4 to demonstrate 'that a man's marriage partner is from the Holy One, blessed be He' (e.g. Gen R. 68.3[on 28.10], R. Phinehas in R. Abbahu's name; cf. B.M.K. 18b; Midr. Teh. 59.2). In B. Sota 9b the Gemara is fully cognisant of the tension. On the one hand it contradicts rabbinic opinion which said that Samson was rebelling, since the text insists it was from Yahweh; but on the other hand, it adds, 'When he went (to choose a wife) he nevertheless followed his own inclination.' In Numbers Rabbah 9.24 (on 5.26f.) R. Eleazar cites Proverbs 3.34 according to *Midrash*: 'If it concerneth the scorners, He scorneth through them, but unto the humble He giveth grace'—apparently meaning that God uses every medium, including Samson's wickedness, for the accomplishment of his will, but that had not Samson succumbed to temptation he would have been given other opportunities to save his people.

2 Samuel 24.1ff. (1 Chronicles 21.1-7)

The targum on 2 Samuel 24.1 offers no significant difference to the MT; but since it is the *anger* of Yahweh, and not Yahweh himself, who incites David, the targumist may have felt this was a sufficient anti-anthropomorphism and not been concerned with any further problem. Quite surprisingly, however, Yahweh is *introduced* into the targum on 1 Chronicles 21.1, *viz.* w'qym yyy *śṭn'* ... ('Yahweh raised up Satan against Israel ...').

R. Eleazer puts the two references together to make Satan the subject of the verb in 2 Samuel 24.1 (P. Ber. 9.8 [Schwab, Vol. i, p. 498]; cf. also B. Ber. 62b).[12] It is the later Pesikta Rabbati 11.5 which comes closest to understanding the text. It pictures David numbering his mighty men (end of 2 Sam. 23) and getting only as far as Uriah the Hittite, the mention of whom evokes divine displeasure: 'again the anger of the Lord was kindled against Israel. Thereupon He moved David to number ....'

1 Kings 8.57-60

On these verses there are no targumic variants or rabbinic expositions of significance to the sovereignty-responsibility tension. But the tension is perhaps too diffuse to occasion mitigating reaction, spread out as it is over several verses. Moreover, the universal language of theistic prayer might blind the reader to the tension unless it were already a live issue with him. Similar remarks hold true for Isaiah 10.5ff.; Jeremiah 29.10-14; and Haggai 1.12-14.

1 Kings 11.11-13, 29-39; 12.1ff. (cf. 2 Chronicles 10.15; 11.4)

The circumlocution *qdm yyy* ('before Yahweh') occurs—e.g. 2 Chronicles 10.15; 11.4 (cf. Judg. 14.4a, *supra*).

Jeremiah 52.3 (2 Kings 24.19f.)

In both passages, Targum Jonathan eliminates the tension by dissolving the connection between Zedekiah's rebellion and its cause in Yahweh's wrath, which becomes the express *result* of the sins of the people.

Joel 2.32

Targum Jonathan makes no significant change. Elsewhere the first part of the verse functions as an encouragement to pray (Midr. Teh. 4.3; 71.3), while B. Sanhedrin 92a and B. Hullin 133a understand the 'remnant' in the last clause to refer to scholars.

Psalm 105.24f.

The targum on 105.25 opens the verse with the *hithpa'el*: *'thpyk*. ... The Aramaic tendency to use *hithpa'el* with passive significance (equivalent to MT *hoph'al*) makes this change seem to be a reflection of the tendency to flee from divine ultimacy whenever such ultimacy is in danger of ascribing evil to God—especially evil directed against Israel. It is possible to understand MT's *qal hpk* in a passive sense (cf. Ps. 78.9); but it was earlier shown that the active sense is most probable in this context. Interestingly enough, the targum has no difficulty following the MT four verses later, in 105.29, where the same verb is used.

Exodus Rabbah 1.8 (on 1.8) argues that God incited the Egyptians to hate Israel for Israel's good. Since circumcision

had to be re-instituted by Moses when the people left Israel, it
is argued that the covenant of circumcision was abandoned
when Joseph died, and so God turned the hearts of the
Egyptians to hate his people in order to prevent assimilation.
Midrash Tehillim 105.8 (on 105.25), however, makes *Pharaoh*
the subject: 'Pharaoh turned their heart to hate His people', i.e
by issuing new laws, Exodus 1.2ff.

Summary and conclusions

There is no simple pattern of the sort that can predict what a
particular targum will do with the next tension-passage, much
less conveniently classify the rabbinic material. Some of the
changes in the targums doubtless reflect other interests than a
desire to ease the sovereignty-responsibility tension; but still,
when the tension reaches its most pronounced form in concen-
trated passages (e.g. Gen. 50.19f.; Lev. 20.7f.; Judg. 14.4;
2 Sam. 24.1ff. and parallels; Jer. 52.3 and parallel) then at least
some of the targumic and rabbinic witnesses inject significant
changes or casuistical expositions. In some cases it is the desire
to avoid ascribing evil to God that is primarily responsible for
prompting the change. In Leviticus 20.7f; 22.31f., however,
there can be little question of this mitigating factor. At the same
time, the targum on 1 Chronicles 21.1 *introduces* the tension,
probably by assimilation to 2 Samuel 24.1. Overall there is a
tendency—we can say no more—to break down the tension or,
more accurately, to shift its focal point to the side of man's
advantage: man becomes a good deal more free, and God a trifle
less ultimate.

THE SOVEREIGNTY-RESPONSIBILITY TENSION IN
RABBINIC AND TARGUMIC THOUGHT: A SKETCH

Before attempting to uncover the limitations of God in the
targums and rabbinic literature, it is important to recognise just
how much his sovereignty is emphasised. In the targums, no
limitation is placed on God's knowledge and power when these
are in open view. 'Affirmative statements are changed into
questions, negative statements into affirmations etc., if their
original wording seems to allow for doubts regarding the
omniscience of God, his omnipotence and the like.'[13] In
Genesis 18.14, for example, TJi changes the question, 'Is

anything too hard for Yahweh?' to 'Is it possible for anything to be hidden from Yahweh?' 'The purpose of this alteration was to remove even the slightest hint that God might be unable to do something.'[14] Further, both TO and TJɪ on Genesis 3.5 make it clear that the fall did not catch God by surprise. Divine sovereignty is so extensive that even if the plague rages for seven years, no man dies before his appointed hour (B. Yeb. 115*b*). R. Hanina said, 'No man bruises his finger here on earth unless it was so decreed against him in heaven' (B. Hull. 7*b*; he cites Ps. 37.23 and Prov. 20.24). B. Sukk. 53*a* tells a long story to illustrate the fact that no one can escape his appointed place of death. In sum: throughout the rabbinic literature, God is one, God is unchangingly merciful and just, and God is sovereign.[15]

Simultaneously, God is becoming increasingly transcendent. A. Sperber lists examples from Codex Reuchlinianus to show how anthropomorphisms are avoided, actives (which ascribe to God an actual action) become passives, and extra care is taken to avoid any suggestion that God could have equals.[16] Similar conclusions may be drawn about PT and TO.[17] If MT at Genesis 5.22 says that Enoch walked with God, TJɪ has, 'And Enoch walked in the fear of Yahweh ...' Similarly, at Genesis 7.16, TJɪ, TJɪɪ, and TO employ different expressions to eliminate the offending anthropomorphism. We read that 'it repented Yahweh *in his word* that he had made men on the earth' (TJɪ Gen. 6.6; cf. Gen. R. 27.4). That God is both sovereign and yet in some way distant is reflected by the answer to the question, Who instructed the children before the destruction of the Temple? 'If you like, you may say Metatron, or it may be said that God did this as well as other things' (B.A.Z. 3*b*).[18]

As in Jewish apocalyptic, God's sovereign reign is not monolithic: there is an age to come in which will be culminated both God's judgment and his soteriological purposes for his people. The structure of rabbinic eschatology[19] is less rigid than its apocalyptic counterpart. It allows more room for blessings in this life, not leaving all reward for the age to come (e.g. Ab. 5.19). The overwhelming rabbinic desire to make Torah relevant and applicable in *this* life imposes a natural curb on uncontrolled futurist speculation. Moreover, although some rabbis indulge in calculating ages (e.g. B. Sanh. 97*b*), R. Jonathan could say, 'Blasted be the bones of those who calculate the end. For they would say, since the predetermined time has arrived, and yet he (i.e. the Messiah) has not come, he will never come' (B. Sanh. 97*b*). But when all caveats have been entered, it is nevertheless true to say that rabbinic Judaism adopts the same sort of eschatological *structure* as Jewish apocalyptic.

More fundamental to this inquiry is the rabbinic perspective on some of God's work in creation. The rabbis agree that God created man with two 'inclinations' (*yēṣer*); the anomalous double-*yôd* in Genesis 2.7 providing the explicit exegetical justification for this belief (B. Ber. 61*a*; Gen. R. 14.4. Cf. also Midr. Teh. 14.1 or 1 Chr. 28.9; Gen. R. 27.4; TJi on Gen. 2.7). Some rabbis included evil spirits in the list of things God initially created (B. Pes. 54*a-b*). Bowker notes that Tanḥuma (Buber) 1.30 interprets Genesis 6.6 to mean that 'the Holy One, blessed be He, may His name be blessed, said, "It is I who put the bad leaven in the dough, for the inclination of the heart of man is evil from his youth." So where it says, "It grieved him at his heart", it means "man's heart".'[20]

It is impossible in a few words to do justice to rabbinic teaching on the evil *yēṣer*.[21] Nevertheless it is important to recognise the fullness of ultimacy ascribed to the God whose creative work embraces even the evil inclination. (Perhaps it is the awesomeness of this concept which contributes to the conclusion that in some way even the evil inclination is good, since without it men would never marry, procreate, build a house, or trade (Gen. R. 9.9)). Yet it is precisely at this point where divine ultimacy begins to crumble. A.R.N. 32 divides men into three classes: the righteous who are ruled by the good *yēṣer*, the wicked under the dominion of the evil *yēṣer*, and a middle class ruled now by one, now by the other (Eccl. R. 4.15f. prefers just two classes). But what governs the destiny of the individual? What class will he find himself in? The crucial factor is his view of Torah. God no only created the evil *yēṣer* but also the Torah as its remedy. When a man makes Torah his concern, the evil *yēṣer* does not overcome him (*Sifre* on Deut. 11.18; B. Ber. 61*a*; B.B.B. 16*a*; B. Kidd. 30*b*; B. Sukk. 52*b*; P. Yeb. 4.2; A.R.N. 16). God has given to man power over his own evil *yēṣer* (TJi on Gen. 4.7). Indeed, the evil *yēṣer* appears to have been given so we may receive reward for conquering it (B. Yoma 69*b*; cf. B. Sanh. 64*a*).

Free will, the 'doctrine that volition is self-originating and unpredictable ... was regarded by rabbinical Judaism as a fundamental principle of the Jewish religion.'[22] R. Akiba's oft-quoted dictum, 'All is foreseen (by God), yet freedom of choice is granted; and by grace is the universe judged, yet all is according to the amount of the work' (Ab. 3.16), is patient of several interpretations. It has been taken to mean that human decisions are free, but predictable by God who foresees what they will be; or again, that both aspects of the sovereignty-responsibility tension are fully operative and irreconcilable. Urbach, however, has convincingly shown that the verb 'foreseen' (ṣpwy) always means 'to watch, keep watch' in the Tannaitic period. Moreover:

> The content of the Mishna likewise shows that R. Akiba's intention was not to resolve the contradiction (sic) between [God's] 'foreknowledge and [man's] freewill, but to make man realise his responsibility for his actions. This responsibility is grounded in two factors: in the permission given to man to choose his own way and in the realisation that man is destined to account for his actions before Him who sees and examines his ways.[23]

If Urbach's interpretation is correct (and I believe it is), then the 'grace' by which the universe is judged can scarcely be more than a reference to kindness, forbearance—i.e. God judges according to the amount of the work, but he is gracious in his judging and will not be too severe. Whatever the interpretation of R. Akiba's statement, it is outstripped by the undisputed maxim found in the Babylonian Talmud, and attributed to R. Hanina: 'Everything is in the hands of heaven except the fear of God' (B.Ber. 33b). The same maxim is found in B. Nidd. 16b (citing Deut. 10.12 as authority), where the angel in charge of conception 'takes up a drop and places it in the presence of the Holy One, blessed be He, saying, "Sovereign of the universe, What will be the fate of this drop? Shall it produce a strong man or a weak man, a wise man or a fool, a rich man or a poor man?" Whereas "wicked man" or "righteous man" he does not mention, in agreement with the view of R. Hanina (above).' (Cf. also B. Yoma 38b; Sifre on Deut. 11.26). In other words, the entire sphere of human moral life is explicitly reserved from divine determination.

From all this it is clear that although divine ultimacy is preserved in terms of the initial creation, it is lost in terms of the individual and his moral, existential decisions. God at this point is distant, and man is more or less on his own, however much God may help him when he begins to move in the right direction. By insisting on this absolute freedom of will, the rabbis are trying to preserve human responsibility and maintain the non-arbitrariness of divine justice; but in one important way they are actually weakening both. To postulate a universe in which God directly and explicitly created the evil *yēṣer* cannot but reduce the enormity, the heinousness, of open rebellion, as compared with the Genesis narratives which do not speculate on the relationship between divine sovereignty and the fall. Rabbinic speculation preserves divine transcendence and pure monism at creation, sacrifices divine ultimacy in the existential moral decision, and makes sin, however evil, part of the essence of humanity instead of an entailment from the fall. Once again the sovereignty-responsibility tension is being denied at its soteriological focal point. The divine endowment is, more or less, only the raw material which man must work up to bring to perfection.[24]

Predictably, the insistence on free will affects the rabbinic view of election. Election becomes a crucial issue for the rabbis facing christian apologists who declared that the church was the true people of God. Justin Martyr in *Dialogue with Trypho* 14 and 18 argues that many of the outward signs of Israel's former election were in reality given for purposes of judgment; and the Epistle of Barnabas 9.4 goes so far as to say that circumcision was actually a form of punishment. Christians could always point to the destruction of the Temple: God has forsaken his people. By way of reaction, 'The catastrophe of the year 70 occasioned the richest amplification of the doctrine (of election), as the Rabbis stressed over and over again the eternal, intimate and unique relationship which exists between God and His people.'[25] As long as Christianity was viewed as a sect of Judaism, the central point of disagreement would remain the question of the continuity of the law. With the fall of the Temple, the full provisions of the law *could not* be met. In some measure the law *had* to be abandoned. Christians, seemingly, were winning the argument, and so the disputed point had to be pushed back farther to a deeper question, viz. Who are the real people of God?[26]

It is against this background that the strongest expressions on election must be understood.[27] R. Gamaliel II insisted that the Jews are God's people: God has not cast them off (B. Yeb. 102b). Midrash Tehillim 72.6 (on 72.17) makes Israel one of the seven (*sic*; eight are listed) pre-created things; but the contents of the list (viz., the throne of glory, the name of the Messiah, Torah, Israel, the garden of Eden, Gehenna, repentance, and the Temple) do not suggest that the writer was thinking of a *gracious* election so much as of an eternal, stable position for Israel. R. Hanina ben Akashia said, 'The Holy One, blessed be He, was pleased to grant merit to Israel, therefore he gave them a copious law and many commandments.' The saying occurs in identical form as a sort of doxological conclusion to the Mishnaic tractates Aboth and Makkoth. At first glance it might be mis-interpreted to mean that God was granting 'merit' to Israel out of sheer grace. Closer examination reveals that God is not conferring 'merit' directly, but by the gracious provision of 'a copious law and many commandments'—i.e. by the provision of rules to be obeyed. In other words, God has, out of grace, provided the covenantal structure of commandments and laws, whereby the chosen people maintain themselves in the divine favour.

There was disagreement among the rabbis as to whether Israel's restoration could take place irrespective of her repentance and merits.[28] However, the argument calls in question neither the belief in the divine election of Israel *qua* people, nor the merit theology everywhere assumed. It deals rather with epochal blessings for the people of God, these people who are already privileged to enjoy the covenant and earn reward.

The gratuity of the election of the people is called into question at one crucial point. When the rabbis expressly consider the *why* of God's choice, the conclusion is almost always in terms of Israel's worthiness. I discussed this briefly, including the apparent exception, in connection with Sanders's work; but it remains to provide a selection of examples.

Of all nations, only Israel accepted the decalogue when it was offered (Pes. R. 21).[29] The oft-repeated story of R. Jose's demonstration that God knows to choose what is good is another way of saying that on account of its good works Israel is 'as wheat among the chaff' (Midr. Teh. 1.20 on 1.4):

> A Roman lady addressed a query to R. Jose. She said to him: 'Your God brings near to Himself indiscriminately whomsoever He pleases.' He brought her a basket of figs and she scrutinised them well, picking the best and eating. Said he to her: 'You, apparently, know how to select, but the Holy One, blessed be He, does not know how to select! The one whose actions He perceives to be good, him He chooses and brings near to himself (Num. R. 3.2).

Compared with Israel, all nations are subsidiary (Midr. Teh. 2.13 on 2.12), as is demonstrated by the fact that the commandments concerning circumcision, tassels, phylacteries and Mezuzahs were given only to Jews.[30] In other words, the blessings of election demonstrate moral superiority. Indeed, Israel could boast not only moral but racial superiority: she was given the law because of all nations she was strongest, most 'energetic'.[31] As the school of R. Ishmael taught, no nation could have withstood Israel were it not for the curbing effect of the law (B.Y.T.=B. Bez. 25b). In an atmosphere like this even Amos 9.7 could be re-interpreted to mean that as the Ethiopians are distinguished by colour, so Israel is distinguished from all other peoples by the manner of her obedience to God (B.M.K. 16b). The Holy One chose Israel because she came from genuine seed (Tanḥ. 16a). Even some of the rabbis who teach that Israel was chosen before the creation of the world understand that divine choice in terms of God's foreknowledge of how good the patriarchs would be (e.g. Ex. R. 15.17).

Most rabbis allow that Gentiles can be saved by coming under Torah (e.g. B.A.Z. 3b, 24a; B. Sanh. 105a; Tos. Sanh. 13.2; cf. TJ1 on Gen. 9.27); but others flatly deny the possibility (e.g. B. Kidd. 31a, 32a; B. Git. 45b; Mek. on Exod. 21.30 (Lauterbach, Vol. iii, pp. 87ff.)). Certainly B. J. Bamberger in his book *Proselytism in the Talmudic Period*[32] exaggerates the eagerness of the rabbis for converts and their friendliness toward proselytes. Above all, it is important to observe that where Gentile proselytes are saved by coming under Torah, this action has nothing whatever to do with God's election. They enter by their voluntary, unconditioned submission to the covenant. This should not be too surprising because, as we have already had occasion to observe, election has been restricted to God's choice of the Jewish race as a whole.

In short, an extensive 'merit theology' is on the rise. I use the expression advisedly, acutely aware of the way it has been abused by christian scholars. The argument of E. P. Sanders must be taken seriously. But if we exclude from this term any idea of supererogation, or of a simplistic commercial weighing of merits and demerits, then we must still confess that merit theology is on the ascendancy in the Tannaitic and Amoraic periods, inasmuch as there is an increasing dependence on personal merit as an approach to God, and much serious theological argument surrounding the significance and limitations of merit.[33] Although it is true to say that various elements of this theological structure are contradicted by other rabbis, there is little doubt which way the winds are blowing. B. Sanh. 81a records an important exchange between R. Gamaliel and R. Akiba:

> When R. Gamaliel read the verse [Ezek. 6.9] he wept, saying, 'Only he who does all those things shall live, but not merely one of them!' Thereupon R. Akiba said to him, 'If so, *Defile not yourselves in all these things* (Lev. 18.24).—is the prohibition against *all* [combined] only, but not against one?' [Surely not!] But it means, *in one* of these things; so here too, for doing one of these things; so here too, for doing one of these things [shall he live].

A later expanded version pictures R. Gamaliel replying, 'Thou hast comforted me, Akiba, thou hast comforted me' (Midr. Teh. 15.7 on 15.5). A not dissimilar picture is painted by R. Jose, who argues that if a single violation by Adam brought so much death and suffering, how much greater would the rewards be for the good deeds? For 'which is greater, the attribute of reward (lit. of goodness) or that of punishment? Surely the attribute of reward' (*Sifra* 27a).

The merits of the patriarchs are particularly powerful, even if it is not likely that the Tannaim thought that such merits could be imputed to the descendants of the patriarchs. Abraham is singled out. In magnifying his merit, the rabbis correspondingly magnify the man. R. Levi tells stories of the effectiveness of Abraham's prayers in relieving the ill and the barren

(Gen. R. 39.11; cf. B.B.B. 16b; Gen. R. 44.16 on 15.11). Even Abraham's faith is meritorious (Mek. Ex. 14.31, Lauterbach, 1, p. 253). The following story makes Abraham so great that the previously noted emphasis on divine transcendence is temporarily lost to view:

> R. Yudan said in the same of R. Hamma: In the time-to-come, when the Holy One, blessed be He, seats the lord Messiah at His right hand, as is said, *The Lord saith unto my lord: 'Sit thou at My right hand'* (Ps. 110.1), and seats Abraham at His left, Abraham's face will pale, and he will say to the Lord: 'My son's son sits at the right, and I at the left!' Thereupon the Holy One, blessed be He, will comfort Abraham, saying: 'Thy son's son is at My right, but I, in a manner of speaking, am at thy right': *The Lord* [is] *at thy right hand* (Ps. 110.5). (Midr. Teh. 18.29 on 18.36).

But Abraham is not alone in his merits. R. Eleazar teaches that Israel will be saved through five things: affliction, the cry of prayer, *the merits of the fathers,* repentance, and the time of ingathering (Midr. Teh. 106.9 on 106.44; cf. Ab. 2.2). The merits of the fathers will endure forever (Lev. R. 36.6).

Coming to his own contemporaries, R. Joshua, citing Micah 7.4, said, 'As briers protect a gap so do the best men among us protect us' (B. Erub. 101a). God would have created the world for the sake of a single righteous man (B. Yoma 38b). Conversely, God permitted Hadrian to destroy the city of Jerusalem only because the merits of the people had run out (Lam. R. 1.5; cf. TJ1 on Deut. 7.10).

Rewards may be bestowed in this life on the man who merits them. Longevity was sometimes regarded as proof of a life full of merits (so R. Meir, P. Bikk. 3, near end: Schwab, ii. p. 385),[34] although this was disputed by some (B.M.K. 28a). R. Hanina was saved from sorcery because of his abundant merits. The Holy Spirit is won by merits.[35]

Clearly, the destruction of the Temple forced on the rabbis some radical rethinking about ways and means of atonement. The rising consensus finds apt expression in R. Johanan b. Zaccai, who argued that the Jews should not grieve too much at the loss of the Temple, since they had an atonement equal to that of the Temple, viz. the doing of good works: did not the Holy One say, 'I desire mercy *hesed* and not sacrifice' (Hos. 6.6;

A.R.N. 4.5)? Others (e.g. R. Eliezer b. Hyrcanus) regarded the cessation of the sacrificial cult as an irreparable loss (B. Sot 49a); but the centrality of good works as a means of atonement, along with suffering and death, can scarcely be doubted. In Exod. R. 44.4 (on 32.13), R. Abin in the name of R. Aha tells a lengthy parable whose significance he spells out as follows:

> So, when Israel sinned, God was angry with them and said, 'Now, therefore, let Me alone, that My wrath may wax hot against them, and that I may consume them' (Exod. 32.10). But Moses pleaded: 'Lord of the Universe! Why art Thou angry with Israel?' 'Because they have broken the Decalogue,' he replied. 'Well, they possess a source from which they can make repayment,' he urged. 'What is the source?' He asked. Moses replied: 'Remember that Thou didst prove Abraham with ten trials, and so let those ten [trials serve as compensation] for these ten [broken commandments].

It must not be thought that the rabbis had no regard for humility. Humility is a virtue frequently extolled, although sometimes even humility is seen as meritorious. But, as G. F. Moore rightly says, 'Pride is hard to subdue, and none so hard as the joint pride of piety and learning, and where men have made a painful effort to eradicate their pride they may become inordinately proud of their humility.'[36] Perhaps the story of God at Abraham's right hand *(supra)* is not so anomalous after all. Certainly the mature merit theology of the medieval period brought with it certain spiritual arrogance.[37]

One might almost have expected that merit theology would bring with it the kind of desperate theodicy found in 4 Ezra. In fact, that is not the case. Although there is considerable variation, it is refreshing to discover how frequently the rabbis retreat for their theodicy to an absolute confidence in the sheer justice of God.[38]

This realisation brings us to the supreme irony. Few are as concerned to preserve the transcendence, justice and sovereignty of God as are the rabbis; but by cutting man entirely free in the moral sphere and developing merit theology, they deny an important facet of divine ultimacy and raise man to a position he does not have when he is chosen out of sheer grace, in defiance of demerit. God is theoretically sovereign, but not in the area of salvation (however salvation be construed); he is transcendent, but instead of taking the initiative in this age and visiting his people with saving grace, he merely assists and rewards their efforts. The tension, of course, remains: monotheism cannot escape it. But it has assumed a new shape.

CHAPTER NINE

JOSEPHUS

Because a large part of *Antiquities* covers Old Testament history, it is worth observing not only how often Josephus adheres to the sovereignty-responsibility tension in Old Testament passages, but also some of his remarkable lapses. He usually preserves the tension as found in the Old Testament passages closely examined in chap. 2 *(supra)*. *Ant.* ii.161-4 (cf. ii. 8) maintains the tension of Genesis 45 and 50; but in *Ant.* ii.169, he remarks that Jacob 'reflected on God's mighty power and his benevolence towards him, *albeit for a while suspended*'. God's hand in Samson's marriage (Judg. 14.4a) is preserved in *Ant.* v.286, as likewise in the events surrounding the revolt under Rehoboam in *Ant.* viii.223. Yet on the other hand a notable whitewash is found in *Ant.* vii.38 where David is said to forget the injunctions of Moses (cf. 2 Sam. 24.1). Josephus puts in additions to stories in order to bolster his heroes (e.g. *Ant.* i.166-8; ii.238-53); conversely, he omits certain shameful episodes (e.g. the golden calf, *Ant.* iii.95ff.). At other times his touches are far more subtle. What prompts these changes?

Josephus is primarily an apologist. In *Bellum* he defends the Romans, in *Antiquities* the Jews, and always the proposition that God in his providence rewards virtue. Only with the Zealots is he bitingly sarcastic (e.g. BJ vi.4). In a sense, he is no theologian—at least, not in any self-conscious, systematic sense; but it is difficult to resist the conviction that he holds set theological convictions which he wishes to communicate by his personal retelling of the Old Testament (and other) history, and this he does by literary means.[1] Yet when the constraints of following (in a midrashic fashion) the biblical narrative are removed from him, as at the end of *Ant.* xi, he makes far fewer references to God and his activity than when he is re-narrating the biblical material.

In *Ant.* i.14f. Josephus says that the 'main lesson' to be learned from history is 'that men who conform to the will of

God ... prosper in all things beyond belief, and for their reward are offered by God felicity, whereas in proportion as they depart from the strict observance of these laws ... imaginary good things they strive to do end in irretrievable disasters' (cf. also i.20; xv.60). This succinct statement of a basic tenet of merit theology is worked out in all of Josephus's writings. After all, 'it is surely madness to expect God to show the same treatment to the just as to the unjust' (BJ v.407). Moses himself taught the people that their life would be blissful if they but followed the laws (*Ant.* iii.88). The one source of felicity is the gracious *(sic)* God, for 'He alone has power to give good things to those who merit them and to take them away from those who sin against Him' (*Ant.* iv.180-83; cf. iv.190; vi.21f.; xx.82f.).

Examples abound. Both Elisha and Onias died as men 'renowned for righteousness and manifestly held in honour by God' (*Ant.* ix.182; xiv.22). Josephus attributes his deliverance from John and his men to God, 'for His eye is upon those who do their duty' (*Vit.* 82f.). 'God loved Noah for his righteousness' (*Ant.* i.72) and therefore answered his prayers (99) while he condemned others 'for their wickedness' (*Ant.* i.72). One of the reasons for the longevity of the ancients was their merits (*aretē Ant.* i.106). God told Abraham to move, for Abraham was a man who entertained 'more lofty conceptions of virtue than the rest of mankind' and therefore he (Abraham) 'determined to reform and change the ideas universally current concerning God' (*Ant.* i.154-7). Indeed, God commended Abraham for his virtue and assured him he would not lose his reward (*Ant.* i.183). When Jacob died, it is said of him that he came behind 'none of his forefathers in piety towards God and ... [he] met with the recompense which such virtue deserved' (*Ant.* ii.196). Asanos and his army received great victory from God 'because they had shown themselves righteous and pure and had always acted in accordance with the will of God' (*Ant.* viii.295). Ezra planned a lot of things, 'but that they turned out well for him was, I think, due to God, who judged him worthy of obtaining his desires because of his goodness and righteousness' (*Ant.* xi.139). To say that repentance may be accepted as a virtue (*Ant.* ix.175f.) presupposes merit theology. The Pharisees are said, in effect, to hold to such a theology (*Ant.* xiii.288-90); and it forms the basis of Mattathias's dying charge to his sons (*Ant.* xii.280ff.).

Merit theology is sufficiently developed in Josephus to produce statements attributing assorted blessings to the merits of the patriarchs or of Moses. The signs of the Sinai theophany 'signified the advent of God propitious to the desires of Moses' (*Ant.* iii.80); 'even our enemies', Josephus says, 'admit that our constitution was established by God himself, through the agency of Moses and of his merits' (*Ant.* iii.321). Only rebels mock the belief (*Ant.* iv.4). Elsewhere, we learn that 'the merits of the fathers should be a palliation of the sins of their children' (*Ant.* viii.278), while Nehemiah is made to declare: 'Fellow Jews, you know that God cherishes the memory of our fathers Abraham, Isaac and Jacob, and because of their righteousness does not give up his providential care for us' (*Ant.* xi.169).

The occasional, mildly mitigating passages do not really dent the structure of Josephus's merit theology. For example, Josephus says that Moses himself wrote that he died, 'for fear lest [the people] should venture to say that by reason of his surpassing virtue he had gone back to the Deity' (*Ant.* iv.26; cf. also *Ant.* viii.111f.). Yet the fact that Moses should, in Josephus's perspective, feel the need to avoid potential misunderstanding on this point, is already a reflection of considerable merit theology.

Such theology elsewhere evokes some whitewashing (e.g. *Ant.* i.205; ii.270-75; v.146). It produces even more bragging. Moses 'for grandeur of intellect and contempt of toils ... was the noblest Hebrew of them all' (*Ant.* ii.229); and he, in his defence of the fact that it was really God who had appointed Aaron High Priest, insists: 'For my part, had the weighing of this matter been entrusted to me, I should have adjudged myself worthy of the dignity, alike from that self-love that is innate in all, as also because I am conscious of having laboured abundantly for your salvation. But now God himself has judged Aaron worthy of this honour and has chosen him to be the priest, knowing him to be the more deserving among us' (*Ant.* iii.190-92; cf. iv.22-5, 54-7). Josephus himself repeatedly brags (e.g. *Vit.* 2, 82f., 174.; *Ap.* i. 47ff.; *BJ* iii.143f.).[2]

God stands as the guarantor behind the merit theology system, for he knows all and judges exhaustively and impartially (e.g. *BJ* i.595, 630f.; vii.33, 271; *Ant.* ii.320; ix.3). But he does not set aside man's freedom. 'God has a care for men, and by all kinds of premonitory signs shows His people the way of salvation, while they owe their destruction to folly and calamities of their own choosing' (*BJ* vi.310). Josephus declares: 'Other legislators, in fact, following fables, have in their writings imputed to the gods the disgraceful errors of men and thus furnished the wicked with a powerful excuse; our legislator, on the contrary, having shown that God possesses the very perfection of every virtue thought that men should strive to participate in it ... (*Ant.* i.22f.).' As a reaction against a degenerate and/or fatalistic form of paganism, by a monotheistic Jew, the statement is commendable; but Josephus has tied merit theology in with it.

With this sort of background it is not surprising that there is nothing of gracious election in Josephus, and little enough of any kind of election. The Jews are spoken of as those whom the Deity favours (*Ant.* ii.331-3), 'God having regard for none among men but you and lavishing on you the means whereby you may become the happiest of all the peoples beneath the sun' (*Ant.* iv.114; cf.117). But this does not refer to the *reasons* for God's favour, which, as we have already seen, rest on the merits of the patriarchs. Kings, however, are frequently said to be elected by God (e.g. *Ant.* vi.312; vii.27, 53, 198, 289, 338f., 376, 384f.; viii.276; ix.106, 108, 111) and in at least one case the choice itself is used as an encouragement to piety and a brave endeavour to be 'worthy of providence' (*Ant.* vii.338f.).

That brings us to consider the nature and scope of divine sovereignty according to Josephus. God is creator of all (*Ap.* ii.191f.; *BJ* iii.369f.; *Ant.* i.272). A large number of things are attributed to his providence: rescue at sea (*Vit.* 15), the frustrating of someone's plans for his (Josephus's) own welfare (*Vit.* 48), circumstances which save Josephus from death (*Vit.* 301), the turning of Vespasian's mind to thoughts of empire (*BJ* iii.404), the death of Aaron's sons (*Ant.* iii.208f.), peace (*BJ* v.278), the successful acquisition of Canaan (*Ant.* v.93,107), the birth of Samson (v.277), and the successes of David (*Ant.* vi.196). Not all of these are attributed to divine providence (*pronoia*), but that idea is present in every case. Hence, in the last-cited example, Josephus writes, 'David, being everywhere attended by God whithersoever he went, achieved success ...' Similarly, in *Ant.* viii.42 we read: 'Now so great was *(sic)* the prudence and wisdom which God granted Solomon that he surpassed the ancients, and even the Egyptians ....'

Certain things are repeatedly attributed to God. Success is one of them, especially military success (e.g. *Ap.* ii.48, 55; *BJ* iii.6f., 144; *Ant.* viii.295; x.40. xii.316, xiii.80; xiv.462f.; xvi.318; xviii.308f.; xx.48). Sometimes the bluntest of this language constitutes part of Josephus's apologetic: the Romans are bound to win because God is on their side. 'God, and no other, it was who made a present to the Romans of the wretched Galileans ...' (*BJ* iii.293). The providence of God standing behind Rome is a constant motif (e.g. *BJ* ii.390; iii.494f.; v.2, 367, 378-419; vi. 38-40, 108-10, 370f., 399-401, 411; vii.319). Not only success, however, but judgment, is attributed to God (e.g. *Ap.* ii.143; *BJ* i.81-4=*Ant.* xiii.314f.; *BJ* iii.539; iv.103f., 190, 288, 323; v.19f., 39, 342f.; vi.108-10, 250f.; vii. 325-35, 358f.; *Ant.* vi.307, 312; viii.241; xii.357). Most of the references in *Bellum* refer to the judgment of God on Jerusalem, even on the Temple: Jerusalem is 'no longer God's place' (*BJ* v.19f.). As for the defenders, God blinded their minds because of their transgressions (*BJ* v.342f.), making a Cassandra out of Josephus and his pleadings (*BJ* vi.108-10). In the *Antiquities* judgments often come upon individuals. Alcimus died by 'a sudden stroke from God' (*Ant.* xii.413); while 'Herod's illness became more and more acute, for God was inflicting just punishment upon him for his lawless deeds' (*Ant.* xvii.168-70). Especially is Josephus attracted to punishments which seem to be peculiarly appropriate. Hence he writes, 'I cannot ... but regard the penalty which Apion paid for maligning his country's laws as just and appropriate. An ulcer on his person rendered circumcision essential; the operation brought no relief, gangrene set in, and he died in terrible tortures' (*Ap.* ii.143). Moreover, God's ultimacy behind the most appalling judgment may be so strongly phrased as to provide a shield for the human instruments—even Titus and Caesar (*BJ* v.519; *Ant.* vi.214).

It is essential that people recognise that they owe all their blessings to God's benevolence (*Ant.* i.111f., 115; iv.212). Failure to do this was Sodom's sin (*Ant.* i.194f.); indeed, it is the custom for all who lack virtue to dismiss the possibility of the Deity's intervention in their crimes; but when they are caught they call for his help (*Ant.* xvii.129f.). This is not a blind confidence which Josephus is advocating, for he tells of a number of cases in which Jews appealed to God's care and providence and were disillusioned (e.g. *BJ* iii.28; iv.297; vi.98). The final 'proof' of divine providence is success.

If the final *proof* of the operation of providence is success, then historical success and historical judgment actually testify to God's providence. Hence, the terrible death of Catullus provides a striking demonstration of 'how God in his providence inflicts punishment on the wicked' (*BJ* vii.425f.). Onias took up arms against the usurper, Ptolemy Physcon, and 'the justice of his action was signally attested by God' (*Ap.* ii.52f.). A roof collapsed and failed to kill anyone, and from this incident 'one may see how well disposed God was toward the king [Herod]' (*Ant.* xii.455). (For other examples, see *Ap.* ii.160, 163; *BJ* i.215; v.367; *Ant.* ii.60; xviii.127ff., 284.)

All of these aspects of divine sovereignty are perfectly consonant with rigorous merit theology. One suspects that Josephus pictures divine omnipotence only in its positive implications (cf. *Ant.* v.312), for he does not sense any tension when he writes, 'What more beneficial than ... to be convinced that everything in the whole universe is under the eye and direction of God?' (*Ap.* ii.294).

Josephus actually introduces the sovereignty-responsibility tension into a few passages, but these never have to do with salvation. For example, Judas tells his father Jacob he might as well send Benjamin to Egypt, 'for nothing could be done to him save what God might send, and that was bound to befall even if he stayed with his father' (*Ant.* ii.116). In fact, the thought is somewhat naive; for if God's sovereignty is here taken absolutely, the statement is a non-comforting truism. Does not what befalls Benjamin under God's sovereignty embrace where Benjamin is, *and therefore what decision his father makes*? An analogous problem arises in *Ant.* x.34.

One other piece of evidence demands attention, viz. the many apparently pagan expressions in Josephus which parallel terms like 'providence'. No easy classification seems possible. The following list is simply a representative selection:

Vit. 17: Josephus reminds the Jews that they are inferior to the Romans, 'not only in military skill, but in good fortune' (*alla kai kat'eutychian*).

Vit. 27: 'I merely allude to them [the rising tide of events] here from a desire to convince my readers that the war with the Romans was due not so much to the deliberate choice of the Jews as to necessity' *(alla to pleon anankē)*.

Vit. 138: 'but I, committing my fate to God ...' *(egō de tō theō ta kat' emauton epitrepsas ...)*. The English translation is misleading.

Vit. 402: 'My success on that day would have been complete, had I not been thwarted by some evil genius *(mē empodōn genomenou daimonos tinos)*. My horse stumbled on a marshy spot. ...'

BJ i.11f.: Of all cities under Roman rule 'it was the lot of ours' to attain the highest felicity and plunge to the lowest depth of calamity.

BJ i.233: Malichus dreamed of raising a national revolt. 'But Destiny *(to chreōn)* derided his hopes', and Herod had him assassinated.

BJ i.275: 'Fate *(to chreōn)* ... proved to have outstripped (Herod's) zeal ...'

BJ i.370: 'But while he [Herod] was punishing his enemies, he was visited by another calamity—an act of God' *(epipiptei symphora daimonios allē*—the English translation is again misleading): an earthquake.

BJ i.373-9: Herod seeks to encourage his troops. 'To be disheartened by the visitations of heaven was natural' *(pros men ge tas daimonious plēgas athymein eikos ēn)*. He goes on to say that he views this catastrophe as a 'snare which God has laid' to trick the Arabs into thinking the Jews are done in. In any case, 'no disaster, whether inflicted by God or man' *(out' anthrōpeion ti kakon oute daimonion)* will ever reduce the valour of the Jews. In the parallel passage, *Ant.* xv. 144-46, Herod insists that what happened was not 'a sign of God's wrath, as some believe. These are only accidents and casual misfortunes *(alla tauta symptōmata ginetai kai pathē tina)*; and if they have been inflicted in accordance with God's will, it is clear that they have also come to an end in accordance with God's will ...' He also observes that none of the soldiers was hurt in the earthquake and concludes that God must want the war to go on.

BJ i.665: 'In [Herod's] life as a whole, he was blessed, if ever man was, by fortune' *(tychē dexia).*

BJ iii.144: Vespasian considers that the entry of Josephus into Jotapata is the greatest luck *(megiston eutychēma),* 'God's providential ordering' *(pronoia theou).*

BJ iii.389-91: Josephus draws lots with others in a suicide pact: 'fortune' *(tychē)* will decide. As it turns out, he is left alive alone with one other—'shall we say by fortune or the providence of God?' *(eite hypo tychēs chrē legein, eite hypo theou pronoias* [v.1]³).

BJ iv.297f.: Fate *(heimarmenē)* lulled some of the guards to sleep.

BJ iv.622: Fortune *(tychē)* was everywhere furthering Vespasian's wishes.

BJ v.367: Fortune *(tychē)* had passed to the Romans; and God, who passes empire around the nations, gave it to them.

BJ v.572: Jews were blinded by Fate *(hypo tou chreōn).*

Ant. iv.113f.: Balaam saw concerning Israel 'the indications of inflexible fate' *(atropos).*⁴

Ant. viii.409: It was Fate *(to chreōn),* I suppose, that prevailed and made the false prophet seem more convincing to Achab than the true one, in order to hasten Achab's end.

Ant. viii.412-14: Fate *(to chreōn)* got Achab killed by an arrow shot at random.

Ant. viii.418f. Nothing is more beneficial than prophecy, for it gives us foreknowledge of what to avoid. Yet, with Achab's history before us, we ought to 'reflect on the power of Fate *(to chreōn),* and see that not even with foreknowledge is it possible to escape it.' Note: Josephus is really stretching here. Prophecy gives us foreknowledge of what Fate will bring about so we may avoid it; but Fate is so powerful that we cannot avoid what it brings about!

Ant. x.76: Destiny *(tēs peprōmenēs)* urged Josiah to fight Nechao, 'in order to have a pretext for destroying him.'

Ant. xv.144-146: See on *BJ* i.373-379, *supra.*

Ant. xvi.76: Of Herod: 'In truth, a divine power *(to daimonion)* had given him a great many instances of good fortune *(eutychia)*, even more than he had hoped for, in external affairs, but in his own home it was his sad fate *(symbainein)* to meet with the greatest misfortunes *(dystychēs)* and such as he had never expected.'

Ant. xvi.210: 'For what man, except one who like this son of mine happened to be guided by good angels ... *(tis gar an, ei mē daimonōn agathōn etychen, hōsper houtos ho pais ...)*'

Ant. xvii.122: Fortune *(tychē)* delivered Antipater up to his enemies.

It is worth noting that several of these expressions can refer to both good and bad events (e.g. *tychē, to chreōn*). Even *daimōn* can refer to the help of heaven (*Ant.* xvi.210) as well as to 'fate' in the sense of 'misfortune' (*Vit.* 402). G. F. Moore has argued convincingly that Josephus's use of these terms is still within a monotheistic framework: that *to chreōn*, the 'must-be', is in reality neither fortune, *tychē*, nor fate, *heimarmenē*, as conceived by Greek writers, but the will of God revealed by the prophets.[5] Similarly for the other pagan terms he uses. His opinion gains support from the fact that pagan terms are considerably more frequent in *Bellum*, which has open imperial support, than in the *Antiquities.*[6]

Where, then, shall we place Josephus himself in those four famous passages in which he distinguishes among the Pharisees, Sadducees and Essenes (*BJ* ii.119-66; *Ant.* xiii.171-3; 288-98; xviii.11-25; the last of which also adds the Zealots)? The Pharisees are alleged 'to attribute everything to Fate and to God' *(heimarmenē te kai theō prosaptousi panta)*, holding 'that to act rightly or otherwise rests, indeed, for the most part with men, but that in each action Fate *(heimarmenē)* co-operates' (*BJ* ii.162f.). In this passage men and providence co-operate, according to the Pharisees; but in *Ant.* xiii.171-3, the division is in the events themselves: some are the work of Fate, but others depend on ourselves whether they take place or not.[7] *Ant.* xviii.11ff. appears to revert to the idea of a 'fusion' of the will of

man and Fate. Uniformly are the Essenes said to ascribe
everything to Fate. The Sadduceans do away with Fate; men
are responsible for their own well-being, while they 'remove
God beyond not merely the commission, but the very sight, of
evil' (*BJ* ii.164f.).[8] According to his own classification, Josephus
himself seems to fit more into the Pharisaic group than into any
other—which is, of course, where one would expect to find him.

To sum up: With lip service Josephus pays considerable
respect to divine providence; but closer examination limits such
providence to the convenient cases. Although he professes to
believe in 'Fate', in the last analysis the important *personal* and
moral decisions belong to men, and God acts as Judge. Inherent
in this pattern is the thought that God's rewards and punishments are distributed on the same principle: men get what
they themselves deserve. Hence history itself can at one and the
same time be used to testify to God's providential ordering and
to pronounce the moral rightness of the forces behind long-term
success.

CHAPTER TEN

CONCLUDING OBSERVATIONS

This short chapter is less concerned with summarising the material of this part of the book, than with highlighting several important findings which have fallen out of the study so far.

The first is the most obvious. Despite all the diversity which enriches intertestamental Judaism, certain trends are so clear they can scarcely be ignored. With the partial exception of the Dead Sea Scrolls, legalism is on the rise, and with it merit theology. T. F. Torrance makes a percipient remark when, though focusing his attention on a later age, he comments that 'legalism always [leads] to the growth of Pelagian notions of merit and of fulfilled duty'.[1] Whether this merit theology adopts, for instance, the garb of Jewish apocalyptic or of rabbinic discussion and legal formulation is not too important from the point of view of this study. Much more crucial are the formulated free will, the 'election' that is more response than grace (despite retention of the latter word), the emphasis on merit, the subtle fences built around God to protect him from charges of either finitude or of involvement with evil.

Some of the distinctions from corpus to corpus bear more significance for this work. The eschatological structure embraced by apocalyptic insures that God's present reign is to be sharply distinguished from his coming reign. The DSS preserve a curious independence from the main-stream trends surrounding them.

Yet it is extremely important to recognise that *none of this literature resolves or evades the question of divine sovereignty and human responsibility.* Implicitly or explicitly, the tension returns, in one form or another, to haunt us still. Individual writers may succeed in eliminating it from a particular passage or even from a particular theme; but this merely changes its shape. For example, formulated free will, understood to include power to contrary, may now absolve God from any apparent complicity in human evil; but then questions must be raised concerning the source of the human capacity for evil, or the manner in which God sovereignly controls history if he does not in some way control human decisions of a moral nature. Elimination of the tension in the arena of human moral responsibility or in the realm of soteriology does not eliminate the tension *per se. But it does radically transform its shape.*

It is the failure to recognise this which mars the otherwise excellent work of E. P. Sanders,[2] and entices him into too uniform and monolithic a presentation of the intertestamental literature. Again and again he observes that human decision stands side by side with divine 'grace'; but he never remarks that 'grace' is undergoing a major semantic shift. He draws attention to passages on election, but minimises the evidence which transforms 'election' almost into reward. I hasten to add that I agree with the thrust of his work and admire his massive competence in the sources; but in my view his polemical aim prevents him from being sufficiently sensitive to the changing face of the sovereignty-responsibility tension.

PART THREE

THE SOVEREIGNTY-RESPONSIBILITY TENSION IN THE GOSPEL OF JOHN

CHAPTER ELEVEN

THE BROAD DIMENSIONS

If the fourth Gospel begins with the *logos*, the Word, it begins equally with God. God was always with his self-expression *(logos)*, and this self-expression was God. God was the creator of all things, even if the evangelist's main point is that the act of creation was by means of the Word. The life which was the light of men (1.4) also finds its source in the *logos*, and thus in God. At this point (1.4) there is no question of the incarnation (which, in my view, finds its first definite mention in 1.9), but only of the source and mediation of all life. The life was also light, a light opposed, but not overcome,[1] by darkness. Thus in a few terse sentences, God and his *logos* together stand above the universe as Creator/Sustainer, and yet opposed to all in it that is contrary to light. The origin of the darkness is not mentioned.

It is not surprising, therefore, to find in the fourth Gospel examples of God's sovereign control over men and events, without the compromise of God's character. It is worth studying a few choice examples before examining how the sovereignty-responsibility tension is related to some of the major johannine themes.

SOME SPECIFIC EXAMPLES

John 3.27

'No one can receive anything except what is given him from heaven.' Several attempts have been made to limit the force of this verse. Brown thinks that in its context it means either (1) if only a few come to John the Baptist, it is because that is all God has given him; or (2) if many come to Jesus, it is because God has ordained it thus.[2] But the verse surely embraces both meanings. M.-E. Boismard offers an even narrower distinction: either (1) *autō* ((to) him) refers to the believer, and *dedomenon* (what is given) to the privilege of coming to Jesus (cf. 6.65), or (2) *autō* refers to Jesus, and *dedomenon* to the believer who is given to Jesus (cf. 6.37).[3] Of the two, (2) is more likely; but it offers no reference to John the Baptist at all, fitting only Brown's second alternative *(supra)*, and is too narrow an interpretation of the text. Lindars compares 3.27 with 19.11, in which the neuter *dedomenon* refers not to *exousia* (power) but to the whole verbal idea, and suggests 3.27 means that no one can receive anything unless the *capacity* to receive it be given to him.[4] But unlike 19.11, 3.27 has no conflict of gender (*hen* and *dedomenon* are both neuter, as indeed are the people whom God has given to the Son, when considered collectively: e.g. 6.37). Moreover, even the neuter *dedomenon* in 19.11 probably does not refer to the *capacity* to receive, but to the fact that the handing over of Jesus into Pilate's hands was determined by God. Lagrange, following Augustine, insists that the Baptist cannot be advising his disciples 'to recognise in success a gift from God', which would be 'a Gamaliel-style maxim (Acts 5.34ff.)'.[5] Therefore he takes the verse to mean that John the Baptist will not presume to take what the Father has not given him. However, the context (3.26) suggests that John, far from restraining himself and cutting back in his ministry so as not to overstep prescribed bounds, is faced with the fact that Jesus' popularity is soaring while his own is waning, and he must come to terms with what he cannot control.

The aphorism is very general: A man can receive only what is given him (i.e. granted him)[6] from heaven. The wide range of meanings attributed to the verse by exegetes reflects the possible ways it might be understood in this context; but the essential meaning of the maxim, and thus the power it has within its context, is not restricted by contextual limitations. In a theistic universe the maxim must be true (cf. 1 Cor. 4.7); but the Baptist uses this universal principle to explain his own peculiar position, giving ultimate significance to the movement of people from himself to Jesus.

Bultmann rightly notes that this principle says nothing about the right or wrong of the situation, and that even a robber could not take his spoils unless God so disposed (cf. 19.11).[7] He seeks to avoid the obvious difficulty by writing, 'The statement points beyond the sphere of moral judgment—which has its justification elsewhere; it justifies events, not persons.'[8] But would John recognise so sharp a dichotomy between *Person* and *Geschehen*, especially when he is considering what *a man* can receive (cf. 3.30)? This does not mean the Baptist is reduced to puppet status, for there is indeed a moral question for him to face: it concerns his response to his disciples' protests (3.26). The Baptist responds thoughtfully and humbly to the circumstances he cannot (and would not) change.

John's maxim about divine sovereignty, broad as it is, thus has several functions. It grounds his own magnificent humility (3.28-30), provides encouragement for his disciples who face discouraging circumstances they cannot control, and within the context of the fourth Gospel as a whole provides the ultimate rationale for this development in salvation history.

John 5.14; 9.1-3; 11.4

More difficult is the relationship between sin and sickness. Some scholars hold that 9.1-3 is normative for the johannine viewpoint, and argue that 5.14 does not expressly condemn the cured man for past sins, but warns him about the danger of persisting in sin in the future.[9] However, the natural implication of 5.14 with its present tense prohibition and comparative 'nothing worse', is that some explicit behaviour was the direct cause of the thirty-eight year paralysis. Indeed, although the New Testament as a whole dissociates disasters from particular sins, several passages forbid the conclusion that there is *never* a direct connection (e.g. Acts 5.1-11; 1 Cor. 11.30; Jas. 5.15?; 1 John 5.16).

In the case of the blind man, however, this is not the case (9.1ff.). The fact that the blindness was congenital provokes the question of 9.2. The disciples, far from being harsh, are most likely voicing opinions held by some of their contemporaries. But Jesus in this case rejects both alternatives offered him and says that this tragedy occurred 'that *(hina)* the works of God might be made manifest in him' (9.3). It is not clear whether *hina* introduces a purpose or a result. The latter view, held by few, suggests that God simply deflects the tragedy into something else; the former sees God's sovereignty operative in the tragedy itself, which has its *raison d'être* in the fact that it is about to be relieved, so that God's work might be displayed by this relief. Comparison with 11.4 renders unlikely any ecbatic view: Lazarus' illness is 'for the glory of God'. 'In any case John could not suppose that the man's birth and blindness were outside the control, and therefore the purpose, of God.'[10]

Nevertheless, Brown is right when he remarks, 'Jesus was asked about the cause of the man's blindness, but he answers in terms of its purpose.'[11] Jesus' reply locates the tragedy within God's control, but in terms not of mere cause-and-effect, but of purpose; and the purpose in view is the manifestation of God's works, of his glory (11.4), as a witness to the light, before men. In this sense John 9 goes beyond Luke 13.1-5, which equally refuses to forge a rigid link between personal disaster and personal sin, but which then diverges in application: Luke 13.1-5 concludes that all men are guilty and all will perish unless they repent, while John 9 discusses what seems to be a personal disaster, in terms of God's sovereignty being exercised for purposes of God's self-manifestation.

John 11.49-52

The prophecy of Caiaphas raises the sovereignty-responsibility tension a notch higher. If John 3.27 speaks of God's sovereignty in sweeping strokes but applies it in terms of salvation history, and if the sickness-and-sin passages (especially 9.1-3) connect divine sovereignty with personal disaster, now (11.49-52) God in some sense actually stands behind a sinful man and his sinful words.

Caiaphas was High Priest 'that (fateful) year': these words, far from betraying ignorance of the customs,[12] help to account for the unconscious prophecy of 11.50f.[13] Caiaphas did not utter these words 'of his own accord'. This does not mean that God was using the High Priest like a puppet, or like Balaam's ass. Caiaphas was giving his considered if callous opinion. The emphatic and contemptuous words, 'You know nothing at all', scarcely suggest good manners and noble reflection. His solution is repelling in its cynicism: he is interested neither in the moral issue, nor in the pragmatic best for the nation, but only in whatever is expedient to preserve the position of the aristocracy (11.48,51).

Johannine irony reaches a peak here. Jesus was put to death, and politically the people perished anyway, and the leaders lost their place. Yet he died 'for the people', and those of the nation who believed in him did not perish but received eternal life (3.16). Caiaphas meant that Jesus should die instead of the people as a political scapegoat; in fact, God stood behind Caiaphas' prophecy (quite unknown to him), ordaining that

Jesus was to die instead of the people in a redemptive sense. Whereas Caiaphas is thinking in terms of expedience, God is thinking in terms of salvation. So crucial a saving event as the death/exaltation of Jesus Christ could not be thought to turn on the whim of a sinful man: God himself was behind it, the God who loved the world so much tht he gave his unique Son (3.16). When Caiaphas spoke, it was God who was speaking, even if Caiaphas and God were not saying the same things. John presupposes that God never relinquishes his absolute sovereignty, and, by exercising his mysterious control, brings his purposes to pass.

John 19.10f.

God's sovereignty over Pilate (19.10f.) raises the tension again. There is a touch of incredulous arrogance in Pilate's question: 'You will not speak to *me* ('me' is emphatic in form and position)?' Pilate's own recognition of his authority 'makes nonsense of all the shifts to which he resorted in the attempt to avoid making a decision.'[14] Jesus' reply does not deny Pilate's authority, but insists that the Procurator would not have had[15] any authority at all over him had not the entire handing over of Jesus[16] been determined 'from above', i.e. by God. For this reason *(dia touto)* the one who handed Jesus over bears the greater guilt. This does not exonerate Pilate: if the sin of the one who hands Jesus over is greater, Pilate's sin is only relatively less.

The thought sequence from 19.11a to 19.11b is not obvious, and the obscurity has led some commentators astray. Morris, for example, plausibly selects Caiaphas as the betrayer, but implausibly accounts for his choice: Caiaphas he deems to be 'ultimately responsible' since Judas was a 'tool'.[17] But Judas was a *culpable* tool—both of Satan and of God (although John avoids such deterministic terminology for both Satan and God); and in this Judas does not stand alone, for neither Caiaphas nor Pilate is exempt from God's control (11.49-52; 19.11). We may compare Acts 4.27f. in which not only Pilate is regarded as a 'tool' of God, but so also is everyone else connected with the case.

So then, it is not God's overruling which mitigates *Pilate's* guilt, as if God did not overrule in the actions of the betrayer; rather, Jesus is saying that the handing over of himself, although determined by God, was the active plot of the betrayer, while Pilate's lesser guilt developed because Jesus was delivered into his charge. Pilate remained responsible for his spineless, politically-motivated decision; but at least he had not engineered the whole ugly scene. Pilate would have had no authority over Jesus at all, unless in God's purposes Jesus had been handed over to him. For this reason the one who actually handed Jesus over was more guilty than the Procurator.

Again, then, the saving event of the death/exaltation is specifically preserved within the sphere of God's acts, confirming Jesus' authority to lay down his own life as his Father commanded (10.18). Not less important, it is clear that divine sovereignty in no way mitigates human responsibility, while human guilt in no way contaminates divine holiness; yet the human moral choices are not fenced off from divine control.

Judas Iscariot

A final instance of note is the account of the fall of Judas Iscariot. As early as the closing verses of John 6, Judas's role as betrayer is identified. Peter's confession, tinged with over-confidence,[18] is gently put down by Jesus. He claims, by a rhetorical question, that he, not they, did the choosing (cf. 13.18; 15.16), and suggests further that Peter should speak only for himself, because one of the 'we' (6.68), one of the Twelve, is a devil (6.70).

Thus far, it is simply a question of Jesus' foreknowledge of Judas's course. But in 13.2, 18, 27, the picture changes. The relationship among these verses, particularly between 13.2 and 27, is complicated by two textual problems which cannot be ignored but must be carefully weighed. (1) *ginomenou* is attested by ℵ* BLWX Ψ *al.*, and *genomenou* by (p[66] *genamenou*) ℵ‘ AD[gr]K Δ ΘΠ f1,f.13 *al.* The aorist tense is the *lectio difficilior*, because the supper was still in progress (13.4,26); but even so it could be interpreted as ingressive, 'supper having been served'. (2) There are several variations touching *Ioudas Simōnos Iskariōtou*, the crucial difference being between the genitive *Iouda* (AD Δ Θ f1 *al.*) and the nominative *Ioudas* (p[66] ℵ BL WX *al.*). The latter entails translation to the effect that the devil had already put it into the heart that Judas should betray Jesus. The question is, Whose heart? Either the devil had put it into his own heart—i.e. he had decided; or he had put it into Judas's heart—an awkward way of saying what the genitive reading means. There are examples of the idiom 'putting into the heart of'.[19] On this basis Barrett argues the text means that Satan had put (the idea) into his *own* heart;[20] but as Lindars notes, 'this makes nonsense of the word *put*.'[21] Presumably *beblēkotos* would have to be *beblēmenou*. On every count, then, the *lectio difficilior*, which also has the superior external evidence, is best interpreted to mean that Satan had put into Judas's heart the idea of betraying Jesus. The awkwardness of the expression accounts for the variants; and moreover, Bauer rightly points out that the sentence, composed this way with the name of the betrayer at the end, provides striking, dramatic impact.[22]

Some see an irreconcilable contradiction between 13.2 and 27; but the contradiction is more in the eye of the beholder than in the text. If by 13.2 Satan has already put the evil suggestion into Judas's mind, it is not until 13.27 that Satan himself enters Judas. This step is touched off by Judas's personal acceptance of the 'morsel' (13.26f.): Judas has chosen for Satan.[23] Yet even after Satan's victory, Judas remains more than a robot, a puppet on a satanic string, for Jesus addresses *Judas* as the one who will act: 'What you are going to do, do quickly.'

Jesus' dismissal of Judas, however, suggests that it is he, not Judas, who determines the time of the passion. This observation recalls 13.18, where Judas's action is in some sense a fulfilment of Scripture. Jesus testifies, 'I know whom *(tinas)* I have chosen.' The pronoun *tinas* may be interpreted to mean either: (1) the *kind* of men—i.e. Jesus chose Judas knowing full well the sort of fellow he was; or (2) 'I know *whom* I have *really* chosen—and Judas is not among them.' Against (2) is 6.70. This prompts Barrett to opt for (1), and supply a lengthy ellipse before *all' hina*: 'therefore I know that Judas is a traitor, but I have chosen him in order that ...'[24] Others argue for an imperatival *hina*: 'But let Scripture be fulfilled ...'[25]

Purposive or imperatival, the clause insists on the sovereign control of Jesus, or of God (in fulfilling Scripture), respectively. In either case the necessity that Scripture be fulfilled is presupposed. The Scripture in question is Psalm 41.9, and it is cited in a form closer to the MT than to the LXX. The difficult expression 'has lifted his heel against me', however interpreted, casts Judas in the reprehensible role of being a close friend of and he is responsible; yet it comes about because God in his ultimate control has arranged things that way so Scripture may be fulfilled. Elsewhere we learn that Judas is 'the son of perdition' (17.12); and whether or not this expression itself implies that Judas was destined for perdition, its context requires that view. If he perished, it was not that Jesus' keeping power was insufficient, but that Scripture might be fulfilled. Judas is responsible for his treason (cf. 12.4-6; 18.2f., 5), and in this sense 'acted freely'; but it is contrary to the theology of the fourth Gospel to conclude from this that God 'merely used his evil act to bring about His purpose.'[26] Such a formulation makes God the one who *a posteriori* merely deflects Judas's sin, or manipulates it, to achieve his own ends; but the teleological nature of the fulfilment-motif renders such a formulation too easy.

In the case of both Caiaphas and Judas, therefore, divine ultimacy even behind evil actions is presupposed. But divine ultimacy operates in some mysterious way so that human responsibility is in no way mitigated, while the divine being is in no way tarnished. In particular, Judas is responsible even when Satan is using him; but over both stands the sovereignty of God. The mysterious ultimacy in this divine sovereignty conclusively limits johannine dualism and makes John savour more of the Old Testament than of Gnosticism. Already it is clear that 'the doctrine of predestination is apparent at every point in the Fourth Gospel, every incident being viewed *sub specie aeternitatis* as predestined in the mind of God.'[27]

FULFILMENT MOTIFS

The case of Judas has already underlined the importance of fulfilment motifs as an indication of God's sovereignty. This one instance can easily be multiplied by sketching the way the fourth Gospel uses the Old Testament, both in general terms and in specific quotations.

The fourth Gospel is full of the Old Testament, which it treats, not primarily as a source for proof-texts, but as the foundation for all that takes place in the revelation of God in Jesus. This has been well-documented, and need not be reviewed here. But it is worth pointing out how, from the perspective of the fourth evangelist, the Old Testament must be interpreted in a christocentric way, if it is to be interpreted aright (5.39f., 46f.). Not only did Moses and the prophets write about Jesus (1.45; 5.46f.), but Abraham saw his day (8.56) and Isaiah his glory (12.38). Jesus is the *logos*, whose introduction in the Prologue evokes thoughts both of Wisdom and of Genesis 1. Even the replacement motifs—e.g. Jesus not only cleanses the Temple but replaces it (2.13-22; cf. 4.21ff.);[28] replaces Moses, in part by surpassing him;[29] displaces the Jewish feasts and appropriates their cardinal symbols (2.13, 23; 5.1; 6.4; 7.2, 37, etc., and contexts)[30]—guarantee the christocentricity of this Gospel. These motifs are established by way of predominantly *pesher* exegesis which presupposes new revelation[31] enabling the identification of Jesus with the roles alluded to from Old Testament pages.

John's selection of the events he relates is not haphazard. Jesus came into the world to fulfil specific roles. Thus the disciples eventually understand *from the Scriptures* that Jesus *had* to rise from the dead (20.9). Specific references to Old Testament passages are most frequent in connection with Jesus' passion; and it is just here that such references become more and more connected with *hoti* (12.39) and *hina* (12.38; 13.18; 15.25; 17.12; 19.24, 28, 36f.; instead of *kathōs*, 1.23; 6.31; 7.38; 12.14).[32] What A. Richardson has said of the passion narrative in the Gospels in general holds for the fourth Gospel in particular:

> The vivid details of the Passion narratives, such as the casting of lots by the soldiers or the vinegar on the sponge, are not recorded by the Evangelists because they were good story tellers with an eye for pictorial effect, but because these incidents demonstrated the principle, *touto to gegrammenon dei telesthēnai* (Luke 22.37). The scandal of the cross ... was predetermined in all its details by the will of God.[33]

Two or three specific examples will clarify this point. John 15.18-24 ascribes to the world hatred, culpable ignorance, wilful blindness, and removes all excuse for such sin; yet 15.25 insists nevertheless that all this took place to fulfil[34] the Scripture which says, 'They hated me without a cause.' In context, Jesus is assuring his disciples that the sad state of affairs just described, far from indicating that plans have gone awry and circumstances are now out of control, is taking place precisely in accord with the very Scriptures of those who are hateful. As Lindars remarks, although the text is given to encourage the disciples, it 'has the effect of making the words apply to the inevitability of our Lord's sufferings, rather than just providing scriptural warrant for them.'[35]

In 19.23f., a similar point is made. John is interested in the gambling of the soldiers for Jesus' tunic, not because of alleged allegorical interest, nor because he wishes to depict the soldiers as greedy, insensitive men (although he probably takes that for granted), but because he wants to show that the Scriptures (Ps. 22.18) had to be fulfilled. So then (*men oun* occurs in John only here and at 20.30), the soldiers did these things. The same emphasis on the inevitability of the fulfilment of Scripture is found in 19.28.

For the first century believer, of course, where Scripture speaks, God speaks. Therefore it is the more remarkable that after this stress on the fulfilment of Scripture, John also emphasises the fuifilment of Jesus' own words (18.9, 32). Jesus repeatedly predicts his death (8.28; 13.18f.; 15.18ff.), and, as G. Reim points out, this prediction is connected with Jesus' identity as the 'Ego Eimi' of Isaiah.[36]

The main point to be learned from this survey of johannine fulfilment motifs is that among the factors which have gone into John's use of the Old Testament are 'the Christian conviction of eschatological fulfilment and messianic presence.'[37] These developments, far from being seen as fortuitous, are recognised as the necessary unfolding of *Heilsgeschichte* according to God's plan. 'Anything less like the heroic redemption of a bad situation by some desperate and improvised measure can hardly be imagined ... What has happened is only the emergence into history of what was eternally laid up in the[d]etermination of God.'[38]

JOHANNINE ESCHATOLOGY

The student who turns to this area of johannine studies is plunged into a vortex of questions. In this section I shall limit myself to discussion of the following points: (1) The hour. This is important for our study because it provides the evangelist with another way of picturing the fixedness of God's purposes, and the unfolding of historical events according to divine timing to bring about divine ends. (2) Literary and historical reconstructions which deal with the tension between realised and future eschatology in the fourth Gospel. Eschatology is crucial to this discussion, because it deals with new developments in the reign (i.e., the exercise of the sovereignty) of God. If the conceptual structure of a book revolves around future eschatology, then that structure will approximate to the Jewish apocalyptic pattern; but where realised eschatology is on the ascendancy, new patterns of the tension between God's sovereignty and man's responsibility necessarily emerge. (3) Theological constructions which deal with the tension between realised and future eschatology in the fourth Gospel. The most common approaches need to be surveyed rapidly to see what light they can shed on the sovereignty-responsibility tension. (4) The *terminus a quo* of the eschatological age, according to John. It is necessary to determine this, because it is *from that point on* that the tension takes on new forms. (5) Towards a new synthesis—one which treats johannine eschatology with sensitivity concerning the relationship between such eschatology and the sovereignty-responsibility tension.

1. The hour

The emphasis upon fulfilment in the passion narratives, as we have seen, stresses the inevitability of the death/exaltation event. This inevitability finds explicit confirmation in the 'mustness' *(dei)* both of Christ's death (3.14; 12.34) and of his resurrection (20.9); and these things constitute the 'hour', toward which the fourth Gospel moves and with which it climaxes. At the beginning the hour has not yet come (2.4; 7.30; 8.20); by the end it has arrived (12.23; 13.30,32; 17.1), the hour which embraces the purpose of Jesus' coming (12.27). Until the arrival of that hour it is impossible for anyone to take Jesus' life (7.30, 44; 8.20). Not just the passion, however, but all of Jesus' life is governed by express submission to the father's schedule (2.4; *kairos*, 7.6, 8). This view may even be supported by John's specific time references ('it was such-and-such an hour').

That Jesus can speak, in 12.23, of the hour as having arrived, and then continue to do so all the way to 17.1, suggests a theological motif which climaxes at the cross but which is present incipiently throughout Jesus' ministry. For this reason, Jesus can speak of the hour coming, but being present now (4.23; 5.25), i.e. in his ministry. Beyond each of the exchanges within that ministry lies the climactic 'now' (12.31; 13.31) of his death/exaltation.

The fixedness of Jesus' 'hour' does not turn on impersonal fatalism, but on the will of the Father, to which Jesus submits—unlike other men (7.6, 8; 12.23, 27f.). God's personal rule is thus related both to the arrival of the eschatological hour, and to the obedience of the Son. Johannine eschatology and christology must therefore be examined in connection with God's sovereignty.

2. Literary and historical reconstructions which deal with the tension between realised and future eschatology in the fourth Gospel

Rudolph Bultmann excises apocalyptic elements from the fourth Gospel (in particular, all or parts of John 5.28-30; 6.39f., 44, 54; 11.24; 12.48; 21.22), attributing them to an ecclesiastical redactor; but in doing so he has been followed by few and opposed by many. Others have also tried to detect diverse communities or some other cause as the reason for what some take to be disparate literary strata. I have argued elsewhere, however, that although one may, a priori, suppose it likely that the fourth evangelist did indeed use literary sources, nevertheless current source-critical theories are methodologically deficient and therefore unconvincing.[39] Therefore in this chapter and the next I choose to treat the fourth Gospel as it stands.

Nevertheless the crux of the problem raised by the source critics transcends the question of method: it concerns as well the Gospel's place in the christian tradition, as indexed by its eschatology. Numerous views have been expounded. C. H. Dodd, for example, holds that John in this respect more accurately preserves the teaching of Jesus than do the Synoptics, which introduced apocalyptic motifs into the earliest kerygma, and that in John these lingering apocalyptic motifs are completely absorbed by realised eschatology.[40] E. Stauffer agrees that the imminent expectation of the kingdom formed no part of Jesus' teaching, and that the fourth Gospel is protesting against the persistently ascendant view of apocalyptic.[41] The dominical view, according to J. A. T. Robinson, was that the kingdom came with Christ, and that the subsequently developed delayed-return doctrine eventually burned itself out in disappointment and then identified the bestowal of the Holy Spirit, without remainder, with the return of Christ.[42]

These views seek to explain the eschatology of the fourth Gospel in terms of reconstructed primitive church history. What Bultmann excises, these reconstructions regard as residue. None of these reconstructions gives enough weight to the stubborn fact that John *does* include the basic elements of the two-age structure. It is more accurate to acknowledge that the Gospel of John takes its place along with other New Testament books in bearing witness to the tension between the 'already' and the 'not yet'. Indeed, this feature has virtually become the *Mitte* of one of the most recent New Testament theologies.[43] In this substantially accurate model, the age to come has already arrived in the person and work of Jesus, but awaits the consummation at his return. This interim invests christian apocalyptic with numerous elements not present in its Jewish forbear, not least the tension between the 'already' and the 'not yet'.

But the observation that John preserves the tension, true though it is, does not explain why he reflects so high a degree of realised eschatology. The excisions and historical reconstructions not being convincing, numerous synthetic theological solutions have been proposed.

3. Theological constructions which deal with the tension between realised and future eschatology in the fourth Gospel

Opposed to those who see in the realised eschatology of the fourth Gospel a reaction against the apocalpytic enthusiasm of the early church is L. van Hartingsveld, who, himself over-reacting, argues that futurist eschatology predominates in John.[44] Van Hartingsveld goes so far as to insist that eternal life is an eschatological gift of salvation only promised, and appropriated in a preliminary way by faith.[45] He thus solves the problem of the high degree of realised eschatology in John by denying it is there. Resurrection life and judgment experienced in the present he takes to be examples of language being used to divide the committed from the uncommitted.

O. Cullmann's explanation for the fact that 'the "already" stands in the foreground more dominantly' is that 'the whole perspective of the Gospel puts the historical life of Jesus in its

place as the decisive mid-point of history more emphatically
than any other Gospel does.'[46] However, besides the fact that he
has overstressed *Heilsgeschichte* in John, this still does not
explain *why* Jesus should be more emphatically presented as
'the decisive mid-point of history' in this Gospel.

Cullmann's student, P. Ricca, likewise stresses *Heilsgeschichte* with a real *parousia* to look forward to, even if the
word isn't used.[47] But because no final conflict is mentioned,
Ricca argues that the *parousia* has significance only for the
church; and when it happens, for believers life will be crowned
with resurrection. But at this point Ricca balks, for he cannot
see how the new glory will differ from the old; and if it does not
differ, the two are indistinguishable. Ricca is reduced to saying
that the church is a *continuum eschatologicum*, a continuing
parousia in which the Lord's presence is as real as in the days
of his flesh and as real as on the last day. For Ricca, this is the
key to the problem: eschatology is christology. The End came,
has come, will come; and all is dominated by Christ, who came,
has come, and will come. There is but one eschatological event:
Jesus himself. All that Ricca has granted with one hand he has
taken away with the other. What begins as an excellent study
degenerates when his key to the problem conflicts with his
earlier exposition.

For J. Blank, too, eschatology is a function of christology.[48]
Christ confronts men and brings salvation; but strangely, Blank
argues that judgment is not a function of Christ but of sinful
men who reject Christ's offer of salvation. He rightly maintains
that realised eschatology predominates in the fourth Gospel, but
comes closer than he thinks to Bultmann's anthropological
interpretation *(infra)*.

A. Corell follows the lead given by Scandinavian scholars
who see a connection between eschatology and the Church.[49] He
sees the Church as a projection of the earthly life of Jesus, yet
also an anticipation of the final fulfilment. To make John thus
sound like Paul, he rides some of John's symbols very hard, and
quite misses the accent on individualism in the fourth Gospel
observed by C. F. D. Moule.[50] But Moule's explanation—that
realised eschatology is the correlative of an accent on
individualism (cf. especially 14.23) as futurist eschatology is of
corporate thinking—although at first sight attractive, founders
on several verses in the sixth chapter, viz. 6.39f., 44, 54. In 6.39,

what Jesus will raise on the last day is *auto*—i.e. all (whom) the Father has given him; but in 6.40, 44, 54, the object of Jesus' resurrection power is *auton*, the *individual* believer. In other words, there is evidence for the combination of futurist eschatology and individualism.[51]

One of the most recent efforts to explain the high degree of realised eschatology in the fourth Gospel comes from D. E. Aune.[52] He argues for a *Sitz im Leben* in which christian pneumatic prophets were giving words accepted as those of the Risen Christ (he could not have seen the most recent telling attacks against this common theory),[53] and explains that the exalted Lord is both expected and experienced in the cultic worship of the johannine community. Aune regards 1.51 as the *crux interpretum* of his hypothesis that the *visio Christi* is the central point of the johannine cultus, and adduces parallels of angels involved in the corporate worship of God's people. He argues that 1.51 reflects a stereotyped revelation-form common in late Judaism and early Christianity, and regards the cumulative force of these observations as a 'decisive clue' that the evangelist means by 1.51 'the kind of event which the Johannine community experienced pneumatically within the context of the community at worship.'[54] It is always risky to build one's case on a difficult and highly disputed passage; and the rest of Aune's speculative exposition never succeeds in replacing the lost conviction. If the cultus is the explanation of the realised eschatology of the fourth Gospel, the evangelist has hidden the fact extraordinarily well.

The best known, yet most difficult to understand, theological reconstruction is Bultmann's. Bultmann's chief hermeneutical principle, reliance on *Sachkritik*, coupled with his philosophical lode-star, a form of Heideggerian existentialism, lead him to collapse Easter, Pentecost, and the *parousia* into the moment of proclamation.[55] He does not argue that the eschaton is the present (in the sense that the age to come has in some sense overlapped the present age), but that the eschaton is present in the moment of the existential encounter. The eschatological, for Bultmann, is that which transcends world history—an abuse of language.

Bultmann emphasises the vertical dualism in John, at the expense of the eschatological (horizontal) dualism. The Son of man comes down from heaven (3.13): the Word has become flesh (1.14). The culmination of his life is in his death exaltation: he is 'lifted up' (12.32). The constant contrast between what is from above and what is from below (3.3, 31; 8.23), between the realm of spirit and the realm of flesh (3.6; 6.63), reflects the same stance. The world and its ruler (16.11) are in darkness whereas Jesus is the light (8.12). He enables men to become sons of light (12.36; cf. 9.5; 11.9; 12.35, 46). Jesus' kingdom is not of this world (18.36), and so if anyone is to 'see' it or enter it he must be born from above (anōthen;[56] 3.3, 5). This vertical dualism is not absolute: the world was made by the Word (1.3) and is still loved by God (3.16), even if it is now characterised by wickedness (7.7). But the strength of the vertical dualism must not be minimised.

At the same time, John reflects a genuine eschatological dualism. Cullmann is right in so far as he shows that the world from above comes to us in the context of redemptive *history*. Hence, as Brown puts it, 'Jewish history has been the preparation for this climactic era (iv 21-23).'[57] Moreover, although the new age has dawned, bringing both life and judgment in the present, the full gift of life does not come during Jesus' ministry but only afterward through the resurrection of the last day. The transition from 'life' in the first sense to 'life' in the second sense is unmistakable in 5.21-30, and in the reverse order in 11.24-6. Not only is there a future element in christian life—even Bultmann admits that—but the basic structure of the two ages is also present (5.28f.; 6.39f., 44, 54; 12.48; possibly 14.2f.; and in the epilogue, 21.22f.).

Despite this criticism, Bultmann, Dodd, and Blank are correct in insisting that the main emphasis in the fourth Gospel is on realised eschatology, even if they do not accord the apocalyptic structure its rightful place.

4. The terminus a quo of the eschatological age

Granted a form of the two-age structure, it becomes imperative to discover just when the eschatological age first dawns. There are three inter-locking puzzles which contribute to this problem. These puzzles begin with the theological unity of the saving event—Jesus' death/resurrection/exaltation/bestowal of the Spirit—and weigh this theological unity against: (1) the place of *Heilsgeschichte* in John; (2) the problem of the so-called 'johannine Pentecost' (20.22); (3) the status of the disciples before and after the saving event.

The unity of the saving event itself is underscored by John's distinctive use of 'to glorify' and 'to lift up' (as commentators now recognise) taking place at the decisive hour (*supra*). Chronologically, Jesus' death, resurrection, exaltation and bestowal of the spirit are separated; but theologically John sees them as one. If this perspective be pressed: (1) genuine *Heilsgeschichte* must be reduced to a minimum; (2) there is a strong case for viewing 20.22 as John's version of Pentecost;[58] (3) there are true believers only *after* the saving event. But in each case major qualification is necessary.

On (1), as I have pointed out already, O. Cullmann has made a strong plea for a good deal of *Heilsgeschichte* in John; and even if he has over-stated his case, he cannot be dismissed. But there is nothing that prevents John from making theological capital while preserving his historical framework. This point is best seen in John 20, where the time lapses in vv. 1, 19, 26 preclude a *merely* theological understanding of the chapter; yet at the same time there is the genuinely theological question of the relationship among 20.17, 22, 27.

This brings us to (2). Because John elsewhere argues that the Paraclete cannot come until Jesus is glorified (7.39; 16.7), it is frequently argued that 20.17 urges the unity of the resurrection and the ascension, which must therefore have taken place between 20.17 and 20.19, because the Spirit is given in 20.22. This argument, it is thought, is strengthened by the different approaches to touching the resurrected Jesus in 20.17 and 20.27.

Against this position the following points are worth considering: (a) C. F. D. Moule explains the differences between 20.17 and 20.27 in terms of the different needs of two disciples. (b) He has also pointed out that 'I am ascending' (20.17) is located in the message Mary is to convey, not given as the reason for her not to 'touch' him.[59] The words 'I have not yet ascended' do not imply that Jesus was in the process of ascending, but only that Mary need not cling since Jesus has not ascended. (c) The very physical demonstration of 20.27 surely argues that Jesus has not yet ascended.[60] The contrast between seeing-believing and not-seeing-believing (20.29) confirms this point by presupposing that Jesus ascended sub-

sequent to 20.28. Attempts to avoid this point are unconvincing.
(d) Those who stress the theological unity of the events must
admit *some* time lapse ('not yet', 20.17) in any case. (e) Under
their scheme, they must think it strange that Jesus' dying word
was 'It is finished' (19.30), instead of the more appropriate 'I
am ascending'. (f) J. D. G. Dunn points out that the different
responses in 20.16 and 28 probably have no significance 'in
view of the identity of the responses in vv. 18 and 25.'[61] (g)
Moreover, those who see 20.22 as the johannine Pentecost, yet
who do *not* think that Jesus has yet definitively ascended, have
even less ground to stand upon, since the bestowal of the Spirit
could not have taken place until this step in Jesus' glorification
(7.39; 16.7).

Common to these approaches is a misapprehension of the
relationship between theology and history in the fourth Gospel.
John is undoubtedly selecting and moulding and explaining the
history he reports, but he is not trying to write a theological
treatise which uses history in purely symbolic ways.[62] On the
other hand, although he acknowledges the temporally sequential
nature of Jesus' ministry/death/resurrection/bestowal-of-the-
Spirit, he sees them as theologically unified. It is not so much
that 'for John the gift of the Spirit is a direct *consequence* of the
death of Jesus, like the Ascension, not a separate event,'[63] as
that for John the gift of the Spirit is a direct *consequence* of
Jesus' glorification, *even though* a separate event.

Because the totality of the saving event emerges as a
theological unity, Jesus greets the advent of the hour (12.23)
before he has even eaten the last supper. This is the whole
purpose of Jesus' coming; and so as early as 10.18 he can say, 'I
lay [my life] down of my own accord', just as he can say,
equally in the present tense but with reference to the future, 'I
am ascending to my Father and your Father' (20.17); and in
both cases it rather misses the point to ask with a straight face,
'Right away?' The sequential arrangement and time lapses
relate to history; the unity of the saving event relates to
theology. True it is that 'the theological motif can be adequately
highlighted without obscuring the chronological outline.'[64]
Theologically, the constituent parts of this saving work of Jesus
are not 'chronologically disposed',[65] while historically they are.

To conclude that John 20.22 is not a 'johannine Pentecost',
however, raises more acutely the question of what the verse *does*

mean. Must we really conclude that John thought the gift of the Spirit was given by Jesus' 'insufflation'? Perhaps the word 'insufflation' is misleading: Schonfield's 'he expelled a deep breath' is attractive. As far as I have been able to determine, the verb *emphysaō*, a New Testament *hapax*, occurs absolutely in the active voice only in John 20.22, never elsewhere in either classical or hellenistic Greek. The LXX, for instance, offers many diverse constructions (e.g. Gen. 2.7; 3 Reigns 17.21; Tob. 6.8. *(v.1.)*; Ezek. 21.36; Ecclus. 43.4; Nah. 2.2); but no absolute usage. BAG, p. 257, cites John 20.22 as an instance of absolute usage 'for the purpose of transmitting the Spirit'; but of its alleged parallels none presents an absolute parallel. At very least John's usage is strange, which accounts for the late addition of 'on them' (Tatian's Diatessaron, D syr^{cur}). If John purposely does not want to go so far as to say that Jesus was actually bestowing the Spirit at that time, he might well have avoided adding 'the Spirit' or 'into them'.

Is it not possible to take this 'exhalation' as an acted parable picturing the gift of the Spirit within the theological unity of the total saving event, without insisting that John thinks the Spirit was acutally bestowed at that moment? Jesus' action speaks of the gift of the Spirit to come, but within a context which relates it to the other elements of the 'hour'. John 20.22 is the acted equivalent not of Acts 2.1ff. but of Luke 24.45-9. This 'giving' of the Spirit is not a gift different from the one in Acts, nor a sort of private proleptic downpayment, but an acted parable pointing ahead. A suitable johannine analogy is the washing of the disciples' feet (John 13.1ff.). Even Jesus' words 'Receive the Holy Spirit' do not conclusively demonstrate that 20.22 is meant to portray the bestowal of the actual gift. Elsewhere in the fourth Gospel Jesus gives commands which in the nature of the case cannot be obeyed at the time: cf. especially 7.37-9. Although this explanation of 20.22 seems incapable of final proof, it enjoys the advantage of avoiding the shortcomings of the other options (e.g., the stubborn fact that Thomas is not present), while according well with the interplay between history and theology in this Gospel.

Consideration of point (3) follows as a matter of course. To ask what is the *terminus a quo* of the eschatological age in John invites a double reply. Theologically, the eschatological age is introduced by the saving work of Christ from incarnation to bestowal of the Spirit, seen as one unified event, with perhaps special emphasis on his death/exaltation. Historically, however, the situation is more ambiguous, since on the chronological plane the believers are living through a unique and unrepeatable transition between the dispensations.

> Now, if we understand the significant events of John in a chronological scheme which links up with Acts, we have to say that the transition period between the dispensations lasted from Jesus' death to Pentecost, if not from the beginning of his ministry to Pentecost, if not from his birth to Pentecost. What we now call full Christian experience was possible only after the ascension and Pentecost, when the 'advocate from heaven' came to represent and act for the 'advocate in heaven'. Likewise, the experience of the new birth and new creation was possible only after the sin-bearing death of the Lamb of God and his resurrection.[66]

This suggests that there are true believers in a *full* christian sense only *after* Jesus Christ has performed all the steps in this climactic saving event. That means there are no full believers until *after* the setting pictured in the fourth Gospel, while those who read the Gospel *are* full believers or are invited to become such. The inherent ambiguity in this situation has contributed to the ambiguity surrounding just who is, and who is not, a believer among those with whom Jesus has to do. It is the tension between *Sitz im Leben der Kirche* and *Sitz im Leben Jesu*. Not only are the disciples, prior to the death/exaltation, seriously lacking in understanding (e.g. 2.22; 12.16; 20.9; cf. 14.26), but apparent belief in Jesus during his ministry is seen again and again to be quite unstable,[67] a point to which I shall return in the next chapter. Thomas's faith is thus a great leap forward; but even such faith cannot match the faith of later believers (20.28f.).

One might almost speak of a double *terminus a quo*: one that is theologically precise and another enmeshed in transitional history. What can be made of these disparate data?

5. Towards a new synthesis

A major part of the problem lies in its formulation. To begin with, vertical dualism and horizontal dualism are too often set over against each other. One recent writer wrongly argues that the dualism of Judaism runs along the horizontal line, and that since John embraces a good deal of vertical dualism, the horizontal perspective is 'in process of dissolution'.[68] H. Odeberg noted long ago that late Judaism makes place for both.[69]

But there are more compelling reasons for synthesis. I have shown that in intertestamental apocalyptic the difference between God's reigning activity in this age, as compared with the age to come, lies in the fact that only the age to come is the setting of God's saving acts and open blessings toward his people, and, concomitantly, his judgment on his foes. The vertical dimension in apocalyptic tends to be restricted in this present age to the private experience of the seer. Therefore, the greater the degree of realised eschatology, the more likely are we to find *in history* the open reign and blessings of the transcendent God. If John betrays more realised eschatology than do the Synoptic Gospels, it is only to be expected that he will have more vertical dualism as well. Emphasis on the vertical dualism increases in proportion with the stress on realised eschatology, not in inverse proportion with the accent on horizontal dualism, from which it is quite independent.[70]

We may go further. In simple apocalyptic, God introduces the age to come without so much as a 'by your leave'. There is no question of man's will co-operating with God at that point: God acts. The christian parallel is the *parousia*, the last day. But New Testament eschatology (including John) has appropriated the two-age structure in such a way that the age to come has already arrived in a preliminary way. Some of the features of the next age emerge now, and others, obviously, cannot. The ultimate finality of resurrection life and judgment await the 'last day'; but men experience life and judgment now. The delay means there is still opportunity for men to respond to God; and yet, because the age has dawned, everything seems much more urgent than before. That it is *God's* activity stands out the more sharply; and so *a priori* one would expect greater stress on God's unconditioned sovereignty in saving men. The marked degree of realised eschatology entails the greater unveiling of God's salvific activity, i.e. more vertical dualism. But the converse is also true. The greater the emphasis on vertical dualism operative now, the greater the degree of realised eschatology.

These conclusions can be tied together with remarks about

the double *terminus a quo* of this new age, one that is theologically precise and the other enmeshed in transitional history. John's readers are not to see themselves in the same position as those whose lives were touched by Jesus within the Gospel itself. They live *after* that transitional history, and *after* the unified saving event. But the emphasis on the theological unity and cruciality of this saving event has the effect of insisting that subsequent history be seen in its light. The saving event has taken place, and the new age has dawned. Realised eschatology is therefore stronger in the fourth Gospel than in the synoptics because of John's more developed theology of Jesus' death/exaltation, in which God has come down and acted decisively. Of course, if theology were to take over completely, it would be impossible to speak of a crucial 'saving event'. One would be reduced to speaking about eternal truths. The event must be historical. But a merely historical description of the saving event, giving little more than the bare bones of what happened, would fail to present the uniqueness and significance of that event, and therefore its evangelistic implications, in the most forceful way. John's readers must realise that God has already acted; Christ has descended, died and been exalted, and now they must approach the historical Jesus from the perspective of faith.

JOHANNINE CHRISTOLOGY

If Jesus is understood to be both God and man, then in him, if anywhere, the tension between God's sovereignty and man's responsibility will come to its sharpest focus. This section, then, seeks to explore the relationship between the sovereignty-responsibility tension and the distinctive way in which the fourth Gospel presents Jesus. It does not attempt to survey the titles ascribed to him, and thus avoids, for example, the knotty problem of the Son of man sayings, except in so far as it impinges on the immediate topic.[71]

1. A survey of the evidence

The fourth Gospel, perhaps more insistently than any other New Testament book, ascribes deity to Jesus. The *Logos*, identified with Jesus Christ (1.14, 17), was not only 'with God', but 'was God' (1.1). The *Logos* joined God in the work of creation (1.3). In the three most common critical editions of the

Greek New Testament,[72] Jesus himself is called *monogenēs theos*, 'the unique God', or the 'unique One, God' (1.18; the latter word is probably in apposition). The staggering element to do with Thomas's confession (20.28) is Jesus' reply (20.29); and this confirms Barrett's observation on 1.1: 'John intends that the whole of his gospel shall be read in the light of this verse. The deeds and words of Jesus are the deeds and words of God; if this be not true the book is blasphemous.'[73] In short, John provides us with three references in which the title 'God' is explicitly given to Jesus (1.1, 18; 20.28); and, as has often been noted, John inserts them with considerable deliberation: the pre-existent *Logos* is God (1.1), the incarnate *Logos* is God (1.18), and the resurrected Christ is God (20.28).

Jesus' deity, however, does not depend only on the direct ascription of *theos* to him. Jesus insists that to believe in him is to believe in the one who sent him (12.44), to look at him is to look at the one who sent him (12.45; 14.9), to hate him is to hate the Father (15.23). He says that all must honour the Son even as they honour the Father (5.23), that he and his Father are one (10.30). We not only learn that the Son cannot do anything except what the father shows him, but that the Son does *whatever* the Father does (5.19). At least one scholar thinks the word 'work', when applied to Jesus in the fourth Gospel, reflects the inner unity between the Father and the Son. The 'I am' statements, in particular the absolute ones (cf. especially 8.58), are claims not only for pre-existence but for deity.[74] Pre-existence does not entail deity; but in the johannine view of things it certainly entails more than ordinary humanity. Pre-existence is repeatedly ascribed to Jesus (1.1, 15, 30; 8.58; 15.5, 24), and it is implied by the ideas of Jesus having come (5.43; 6.14; 7.28; 10.10; 11.27; 15.22; 18.37; etc.), being from God (6.46; 7.29; 9.33; 16.27f.; 17.8), and being sent by God (3.17, 34; 4.34; 5.23f.; 6.39f.; 7.16; 8.16, 18; 9.4; 10.36; 11.42; 12.44f.; 13.20; 14.24; 15.21; 17.3, 8, 18, 21, 23, 25; 20.21; etc.). Not one is before him. Certainly the Jews are represented as hating him precisely because he made himself equal with God (5.17f.; 10.33; 19.7).

At the same time, John refers to Jesus as a 'man' (1.30; 4.29; 8.40; 9.11f., 16; 10.33; 19.5)[75]—even on the lips of Jesus himself (8.40). Admittedly, these references are incidental. However, whatever the attributes of the Word, 'the Word became flesh' (1.14); and despite the efforts of E. Käsemann (on which see *infra*) this clause is best understood within a pattern of humiliation from which the Son is glorified by exaltation to the position he once possessed (17.5), but temporarily relinquished. Although the *Logos* springs from God, 'the Salvation' (=*hē sōtēria*: a title?)[76] is of the Jews (4.22). If this is a title, then the text can only mean that Jesus springs from the Jewish race—a decidedly human phenomenon. Pilate's words 'Here is the man!' (19.5) may have been uttered in coarse jest, or to arouse feelings of contempt if not pity; but coupled with 'Here is your king!' (19.14), it is hard to resist the conclusion that the evangelist himself, a master at double meanings, saw Jesus as a man in the depths of humiliation and yet the king.[77] Jesus grew tired and thirsty (4.6f.; 19.28), loved and wept (11.5, 35). He was tempted (6.15, 31; 7.3f.; although this is not stressed). Moreover, whereas he sometimes manifests supernatural knowledge (e.g. 1.48; 2.25; 5.42; 6.6; 6.15?; 6.64; 13.21; 14.29; 16.30; 18.4), there are occasions when he appears to learn things like other men (4.1; 5.6; 7.1; 11.3f.). When he dies, from his side flow blood and water (19.34).[78]

But above all, John presents Jesus as completely and utterly dependent on the Father—for his power (5.19, 30; 8.28; 10.37; 14.10), knowledge (5.30; 8.16), his entire mission (4.34; 6.38; 17.4). These references could be multiplied, and have been well presented, if overstated, by J. E. Davey.[79]

It is possible from such passages as 15.18; 17.16, 21 to conclude that there is no intrinsic difference between Jesus and other (christian) men: they are not of the world, just as he is not of the world, and his prayer for them is that they be one, just as he and his Father are one (although this last petition equally points to Jesus' distinctive unity with the Father). Such an approach plays with the evidence selectively, for nothing is clearer in the fourth Gospel than Jesus' uniqueness. Even in the passages cited, there are qualifying factors. In 15.18f. Jesus has *chosen* his disciples out of the world; in 17.24 they will be rewarded with seeing Jesus' glory. The oneness which Jesus enjoys with his Father can pertain to moral and functional categories, and thus be shared by his disciples (as in 8.42; 17.21; cf. most commentaries on 8.38ff.—e.g. Barrett, Brown, Lindars, Morris), but it is not restricted to such spheres. In John, men may become *ta tekna* of God, but only Jesus is *ho huios*—

indeed, *ho monogenēs huios*. Although a man, no man ever
spoke as he (7.46), who surpasses John the Baptist (1.15, 27,
30; 3.27ff.) and even Moses (1.17). His relationship with the
Father is special (2.16); he is 'from above' in a unique sense,
and is therefore above all (3.31).[80] He sets the pattern for
humility (13.12ff.) but he stands alone in his claim for
supremacy and honour (e.g. 5.23; 12.8). He is *the* Son of God
(1.49); and whereas he chooses men, he is himself exclusively
God's Chosen One, God's Elect (1.34).[81]

By any reckoning, Jesus is in some sense God, in some sense
man, and in some sense unique. How may these things be
integrated with each other and with johannine theology? And
what understanding of the sovereignty-responsibility tension is
betrayed by these data?

2. A selection of proposed solutions

The following list is not meant to be exhaustive; but it does
represent a fair selection of modern thought on the christology
of the fourth Gospel. I should add that the various categories
occasionally overlap somewhat.

(i) The most common modern approach to johannine
christology is to fence the evangelist's language off from
ontological categories when in one way or the other he ascribes
deity to Jesus. This method develops in different ways, but it is
found in writers from Cullmann to Bultmann[82] (and even in
one as conservative as A. M. Hunter),[83] and usually pictures
Jesus' deity as God-in-revelation. M. Appold[84] insists that
Jesus' oneness with the Father is not to be explained in moral,
metaphysical, or philosophical categories. Rather, it is a oneness
of 'equivalent relationality' *(sic)*, which, if I understand him
aright, is a functional category. J. A. T. Robinson's argument
'places Jesus on exactly the same metaphysical level as every
other son of God yet attests him functionally unique, because he
alone "always does what is acceptable to God"'.[85] In discussing
the matter, R. Kysar prefers to adopt the terminology 'function'
and 'person', instead of 'function' and 'ontology';[86] but I doubt if
this refinement substantively changes very much. In any case, it
is far from clear that absolute distinctions between what is
'functional' and what is 'ontological' can legitimately be made.[87]
'It is questionable whether St John gave any thought to the
ontological nature of the sonship', writes T. E. Pollard;[88] to

which the appropriate initial rejoinder is: 'It is doubtful whether St John gave any thought to the functional nature of the sonship.' Beyond that, it is of utmost importance to recognise that both ontological and functional categories can be found in John, a point inconsistently recognised by Pollard himself in the same paragraph, when he cites 7.19 and 14.9 and concludes, 'Jesus claims to reproduce not only the Father's thought and action, but also his very nature.'[89]

(ii) Many of those who appeal to the functional elements in the deity of Christ in John's Gospel also make recourse to hellenism. Fuller does this, and of course Bultmann. Lindars takes the same approach, arguing that the ascription of *theos* to Jesus shows that 'the restraining influence of rigid Jewish monotheism is beginning to weaken'.[90] The habit of calling Jesus *kyrios*, it is argued, led naturally to calling him *theos*, by analogy to 'the Lord God' in the LXX. Referring to Jesus as God subsequently becomes very common in the epistles of Ignatius, a further step in the hellenising process.

Too many objections may be raised against this easy answer. First, as B. A. Mastin has shown,[91] Ignatius's ascription of *theos* to Jesus is quite in contrast to the careful reserve exhibited by John. Ignatius repeatedly speaks of Jesus as 'our God'; he writes of 'the passion of my God', and 'the blood of God', and so forth. Second, I have already indicated how common it was in Jewish circles to speak of divine-like beings. In particular, R. N. Longenecker has pointed out that six of the New Testament passages which call Jesus God appear 'in the writings representative of the *Jewish* cycle of witness', whereas only two or three can be identified in the Paulines. Longenecker argues—and Mastin agrees—that ascribing deity to Jesus in a Gentile setting would suggest he was one god among many; whereas ascribing deity to Jesus in a Jewish setting would lead to 'a rethinking of traditional monotheism in an attempt to include the idea of plurality within a basic unity'[92]—unless it led to a charge of blasphemy.

(iii) In an earlier essay,[93] Mastin suggested that ascription of deity to Jesus in John 20.28 was prompted by the imperial cult under Domitian. Suetonius tells us Domitian was addressed as *dominus et deus noster*, to which Christians might well reply that Jesus alone was Lord and God. However, it is by no means universally agreed that the fourth Gospel was written at so late a date. Moreover, it seems strange that the christian response (if such it be) is not framed as a plural confession to parallel the imperially prompted confession (the book of Revelation provides better parallels). Even if John 20.28 were in any way called forth as a response to the imperial cult, that cult can scarcely account for John 1.1, 18. Besides, this fourth Gospel, in contrast to the Apocalypse, does not smack of conflict between Christianity and the imperial cult.

(iv) A fourth explanation has been offered by R. E. Brown. Brown argues that the passages in the New Testament (including the fourth Gospel) which specifically give Jesus the title *theos* are either in hymns or doxologies, and he supposes that this is an indication that the title 'God' was applied to Jesus more quickly in liturgical formulae than in narrative or epistolary literature.[94] Brown, in agreement with many others, regards the Prologue (which embraces the first two crucial references, 1.1, 18) as a hymn that was edited before insertion into the fourth Gospel. Moreover, he regards 20.28 as a response evocative of an early christian liturgy, Thomas speaking on behalf of the entire christian community. He thinks Revelation 4.11, 'Worthy art thou, *our Lord and God*', a confirmation of his interpretation.

There is some truth in what Brown is saying; but his general theory fits the fourth Gospel less convincingly than it fits other parts of the New Testament. J. T. Sanders is willing to concede that the johannine Prologue is 'religious poetry', but, on formal grounds he argues that it is not a hymn in the same sense that the other passages he studies are hymns.[95] C. K. Barrett, in an important essay,[96] insists that the Prologue is not verse, but rhythmical prose, written originally in Greek, and by the evangelist. Not all of Barrett's arguments are convincing, but his main thesis is eminently defensible. Moreover, Mastin has pointed out that the definition of 'doxology' becomes a little vague if John 20.28 and Revelation 4.11 are both lumped together under this rubric. To serve as evidence that they both reflect the same liturgical/doxological response, they would have to be identical in form and they are not. On the face of it, John 20 is prose narrative; and in Revelation 4.11 the words 'our Lord and our God' simply identify who is worthy to be praised. In any case, our massive ignorance of first century christian liturgy makes theories which depend on early and well-developed liturgy more speculative than most others (and for the same reason, more difficult to disprove!).

(v) B. A. Mastin, in his recent article, already referred to,[97] sides more or less with those who see Jewish background as the dominating influence on the fourth Gospel. However, he suggests that it is the church-synagogue clash which calls forth the ascription of deity to Jesus. As the synagogue minimises the significance of Jesus, so the church is helped to see his significance. In particular, he cites the johannine passages in which Jesus is in conflict with the Jews, in conflict which turns on Jesus' identity (cf. especially 5.17f.; 8.58.; 10.30ff., and their contexts). By way of reply, however, certain things must be observed: (1) The three passages which unambiguously ascribe the title *theos* to Jesus are *not* in settings of Jewish/ christian controversy. (2) Mastin's theory approximates more closely than he thinks to the thesis that Jesus was deified in proportion as christianity drew away from Jewish monotheism and towards hellenistic polytheism, despite the strictures he imposes on the latter. *Both* see Christianity's withdrawal from Jewish thought as in some sense the pre-condition for the ascription of deity to Jesus; and therefore *both* fall under the stubborn evidence adduced by Longenecker and others. (3) I am unhappy with the way church/synagogue disputes are getting blamed for everything in the fourth Gospel these days. The subject is so vast, I can here barely mention it. Nevertheless I must say that Leistner's insistence[98] that John is not as anti-Jewish as some suppose makes a great deal of sense to me; while the circular reasoning which crops up repeatedly in a work like J. Louis Martyn's[99] engenders suspicion that a clever theory is being foisted on the evidence.

(vi) C. K. Barrett frames the problem in terms of a dialecti-cal christology.[100] He rejects as anachronistic the efforts to detect 'two natures'—e.g. to see the subordinationist passages (especially 14.28) as a reference to Jesus' humanity—as he rejects majority patristic and some Reformed attempts to find distinctions between Father and Son independent of the incarnation. His own approach is to focus on one point at a time, and thus to discover the fourth Gospel is christocentric in confronting men, but that even the christocentricity is theo-centric, the ultimate goal being to worship *God* in spirit and in truth. At the same time, although he admits that even those passages affirming Christ's deity *accommodate* a distinction between Jesus and God (e.g. 1.1-18; 5.1-47; 10.22-39), he strenuously insists that this is *accommodation*, not *obliteration*. I think his analysis is essentially correct. My criticisms are threefold: (1) The word 'dialectical' is extremely slippery, being used by Barthians, Marxists, and Bultmannians in quite distinctive ways. It is better avoided. (2) Barrett puts too many johannine contrasts under this category in any case—a point to which I must return. (3) His analysis does not explain the genesis of this 'dialectic'.

(vii) K. Haacker's stimulating dissertation argues that the high point in the Prologue is not 1.14, but 1.17: Jesus is the *'Stifter'* (founder) of a new religion, replacing Moses and his religion.[101] In showing how Jesus outstrips Moses, the evangelist must show how Jesus' revelation comes from God in an unprecedented fashion, a way that surpasses all that Moses or any other predecessor brought. Haacker argues that the motifs of the 'sending' and the 'descent' of Jesus are introduced to establish Jesus' superiority;[102] and that even

> the presentation of his pre-existence is, like Christ's descent, a derivative of the revelation motif. In any case, this is so whenever revelation takes on soteriological significance for the whole world. Pre-existence is the model *(Umsetzung)* of the divine origin in the time category, just as the descent motif is the model of the divine origin in the spatial category of primitive cosmology.[103]

Moreover, in Jewish thought even pre-existent things like Torah, and in some cases Moses, were nevertheless created; but the fourth Gospel ascribes absolute pre-existence to Jesus Christ, again to establish his superiority.

Haacker's analysis, though impressive, stumbles on his method. The superiority of Jesus and his revelation over all predecessors can indeed be plotted throughout the fourth Gospel; but it is not so all-embracing a motif as Haacker thinks. To make any one verse in the Prologue (1.14 or 1.17) so controlling a factor blinds the interpreter to other strands of thought. Most of the texts which Haacker cites concerning Jesus' pre-existence, descent, and the like, are not obviously in contexts which relate to a contrast between Jesus and previous 'founders'.

(viii) Of other proposed solutions to johannine christology, none has created as much stir in recent years as that of E. Käsemann.[104] Although not the first in this generation to argue for a docetic christology in the fourth Gospel,[105] Käsemann has put the case so forcefully that he has called forth a barrage of protest. Somewhat ironically, while for Bultmann and Cullmann Christ's deity is nothing but God in revelation, for Käsemann christ's humanity, his 'flesh' in 1.14, 'is for the evangelist nothing other than the possibility for the Logos, as Creator and Revealer, to communicate with men.'[106] He understands Jesus' humanity, not his deity, functionally. As is well known, Käsemann views 1.14a as 'the absolute minimum of the constume designed for the one who dwelt for a little while among men',[107] needed only to make 1.14b possible; while most of the subordinationist passages serve only to establish Jesus' authority.

Most of Käsemann's critics have focused on the fact that he has blown up one side of the evidence and seriously ignored the other.[108] At least one has called his position 'nothing more than absurd'.[109] Another concedes Käsemann's point for the body of the fourth Gospel, but thinks 1.14 is a late anti-docetic addition.[110] K. Berger argues that the verb *ginomai* ('to become'; 1.14) would have to be *'erscheinen'* ('to appear') to suit Käsemann's theory. Berger himself does not see in 1.14 an incarnation so much as a theophany.[111]

3. Towards a better synthesis: the transcendent God personally expounded

Before the exile, the chief problem in Israel was her tendency to drift toward idolatry. After the exile, the problem shifted. We have observed in the intertestamental literature a tendency to stress divine transcendence at the expense of divine personality. Under this over-arching umbrella of sovereign transcendence, the people operated in increasing independence: divine ultimacy was squeezed out of the sphere of human moral decisions. Necessarily, God became, in some ways, a little removed from his people.[112] Free will became formulated for the first time in Jewish writings.

Now if Longenecker and others have shown that the ascription of deity to Jesus was first made in Jewish Christian circles (*supra*), the evidence I have adduced from Jewish intertestamental literature reveals the beginning of a need for such a development in the same circles in spite of their simultaneous emphasis on the unity of God—indeed, almost because of it.

John presents this christology in such a way as to fill this need. Some scholars have recognised this. J. Jeremias, for example, says, that although God had in some ways revealed himself in the past, 'he had remained full of mystery, incomprehensible, inscrutable, invisible'; but at one point 'God took off the mask' and spoke clearly and distinctly: and Jesus Christ is that Word.[113] Another says:

> ... God has quite personally and eschatologically disclosed himself in the man Jesus and has spoken and acted through this man. Thus for John Jesus as 'the Son' is the *full-fledged presence* of God (italics his) ... and God personally meets men exclusively through the man Jesus.[114]

> Being truly God and truly man, and being also the image of God and the archetype of humanity, (Jesus) is an ontological mediator between God and man; he is no less a mediator of true knowledge, and of salvation.[115]

In short, '.He is—as it is once expressed in Col. 1.15—the visible image of the invisible Father.'[116]

Without, for the moment, further pursuing the question of ontology, I propose now to sketch in John's picture of Jesus, focusing attention first on Jesus' God-like functions, and then on his man-like functions.

The Prologue begins with the *logos*, who from the beginning not only was with God, but was God (1.1). The distinction between the *logos* and God *(ho logos ēn pros ton theon)* makes possible his becoming something other than just God (1.14); their identification *(theos ēn ho logos)* makes certain that the revelation is indeed God revealing himself (1.18). The Prologue concludes with the *logos* becoming flesh (1.14), being identified as Jesus Christ (1.15, 17). The invisible God has thus become visible (1.14f., 18). Between the opening and the close of the Prologue, otherwise transcendent features of God's activity are by this means brought near: the same *logos* was involved in creation (1.3), and has come to what is his own (1.10f.). Even the possibility of salvation by becoming children of God is patterned on this bridging of the gulf between God and men

(1.12f.): 'In this way, the necessary and constantly reiterated scriptural affirmation of the infinite distance between God and man, and the affirmation of the coming of the Son of God who bridges this abyss in making believers participate in his divine sonship, are harmoniously related.'[117]

Because Jesus thus bridges the gulf between the infinite God and finite man, the argument can leap with neither warning nor impropriety from Jesus and his words and work back to God and his words and work. Hence, for example, in 3.33ff., the person who receives the witness of *Jesus* 'sets his seal to this, that *God* is true.' Jesus' words are God's words (3.34); that is the reason why the one who receives *Jesus'* witness confirms that *God* is true. Lest there be any suspicion that not all of Jesus' words are God's words, the evangelist hastens to add that God has given the Spirit without measure to Jesus (if we may take the clause that way), and so loved him as to give everything into his hand (3.34f.). This leap from Jesus to God is not exceptional. In precisely the same way, the faith that leads to life hears *Jesus'* words and believes the *one who sent him* (5.24; 14.24). Only Jesus has seen the Father (6.46); but to know Jesus is to know the Father (8.19).

God, then, supremely at the 'hour', glorifies his Son and is thereby glorified in him (17.1; 13.31). By accomplishing the work the Father has given him to do, Jesus has glorified the Father, and will be returned to the glory he once shared with the Father (17.4f.). His work entails passing on God's glory (17.22), the glory of the 'one and only God' (*monogenēs theos*), witnessed by his disciples (1.18). Even the descent/ascent theme presupposed by this perspective stresses the revelation of God to man.

The fourth Gospel thus admirably preserves the distance between God and men, while simultaneously bridging that distance by the incarnate *logos*, the Son of God. His coming corresponds to the vertical dimension in johannine eschatology. If contemporary Judaism was convinced that no one could see God until the age to come, John was announcing that the age to come had arrived even in this respect: the first disciples had seen Jesus. There was more glory still to be seen (17.24); but the divine presence had already been expounded to the believers (1.18; 17.26).

What about all the passages which underline the 'sentness' of

Jesus and his dependence on his Father? On these points, Käsemann has come very near the truth, despite the objections of his critics. Most of the passages which mark Jesus' dependence and 'sentness' function in their contexts as the ground of Jesus' authority (5.17f., 19-30; 6.28, 32f.; 7.16, 18, 28f.; 8.16, 29, 42; 10.17f.; 11.41f.; 12.45, 48ff.; 14.23f., 28-31; 17.2, 7). In speaking God's words (3.34; 7.16; 8.26, 38, 40; 14.10, 24; 17.8), performing only the Father's works (4.34; 5.17, 19ff., 30, 36; 8.28; 14.10; 17.4, 14), and doing the Father's will (4.34; 5.30; 6.38; 10.25, 37), Jesus is 'the voice and hand of the Father'.[118]

In connection with the 'hour' and the fulfilment of Scripture, we have already seen how Jesus is in no way dependent on the whims and decisions of men, but only on the will of the Father. Even the classic subordinationist passage, 14.28, calls for some such comment as that of Loisy: 'It is understood that the Christ, because of his heavenly origin, is in essence divine, since he compares himself with the Father.'[119] Perhaps the omission of some scenes from the synoptic tradition (e.g. the temptation, Gethsemane, the cry of dereliction) finds its reason in this, that to include them might hinder the presentation of the crossing of the barrier between transcendence and finitude.

Supremely, then, Jesus the Son of God is seen in the fourth Gospel as the mediator between the Father and men. The Father is therefore presented not so much in his relation to the world, as in his relation to the Son. Even in 3.16, the Father's love for the *world* causes him to send his *Son*; while in 3.34f. and 5.19f. the Father's love for the *Son* prompts him to show the *Son* all he does, and place everything in his hand. 'To get to the bottom [of johannine thought], it must be recognised that the foundation of the church is the fact, not of a sort of divine philanthropy, but of the personal love of the Father for the Son.'[120] The glory to which Jesus is moving, he already had with the Father before the world began (17.5); but it was given him because of the Father's pre-cosmic love for the Son (17.24). Christians will be especially loved by the Father (14.21-3), but only in their relationship of obedience to the Son. And if the Father is asked to take over some of the functions of the Son (17.11ff.), it is because the Son's work is coming to an end, and the time for the coming of the other Paraclete, for whom the Son himself has prayed (14.16ff.), is drawing on.

All of these features, however, gloss over the stubborn fact that Jesus is consistently presented in a position of subservience and, more specifically, unswerving obedience, to his Father. His food is to do the will of the one who sent him (4.34); and, despite the fact that Jesus' dependence is frequently set in contexts which give him authority, it is real dependence nonetheless. The world must learn that Jesus does exactly what his Father has commanded him, despite the vigorous attack by the prince of the world (16.30f.). This is true not only of the father's words and actions, which the Son takes over, but, as we have seen, of the entire passion: 'the passion belongs to the commission the Father laid on the Son; and Jesus in loving obedience has discharged this commission, right to the last detail'[121] (cf. 18.11, 37; 19.17?; 19.28-30). Thus, even though stress is laid on the fact that the entire 'hour' and its events are predestined by God and foretold by Scripture, equal stress is laid on Jesus' willingness to drink the cup the Father has given him (18.11), to lay down his life of his own accord (10.18). This is the reason the Father loves the Son (10.17; cf. 8.29). The cured blind man was right when he noted that God listens to the godly man who performs his will (9.31). In Jesus, therefore, the certainty of divine predestination and the significant freedom of obedient response meet in a spectacular display.

> It is in the life and death of Jesus Christ that the problem of free will and predestination finds its most poignant expression, and here, too, if anywhere, it must find its solution. The predetermined one freely chooses his appointed destiny: 'not what I will, but what thou wilt' (Mark 14.36). In Christ, the elect of God, perfect freedom and absolute determination intersect; human freedom and divine omnipotence meet and are one. The problem of free will and determination can be solved only in the new humanity of Jesus Christ.[122]

Real freedom for a man is freedom from sin (8.34ff.), that is, a freedom which voluntarily performs God's will, in the way Jesus kept his Father's word (8.54). Or, as C. F. D. Moule has put it:

> Jesus exhibits the nature and character of God in the only way in which they can be absolutely and perfectly exhibited in the context of human behaviour, namely in such a

relationship as properly belongs to man over against God, the relationship of glad and willing filial obedience. To this extent the paradox of glory and humiliation, of equality and subordination, is resolved in that relationship of perfect intimacy and identity of purpose which expresses itself in perfect obedience. Oneness of will is expressed in subordination of will, freedom in constraint.[123]

We have observed that when Caiaphas prophesied (11.49ff.), he did not speak *aph' heautou* ('of his own accord'; lit. 'of himself'). But Jesus can say, similarly, 'The words that I say to you I do not speak *ap' emautou*, on my own authority' (lit., 'of myself'; 14.10). God's sovereignty therefore remains intact whatever the response of men may be; but men are not thereby absolved of their responsibility to do his will. Caiaphas speaks out of arrogance; Jesus speaks out of conscious obedience to the Father.

Another corollary of the stress on Jesus' obedience arises from the observation that responsibility is exercised first of all *towards God.* This does not mean that Jesus does not act graciously towards other men; it means rather that he acts graciously towards them because he acts responsibly towards his Father. He gives his life for the sheep; but this is a command received from his Father (John 10.15ff.). He preserves all the Father gives him and resurrects them on the last day, because this is the Father's will (6.37-40). He washes his disciples' feet in token of spiritual cleansing, for he knows the hour has come for the final act (13.1ff.).

At the same time, this last action becomes a paradigm of self-sacrificing service for the disciples (13.12ff.),[124] constituting in fact the 'new commandment' (13.34), to love as Jesus has loved. The same pattern—Jesus' special sacrifice, followed by its function as paradigm for others—is found also in 12.24f. In his sacrifice, Jesus was first of all pleasing his Father, thus standing with men in the necessity of obeying God. But although the sacrifice was unique, it was nevertheless so self-giving that it becomes a paradigm for others to follow; and in establishing the pattern in a new commandment Jesus stands with God in conscious authority. Thus, Jesus stands alternatively with men and with God. On the one hand, he has kept his Father's word (4.34; 8.29, 55; 15.10), and men are exhorted to follow his example and keep Jesus' word (5.24; 14.21; 15.10; cf. 8.37)—which, on the other hand, is his Father's word (8.28, 38; 12.49f.; 14.24), and therefore binds men with all the authority of God. The position of Jesus Christ in all these patterns may be schematised like this:

GOD

over against man: Jesus stands with God in revelation and authority

(JESUS)

over against God: Jesus stands with man in obedience and dependence

MAN

Thus, the Son can do nothing by himself (5.19, 30), just as the disciples can do nothing without Jesus (15.4). But the Father loves the Son and shows him all he does (5.20), while the Son loves his disciples as the Father loves him (15.9), and has chosen them to go and bear fruit (15.16).

Jesus stands with God and expounds divine transcendence to finite men; he stands with men and demonstrates in his own life the proper relationship between men and God. This structure is called forth by the entire Christ-event, and the church's Spirit-guided understanding of it as the ultimate revelation of the transcendent and holy God to finite and sinful men. Moreover, in the fourth Gospel the sovereignty-responsibility tension has merged with the tension in the divine-human christology, so that the two are virtually one.

THEODICY

The insights gained from studying johannine eschatology and christology contribute to an understanding of John's stance *vis-à-vis* 'evil'. John deals with three aspects of evil: (1) moral wickedness; (2) the suffering of sickness; (3) the suffering that arises from persecution.

In the case of moral wickedness, John attempts no answer as to its origin. God in some way, as we have seen, stands behind it; but equally, he stands over against it, so much so that the *logos* becomes the lamb of God who takes away the world's sin, and the wrath of God is manifest against it (1.29; 3.36). In the case of the suffering of sickness, answers vary: it may be caused by specific sin (5.14), or without reference to sin. When God stands more directly behind illness and death, the accent is on his purpose rather than his causation (9.3; 11.4). That purpose is the manifestation of God's glory. In the case of suffering due to persecution—which receives predominant treatment—the answers come in terms of Christ's example, the bestowal of the Spirit (which is related to realised eschatology), and futurist eschatology.

In the Old Testament, the unknownness of God's ways, and the consequent need to trust him, constitute a major part of the theodicy. However, in John's Gospel, there is a new revelatory stance: believers are 'friends' rather than 'slaves', precisely because they are told their master's business (15.14f.; discussed *infra*). The new age has dawned; but because it dawns in two climactic stages, there is on the one hand a sense of arrival, of solution, of victory; and on the other, and to a lesser degree, a sense of release-still-to come, of long-range expectation.

The realised eschatology promises peace and joy despite trouble (14.27; 15.11; 16.33). This is connected with the promised Spirit/Paraclete (14.16-18, 25ff.; 15.26; 16.7ff.), whose roles include making present the presence of God (14.16f.; cf. 14.23), and teaching the disciples, making known to them what pertains to Jesus (14.25f.; 16.14). Therefore it is best for the believers that Jesus go away, so that the Paraclete may be given (16.7). Moreover, Jesus has chosen his followers out of the world, and therefore the world hates them; but they are to remember that the world hated Jesus first (16.18-20). This is why John's christology is so crucial for this aspect of theodicy. With the coming of the 'hour' has come the most spectacular display of how God himself, in his *Logos*, reacts under fire. Suffering for righteousness' sake as God's will is for Jesus' followers, if not more comprehensible, at least more bearable, precisely because Jesus the Son of God passed that way, and his servants are not above him. Therefore it is no accident that this thought (16.19-20) is expounded right after the declaration that the disciples' status is changed by more revelation (16.14ff.): Jesus *is* that revelation. He has made known everything he learned from his Father (16.15), because he himself has expounded the Father (1.18; 17.6, 26). Theodicy as a personal dilemma (as opposed to a philosophical conundrum) is more bearable in proportion as God is understood to be *for* and *with* his people rather than *against* them or merely *over* them. From Jesus' own example the disciples also learn that suffering according to God's will glorifies God. To point out that the suffering of the disciples may have the same purpose is one of the functions of the epilogue (cf. especially 21.19). Of course, this realised eschatology is not the whole story: the 'last day' and the resurrection of the just and the unjust is still to come (5.28f.).

John is not primarily interested in the problem of theodicy, and it is useless to speculate what else he might have said. But his eschatological and christological emphases have contributed fundamentally to his understanding of the problem, however incidentally he displays such understanding. Certainly he never deploys a naive merit theology to promise an escape which could not materialise.

CHAPTER TWELVE

THE SOTERIOLOGY OF JOHN

HUMAN RESPONSIBILITY

Whatever is made of John's emphasis on election *(infra)*, many elements conspire to convince the reader that John holds men responsible for their plight.

1. Universal sinfulness and its crippling effect

Sin in the fourth Gospel has often been treated in a reductionist fashion which identifies it, without remainder, with unbelief. The root of sin is the failure to recognise God as God, in particular the refusal to acknowledge and receive the *logos* (1.10). But it is more than simple unbelief.[1] It manifests itself in profanation of the Temple (2.13ff.), wicked deeds (3.19f.), adultery (4.16-18), sin which brings illness (5.14), self-complacency in the matter of pleasing God (5.44), gross materialism (6.26), fickleness (6.66), treachery (6.71, etc.), hypocritical 'justice' (7.23f.), murderous intent (7.30; 8.59; 11.48ff.), tyrannous bondage (8.21, 24, 32-6), lying and murder (8.44), rejection of light (9.41), theft (12.6), corruption (12.10f; 19.12f.), religious hypocrisy (18.28), physical violence (18.22; 19.1-3). The lack of detailed ethical discussion is no sufficient index of the scope of the johannine view of sin, 'because the Fourth Gospel does assert the ethical seriousness of Jesus quite as strongly as Matthew, albeit in its own way.'[2] Sin is something with the most ominous consequences (3.36; 5.14, 29), something which the Lamb of God must take away, even while men must give it up, if they are to be free (5.14; 8.21ff., and the weakly attested 8.11). The constant threat of judgment (e.g. 3.18, 36; 12.47f.) demands repentance, even if the word itself is not used.

Another indication of John's view of sin is his use of *kosmos*, 'world'. Some writers attempt to divide John's uses of the word into three categories: positive, neutral, and negative. On such a basis, for example, N. H. Cassem finds that all the positive references are in John 1-12, and that 1 John was written to counteract any suggestion that the *kosmos* could have positive features.[3] His position will not stand close scrutiny. All references designated 'positive' do not give a rosy hue to kosmos, but to God and his salvific purposes. The best value that can ever be assigned to *kosmos* is 'neutral' (e.g. at 12.19; 16.21; 11.9; 17.5, 25; 21.25), and even some apparently neutral usages (e.g. 'He was in the world, and the world was made through him', 1.10), simply pave the way for mention of the heinous crime of unbelief ('yet the world knew him not'). If the *logos* is the true light which comes into the *kosmos* (1.9), it is because the *kosmos* is characterised by darkness. If God sent Christ so that the *kosmos* might be saved by him (3.17), it is because the *kosmos* is lost without him. Similarly, 1.29 says a great deal for the Lamb of God, but not much for the *kosmos*. In short, the *kosmos* hates (7.7). In particular it hates Jesus, because he lays bare the horror of its evil, which exposure it tries to shun (3.20).

Jesus' charge to his attackers, that not one of them keeps the law (7.19), is both inclusive and particularised. Sins characterise all those 'from below' (8.21, 23f.), and surely lead to 'death in sins' apart from belief in Jesus. Jesus' condemnation of them is broken up by their interruptions (8.22, 25), which suggest the people are oblivious to their sin, ignoring it in favour of questioning him. Even when many 'trusted in his name', Jesus 'would not entrust himself to them' (2.23-5, NIV), precisely because he knew what was in *all men*. This negative universalism, to give it a label, is a repeated feature of John (cf. 1.10f.; 2.23-5; 3.19f., 32; 4.48; 6.26f.; 12.39-41). The fact that it is in each case relieved by reference to some who do respond,[4] however inadequately, does not suggest that such people are intrinsically less sinful, but only that they have come out of this background.

Contrary to first impressions, John 15.21-4 likewise presupposed guilt *before* the coming of Jesus. The world (15.18ff.) has not become guilty of sin in an absolute sense, because Jesus came, as if Jesus' coming induced sin in an otherwise pure world. The clause 'If I had not come' (15.22) is not co-ordinate with 'and spoken to them'. This is an instance of the semitic tendency to co-ordinate what is logically subordinate[5] (a point supported by 15.24 where the notion of 'coming' is absent). Equally important is the context. Jesus has been outlining the reasons for the world's persecution of believers(15.18-21): the world acts this way because it does not recognise Jesus' authority (his 'name') nor know the one who sent him (cf. also 16.3). If, having come, Jesus had not spoken to them (i.e., to the members of the world), they would not be guilty of the sin in question, viz. persecuting Jesus and his disciples. But Jesus' word and works do not *induce* sin, so much as show the world up for what it is. The world has never been confronted quite this way before; and now Jesus' words and work simultaneously arouse the animosity of the *kosmos* and rob it of all excuse.

This universal sinfulness manifests itself in an unwillingness to come to Jesus (5.40). It presupposes a self-love which makes men morally *incapable* of belief (5.44). Jesus' opponents do not really love God in their hearts (5.42). The demonstration of this is found in the next verse: 'I have come in my Father's name, and you do not receive me.' One might have expected Jesus to continue, 'If I had come in my own name, you would have received me.' He does not do so, precisely because he is so much at one with the Father it is inconceivable that he could do other than please him (8.29). Thus it is *God's* authoritative revelation that is being rejected. But if another person comes *in his own name*, he will be received, because he does not come with final and ultimate authority which demands instant submission and obedience. As long as the Jews are willing to receive glory from one another (and, implicitly, to give glory to one another), they *cannot* believe any divine revelation which lifts their eyes Godward to make them strive for the glory that comes from the only God (5.44).

This inability to believe is moral, not metaphysical; but it is real inability none the less. It is symbolised in John 9 by blindness from birth: 'The human condition of being born in sin (9.34) is equivalent to being (spiritually) blind from birth (9.1).'[6] The man is healed at *Siloam* or *Apestalmenos* (9.7); and since Jesus is the 'Sent One' the 'blindness is removed with reference to and with the aid of the "sent".'[7] The inability of man in the spiritual sphere may also be pictured by dead Lazarus, whose response to Jesus' loud call (11.43) is due solely to Jesus' power. Faith is not a condition for this resurrection to take place: John 11.40 says rather that faith is a condition for seeing the glory of God. This way of phrasing it prepares the reader for the fact that of those who saw the miracle, some believed (11.45) and thus saw the glory, while others did not (11.46). Lazarus' resurrection is as sovereignly effected as will be the resurrection of the last day (11.23f.), and therefore invites belief (11.14f.) in the one who is himself the resurrection and the life (11.25).

Again, if men do not understand Jesus' *lalia*, his spoken communication, it is because they *ou dynatai akouein ton logon autou*, they cannot hear his word, his message (not, as in RSV, that they 'cannot bear to hear' his word; 8.43). This is shocking: Jesus does not say they fail to grasp his message because they cannot follow his spoken word, his idiom, but that they fail to understand his idiom precisely because they *cannot* 'hear' his message. The Jews remain responsible for their own 'cannot', which, far from resulting from divine fiat, is determined by their own desire *(thelousin)* to perform the lusts *(tas epithymias)* of the devil (8.44). This 'cannot', this slavery to sin (8.34), itself stems from personal sin. Sin enslaves.

The reason the Jews hold they have never been enslaved (8.33) is not that they are oblivious to history's painful facts, but that they regard subjection to God as freedom in the highest sense. That they are thus subject to God is linked in their mind with racial privilege from Abraham. But Jesus, after insisting that the slavery with which he is concerned is bondage to sin (8.34), changes the slave metaphor slightly in order to reject their dependence on race (we may translate, 'the slave has no permanent place in the family', 8.35), and introduce the Son who alone has the authority to set slaves free (8.36). Thus, although they are implicitly invited to (and made responsible to) keep Jesus' word (8.51), their moral evil coupled with this false confidence in their racial heritage renders them so obtuse that 'they can no more believe the truth than they can come to the light (3.19).'[8] Indeed, *because* Jesus speaks the truth, they do not believe (8.45). If a man reacts negatively *because* he hears the truth (not merely *although*), what hope is there for him, unless God takes action for him? In precisely the same way, the world *cannot* receive the Spirit/Paraclete (14.17), because it fails to recognise *(theōrein)* him, fails to know *(ginōskein)* him (cf. 1 Cor. 2.14). On the other hand, the disciples do receive the Spirit, not because they recognise and know him, but because he abides with them and will be (is?) in them. 'Therefore *to know* and *to have* are so conjoined, that not to know is the cause of not having, and to have is the cause of knowing.'[9] Failure to recognise the Paraclete is man's fault, while human recognition of the Paraclete owes its cause to the Paraclete's ministry.

Two conclusions are to be drawn. Since all at one time belonged to the world (15.9; 17.6; which verses explain the shift from 7.7 to 17.16), and the world is morally incapable of recognising and accepting God's salvation, then (1) it follows that no one can come to Jesus unless that coming is granted to him (6.44, 65); and moreover, (2) for John responsibility does not turn on an *absolute* power to contrary. The world chooses, but by itself it cannot (because it will not) choose the revelation of God in Jesus Christ. Responsibility depends more on reasonable obligation than on *absolute* freedom. Therefore, in a sense, the first step the world must take is to admit its blindness (9.41), without which admission there is only continued guilt. This strikes at the very root of merit theology.

2. Men are challenged to desire, believe, obey, come, etc.—and do so

Men are not unthinking puppets in the fourth Gospel. Within the dramatic presentation, the interplay of personalities is obvious. There are coherent requests and semi-rhetorical questions (e.g. 12.21; 19.38). The one who responds positively to Jesus is repeatedly designated *ho pisteuōn*, 'he who believes', or the like (e.g. 1.7, 12; 3.15-18, 36; 7.39; 11.25). Similarly, everyone who drinks the water Jesus gives, has eternal life (4.13f.). The one who really does come to Jesus (6.35f.)[10] will never be hungry; the one who believes has everlasting life (6.47). Again, the one who eats Christ's flesh and drinks Christ's blood, is the one who abides in him and never perishes (6.53, 56). The one who keeps Jesus' word, who believes the one who sent Jesus, shall never see death (8.51; 5.24). 'Eternal life' is for the one who does not love his *psychē*, but hates it (the love-hate contrast is a semitism). As Jesus gave his life, like a *kokkos*, so his followers must die to all self-interest; and those who thus serve Christ will be honoured by the Father (12.24-6). The promised blessing is contingent upon loyal obedience. The same stress on the necessity of obedience is found at the end of a structurally similar passage (13.18), and again in 3.36. The privilege of being granted the power to become God's children depends on receiving the *Logos* (1.12); and, after he has ascended, it depends on receiving the witnesses (13.20).

It might be argued that these demands primarily *describe* the recipients of salvation without much reflection on the question of their responsibility, let alone their ability, to conform. In some passages, that contention has some weight: e.g. 5.29f.; 12.44. But there are two factors which make the suggestion impossible. (1) It ignores the fact that 'the Gospel of St. John is par excellence the Gospel of appeals, or rather one immense appeal from one end to the other'[11] (cf. 20.30f.). The descriptive *ho pisteuōn* phrases, for example, are themselves conditions that must be met, and as such they are implicit invitations, not less insistent than the explicit invitation of 7.37f. The constant alternatives, promised blessing or threatened condemnation, make no sense if this book is not evangelistic. (2) People are not only invited to believe, obey, etc.; they actually do so. On the basis of evidence, whether signs of testimonies or the message of Jesus, men believe, waver, reject (e.g. 1.41, 49f.; 2.11, 22; 4.39, 41f.; 6.66, 69; 8.30f.; 10.37f.; 11.40; 20.8, 28f.). Men take steps of conscious faith. The classic example is Thomas (20.25-8), but there are others. John 9.35-8 pictures the once blind man coming to deeper faith, on the basis of Jesus' self-identification of himself as the Son of man. The man already believed Jesus to be a prophet (9.17), and his question (9.36), whether it betrays puzzlement at the title 'Son of man', or simply asks for positive identification (cf. 12.34f.), indicates he is eager to believe, eager to see spiritually: the *hina*, 'that', (9.36) is elliptical and has telic force. Jesus' answer, when it comes, evokes belief and worship. No matter what emphasis there is in the fourth Gospel on election, men come, see, believe; and 'the seeing is real seeing, the coming real coming, and the believing real believing, man's seeing, man's coming, man's believing.'[12]

But if man's *responsibility* in these matters is unambiguous in John, the question of his autonomous *ability* is less so. John nowhere follows the example of much intertestamental literature in tying together responsibility and *absolute* free will in the sense of power to contrary (cf. T. Jud. 20.1-3; 2 En. 30.15; Ps. Sol. 9.7; Ab. 3.16; B. Ber. 33*b*; B. Nidd. 16*b*; Philo, *Post.* 10f.; *Quod Deus* 45-50; Conf. 177f.; *Spec. Leg.* i, 227). He writes of the need for men to want to do God's will if they are to discover whether or not Jesus' teaching is from

God (7.17), and this challenge is both an invitation and an accusation;[13] but it is not metaphysical speculation about the extent of human freedom.[14] Men must seek the praise that comes from God (5.44), and work for the food that endures to eternal life (6.27); but it is also called a *gift* from the Son of man (cf. 4.10). And when the crowd replies with a question which shows they expect to perform works (plural) in a way which will earn merits (6.28), Jesus replies that the work (singular) of God is to believe in the one God has sent (6.29). The passage thus becomes equivalent to the demand for faith.

3. Further responsibilities

The responsibilities emphasised by John reflect a rich diversity of type. The demand for faith does not require a mere contentless *dass*, but belief in the highest christological propositions.[15] In a similar vein, men are obligated to interpret the Old Testament Scripture christocentrically (1.45; 5.39f., 45-7): Moses wrote of Christ. Nicodemus, the teacher of Israel (a title?), should have known what the new birth entailed (3.10), apparently from the Old Testament. (Perhaps we are to think of such passages as Ps. 51.10; Isa. 44.3; Ezek. 11.19f.; 18.31f.; 36.26; 37.14; 39.29; or, with gentle irony, Eccles. 11.5. Alternatively, Nicodemus should have been prepared for the idea of the direct hand of God in salvation.) Those who come to faith are required to persevere, and, just as they have accepted the various witnesses that point to Christ, so they in turn must bear witness to him (4.35-8; 15.26f.; and possibly 20.23). In this task, examples have been set by the Samaritan woman (4.39), and especially by John the Baptist (1.6f., 20, 31-4).[16] Prayer by Christians is presupposed (14.13f.; 16.23-6). They live under a new commandment (13.34f.) to love one another. It is remarkable that the responsibility to love the brothers is repeatedly presented in the form of commandment: cf. 15.12, 17—although in 13.34f.; 15.12, the responsibility to obey is enhanced by Jesus' example. In both cases, the combination of present and aorist tenses of *agapan*, 'to love', suggests that the believers are to love each other continually as Christ in his death/exaltation loved them supremely (cf. Eph. 5.2). Implicitly, these and other responsibilities are enjoined on every reader of this Gospel.

The emphasis on obedience *to* Christ, exemplified by the obedience *of* Christ (15.10), is not in the least mitigated by the change in the disciples' status from slaves[17] to friends (15.14f.). To the modern mind, perhaps the chief characteristic of the slave is that he must obey; but this characteristic remains intact when the disciples become Jesus' 'friends'.[18] The difference between the two categories in 15.15 turns on knowledge of what the master is doing, not on obedience. Indeed, this new knowledge increases the responsibility of the one who thus becomes a friend of Jesus, for the title can be kept only as long as obedience under this new revelatory stance is maintained. The comparison is not between unbelievers and believers, but between believers who had less knowledge and those who enjoy more (cf. Gal. 4.1-9). Thus, a friend of Jesus (1) has had things revealed to him by Jesus, (2) must obey Jesus, and (3) has been chosen by Jesus. None of these things can be predicated of Jesus with respect to the disciples: the 'friendship' is not reciprocal. Neither God nor Jesus is designated a 'friend' of man. (Of course, neither of them is 'un-friend': cf. John 3.16; 15.9; etc.; but neither of them is a 'friend' in the sense used here.) If God is sovereign and autonomous, and men are responsible to him (and therefore to Jesus as well), it is axiomatic that reciprocal 'friendship' is out of the question. The highest possibility for man is that he be a friend of God, a friend of Jesus. Of course, the title itself invites obedience not so much on the basis of authority as on the basis of Jesus' love in conferring the honour; but the demand for obedience is not less urgent for that. The title hitherto had been given only to the most privileged and intimate of God's servants (Abraham, Isa. 41.8; 2 Chr. 20.7; cf. Jas. 2.23; Moses, cf. Exod. 33.11), usually within a context associated with election (Isa. 41.8; cf. 2 Chr. 20.7) or special revelation (Exod. 33.11).

The new commandment, as we have seen, connects obedience to Christ with love for believers: obedience entails the responsibility to love. John 14.15, 21, 23f. connect love for Christ with obedience: love for Christ entails the responsibility to be obedient. All three of these verses in John 14 are connected with the promise that God will manifest himself to the loving and therefore obedient believer.[19] The first verse (14.15) specified that this divine manifestation is the promised Spirit/Paraclete. Now elsewhere it is made clear that the coming of the Paraclete is dependent on Jesus' 'going away' (16.7; cf. 7.39). John 14.15, 21, 23f. do not so much put in doubt this coming (14.15ff.), this manifestation of Jesus and the Father (14.21, 23f.), as they do the genuineness of the disciples' love, and therefore of their discipleship itself. The question to be raised by John's reader is not, therefore, 'Has Jesus manifested himself, and sent the Paraclete?' but rather, 'Do I love Jesus in such a manner as to obey his commandments, that I may be among those to whom this personal revelation is given?'

John 16.27 goes farther: 'The Father himself loves you, because you have loved me and have believed that I came from the Father.' Does this mean that the believer's love precedes the Father's love, and is in some way the ground of it? The suggestion runs counter to the entire johannine emphasis, in which God is the one who loves the world so much he sends his Son—even this world which refuses to acknowledge him. Nor does Barrett's attempt to resolve the problem by referring to a 'circle of love', with the Father at the centre, really help.[20] Two contextual features provide a clue that resolves the difficulty. (1) The preceding two verses (16.25f.) show that the point at issue is not the difference between the believer and the unbeliever, as if the evangelist were trying to assign to the believer's love the ultimate credit for this distinction; but rather, as in 15.14f. (*supra*), John is making a distinction between the disciples' relation to the Father *now* and *in that day*, i.e. after the hour. The succeeding verse (16.28) shows that hitherto Jesus has exercised a mediating role in the revelation of the Father. But now, with Jesus' glorification, and the bestowal of the Spirit/ Paraclete (16.13f.), there is new intimacy between the believers and *the Father himself* (16.27). The mediating mission of Jesus has thus been successful. (2) The aspect of this new intimacy with which the evangelist is here concerned is prayer.

From these two observations, it must be concluded that verse 27 is not so much interested in assigning ultimate credit as in pointing out that the believer's relationship to the Father, and his effectiveness in prayer, depend on his continued love for and belief in Jesus. And this is his responsibility.

John 3.19-21 likewise comes short of ascribing ultimate credit to man, even while it lays heavy responsibility on him. The light has come (perfect tense) into the world, and this is a perpetual challenge to believe. But with the light has come a verdict of guilty[21] (3.18f., 36). This makes the case urgent, but not hopeless: it persists only as long as there is unbelief (cf.

8.24). The reason for the unbelief, the preference for darkness, is moral: the practice of evil. The reason evil deeds prevent belief is because the one who does evil does not want his deeds exposed and rebuked,[22] and therefore avoids the light. Now at this point, we might have expected in 3.21 the converse thought that the one who does what is true *does* come to the light in order to show that his deeds are good, and be vindicated. Instead, the evangelist refuses to complete the parallelism, and says instead that this man comes 'that it may be clearly seen that his deeds have been wrought in God' *(en theō)*. Barrett, not observing this distinction, sees men divided into two classes *before* they are confronted by the light:

> Men are divided into two classes, those who do evil and those who do the truth. The former will inevitably reject Christ and are rejected; the latter as inevitably accept him. The disjunction between the two groups appears to exist before they are confronted with Christ himself; there seems to be no question of those who do evil being changed into men who will do the truth.[23]

Similarly Schnackenburg[24] uses 3.31 and 8.23 to argue that John means that those who reject God's messenger and his words are a different type of being. But 3.31 contrasts Jesus not just with unbelievers but with everyone (cf. also 3.13), and 8.23b is true of a person only as long as he disbelieves (cf. 8.24). The exceptive clause in 8.24 makes all the difference (contrast the irreversible judgment on the prince of this world, 12.31). To accept the rigid dualism of Barrett and Schnackenburg would mean that those who come to the light do so because of their own intrinsic superiority. But the evangelist balks at completing the antithetic parallelism and introduces a new ingredient, the idea of works done 'in God'. The expression is found in the johannine corpus only here and in 1 John 4.15f. Whether it means that the believer's works 'are wrought in virtue of his fellowship with God',[25] or, better, 'done in fellowship with God' (Lindars points to 3.15, *en autō*, almost certainly to be construed with *echē*),[26] the works are not done without reference to God, by the man alone. John uses this ambiguous expression to reinforce human culpability without supporting human pride, to assert that the one who does evil is morally responsible for his unbelief without allowing that the one who does what is true may take the credit for his belief. Verse 20 unambiguously assigns blame; verse 21, more phenomenological a description, does not assign merit, but obliquely points toward God.

4. The 'cosmic' sweep of God's saving purposes

A major strand of thought in the fourth Gospel pictures God's stance toward the world as both positive and all-embracing. God loved the world so much he sent his unique Son (3.16). The *kosmos* loved by God is not morally neutral, as we have seen; nor will the more subtle approach of Schnackenburg carry conviction:

> Here, as wherever the mission of the Son is spoken of, the notion of 'world' is neither quite neutral nor quite negative. The 'world' is not simply the place where men live, but sinful mankind which has turned away from God. Still, it is not the specific term for mankind in so far as it rejects the divine envoy and pursues him with enmity and hatred. It is the 'world' far from God and yet profoundly longing for him and sensing its need of redemption, the 'world' which is the object of God's infinite mercy and love.[27]

But is the world ever portrayed as 'profoundly longing' for Christ in John's Gospel?! If Jesus is the Saviour of the world (4.42; 1 John 4.14), it is because the world needs saving, not because some receptive part of the world is in view. Similar remarks pertain to 1.29; 6.33, 51. Thus, 'world' in 3.16 refers primarily neither to the greatness of the number of the people nor to those who seek Christ. It is the dark world that loves evil and hates light. God loved the world *despite* what the world was;[28] and that is the measure of his love, which is the ground of his commission to the Son. The expressions 'loved', 'gave', and 'only' all have emotive force, and simultaneously enhance the implicit invitation and magnify the reprehensibility of rejection. God's purposes toward the world in sending his Son were salvific (3.17); but the world is promptly divided up into those who believe and are not condemned, and those who do not believe and already stand condemned (3.18).[29] The same division recurs in 8.12, where, although Jesus is 'the light of the world', only the believer is promised 'the light of life'. (Cf. also 1.9-11.)

Rigid interpretations which make 'world' refer to specific people bristle with difficulties. The possibilities seem to be: (1) 'World' means every person without exception, and therefore all will ultimately be saved. This theoretical possibility is not a real possibility, as far as John is concerned. The world divides into those who believe and those who do not. (Cf. also 17.9.) (2) 'World' means every person without exception, and therefore God's purposes must inevitably be frustrated, since some will not believe. But such a position cannot be squared with either the emphasis on the certainty of the accomplishment of God's purposes, nor with predestinarian passages such as 6.44, 65; 17.9. (3) 'World' here refers to the elect, all those whom the Father has given to the Son. But there is no warrant for taking the word that way, which sounds like a starker form of Schnackenburg's subtlety (supra).

It is possible that 'world', in addition to bearing its connotations of evil, means something like 'all men without distinction' rather than 'all men without exception'. If so, it would be a slap at Jewish racial exclusiveness, and would have important implications for the Gospel's Sitz im Leben. This approach might find support in the use of 'all' in 1.7, 9; 12.32. John the Baptist was a man sent from God, and therefore in bearing witness so that all might believe he was reflecting God's benevolence toward the human race. Jesus reinforced John's credibility for the same reason: so that his hearers might be saved (8.33f.). John's primary mission was to Israel (1.29-31), but his witness was given so that all men—i.e. who came across it—might believe: he, like Abel, although dead, is still speaking. To push the language to make it refer to every man without exception would be silly. Similarly, if 1.9 does refer to the incarnation, the 'every man' on which the light shines is qualified by 1.10f. (cf. on 8.12, supra). Similarly in 12.32: the 'all' whom Jesus will draw, and the drawing itself, cannot both be taken absolutely, because in the succeeding verses it becomes clear that not all are saved (12.35-41). In the context of the arrival of the Greeks (12.20-22), to whose request for an audience Jesus has not so far responded, the 'all' appears to mean 'all' as opposed to Jews only: Jesus does not talk to the Greeks because that which will draw all men is the climactic event of his own death/exaltation.

Although there are some helpful insights in this approach, it is probably inadequate by itself. The evangelist seems rather to present God's stance toward the whole world in much the same way as the pre-exilic prophets presented God's stance toward the wayward Israelites: he punishes reluctantly, loves graciously, and finds no pleasure in the death of the wicked (Isa. 30.18; 65.2; Lam. 3.31-6; Ezek. 18.3-32; 33.11; Hos. 11.7ff.). The primary purpose for which God sent the Son into the world, the primary purpose why the Son came, was to save the world (3.17; 8.15; 12.47), for 'the already condemned world needed no further condemnation, it needed saving.'[30] Moreover, each of these statements not only reveals God's graciousness, but functions as an implicit invitation and a way of laying blame squarely on those who reject God's invitation. But it is untrue to the fourth Gospel (as it is to the Old Testament) to deduce from this evidence that election is ruled out, or that absolute universalism is taught, or that there is no room for a special relationship between God and some part of the world (cf. 17.9), or again that God is frustrated if all the world is not saved. The passages in John which deal with the 'cosmic' sweep of God's purposes not only have contexts which eliminate such interpretations, but function in such a way as to increase human responsibility in the light of God's gracious and available salvation.

5. Final observations

Each of the factors that go into the Old Testament's picture of human responsibility has re-surfaced in the fourth Gospel. Emphases may be a little different—e.g. men are not so much described as seeking the Lord, as exhorted to do so; and God's pleas for repentance now find their most eloquent expression in the incarnation and death/exaltation—but the same ingredients are there.

In addition, several facts have repeatedly come to light: (1) Unlike much intertestamental literature, John does not tie human responsibility to freedom (in the sense of absolute power to contrary). Freedom, for John, is freedom from sin, i.e. the performing of God's will. (2) Human responsibility for John is not incompatible with inability, provided it is moral inability.[31] (3) There is no unambiguous evidence for merit theology in the fourth Gospel.

FAITH AND EXTERNAL EVIDENCE

On what, then, is true faith based in the fourth Gospel? What or who receives ultimate credit when X believes and Y does not? What part does the evidence provided by signs, testimonies (of Jesus and of others), and the Scriptures play in convincing men? How are we to understand John's apparently ambivalent attitudes to the value of external evidence in providing a ground for faith?

In many places John makes it clear that the external evidence, of which the signs are most prominent, does indeed have the purpose of evoking faith. The witness of John the Baptist (1.7), Jesus' questioning and self-revelation to the once blind man (9.35ff.), the eyewitness testimony of Jesus' death (19.35; cf. 21.24), the writing of the Gospel itself (20.30f.),[32] all have the avowed goal of engendering faith. Jesus takes pains to foretell his betrayal and death/exaltation so that these events, far from destroying the disciples' faith, will establish it (13.19; 14.29). He is glad he is not in Bethany when Lazarus is taken ill, so that the disciples may believe by virtue of a sign greater than healing (11.15). Even his public prayer (more accurately, his thanksgiving) at Lazarus' tomb is given for the purpose of evoking faith (11.41f.), as is the voice from heaven (12.28). Again, the Father shows ever greater works to the Son, who performs them, so that the disciples may marvel (5.20). The last public discourse ends with a plea to believe if not Jesus, at least his works (10.37f.), an injunction repeated to the disciples in private (14.11). In other words, men are responsible not only to believe Jesus' words, but to believe because of the signs; and unbelief brings condemnation from both (12.47; 15.24).

On the other hand, some very negative things are said about signs. The people are excoriated for their dependence on signs and wonders (4.48), and indeed regularly manifest precisely that attitude which is here condemned: they want Jesus to perform signs which authenticate him, by virtue of their spectacular display (2.18; 6.30; 7.31; cf. Matt. 16.1; Mark 8.11f.; Luke 11.16), as genuinely from God (John 9.16, 31f.; 10.21). The people thronged to see Jesus because they heard of Lazarus' resurrection (12.18), and this upset the Pharisees (12.19) because Jesus' signs were drawing off the people (11.47f.); yet this movement of the people seems to reflect their love of the sensational, rather than serving as an index of true faith. Did the people believe in signs, then, or not?

John 7.5 provides a clue. Jesus' brothers 'did not believe in him', even though they did believe he could perform his miracles (7.3f.). But belief that Jesus could and did perform 'signs' does not entail understanding of what the signs really point to. The belief is not authentic faith. Thus the crowd in John 6 had seen Jesus' signs in one sense (6.2, 26), but in another sense had failed so miserably to see them that they asked for another (6.30). The people believed the other signs had actually taken place; but their belief was not authentic faith. In the nature of the case, therefore, signs by themselves cannot *guarantee* such faith.[33] Although the people had seen in one sense, they had not seen in the other (6.36;[34] cf. 12.37), a failure for which they are clearly responsible. John 11.40-47 neatly preserves the ambiguity: although many saw the sign-miracle, only those who believed really saw the sign-glory of God.

Other types of external evidence evoke results just as ambiguous. The Jews diligently study the Scriptures but do not see that their witness points to Christ (5.39f., 45-57). They would have concurred that the Scripture cannot be broken (10.35), even though they are accused of not believing what Moses wrote (5.46f.). That is why Jesus can refer witheringly to 'your law' (8.17; 10.34)—not to disassociate himself from it, but to magnify the responsibility of the people to interpret it aright—and yet at the same time lay considerable stress on Scripture and its christocentric fulfilment. This is analogous to the relationship between his negative statement about signs and wonders (4.48), and his own positive use of signs and wonders to engender faith. Similarly, Jesus' self-testimony is given to evoke faith, but is repeatedly not believed (e.g. 3.11, 32f.; 5.37-40). The voice of 12.28f., though for the sake of the crowd, was 'interpreted by the materialists as a clap of thunder and nothing more, and by the more spiritually-minded as an angelic utterance.'[35] The evidence itself could be variously interpreted. The only difference between signs and this kind of testimonial evidence is that the former have the added disadvantage of attracting sensation seekers. But *no* external evidence is sufficient to *guarantee* faith (cf. Luke 16.30f.).

If such evidence is insufficient to guarantee faith in all before whom such evidence is presented, is it sufficient by itself to engender faith in some people? If so, why only in some and not in others? Of whom is the 'some' made up? For example, when we read that some believed in Jesus because of John's testimony (even without a confirming sign, 10.40-42!),[36] while others enjoyed John's light only for a while (5.35), what stands at the root of the different response?

Faith in the fourth Gospel does indeed seem to spring from evidence, whether signs (2.11, 23; 4.53; 6.14), another's testimony (4.39; 10.40-42), Jesus' own testimony (4.41f.; 8.30; 9.37f.), his physical appearance after the resurrection (especially 20.27-9), or, apparently, the unspecified pattern of events (12.42f.). On closer inspection, some of these cases must be summarily dismissed, because there is some contextual caveat. John 2.23 is followed by the rejection implicit in 2.24f. The first steps of faith in 6.14 are followed by 6.15, 36, 66. The Jews who apparently put their faith in Jesus in 8.30 are dismissed in 8.37-44, 55.[37] But even so, on the face of it, the instances in 2.11; 4.39; 41f., 53; 8.37f. are clear examples of faith grounded on evidence.

But again, some doubts must be cast up, two in particular. (1) In 6.66-70 when many disciples turn back and no longer follow Jesus, the Twelve are prepared to stay, because they believe that Jesus is the Holy One of God; but Jesus, although he asks them if they *want* to stay, insists that *he* chose *them*— including the one who is a 'devil'. In other words, when the question is raised why some 'disciples' (6.66) turn back, and others persevere, the answer has more to do with election than with evidence. (2) Again, in 16.29f., in response to Jesus' speech *en parrēsia*, the disciples declare that *by this* their faith that Jesus came from God is established. But Jesus openly questions their faith, because he knows the 'hour' has come, and they will be scattered (16.31f.). They will all therefore come to faith in a deeper sense *only after the resurrection*. Authentic faith is reserved for the period introduced by the eschatological hour. The evangelist thus casts doubt on the faith of the Twelve prior to the death/exaltation (16.31f.), and accentuates faith in the *risen* Lord (20.8, 18, 20, 25, 27-9). This renders coherent the claims to greater insight *after* the resurrection (2.22; 12.16; cf. 14.26).

John is again wrestling with the problem of the best way to present his theological summary of Jesus' life in the most telling evangelistic fashion. He portrays people coming to faith (not only the Twelve but also those in 4.39, 41f., 53; 9.37f.) during Jesus' ministry, but he reserves authentic faith for the new age. Therefore there is reason to suspect that even those instances of faith prior to the death/exaltation, which betray in themselves no mitigating caveats (viz. 4.39, 41f., 53; 9.37f.) are to be understood within the framework of his theological presentation of redemptive history. The evangelist includes these narratives of coming-to-faith, because had he not done so his Gospel could not have had so extensive an evangelistic impact, since the three cases touch Jews (9.37f.), Samaritans (4.39, 41f.) and (possibly) Gentiles (4.53—if he is a military man, likely a pagan: *Ant.* xvii.198).

The faith in John 20 is directly dependent on the climactic evidence of the resurrection; and, although Jesus implies it is not the best sort of faith (20.29), he nevertheless willingly offers the evidence in order to convince Thomas (20.27). But the resurrection appearances are restricted to those who already belong to Jesus, those he has kept, those the Father has given him (e.g. 4.19f.; 17.6, 12). In this they differ from the public nature of most of the (other) signs. The evidence of the resurrection evokes faith in those who are already in some sense peculiarly Christ's.

The fourth Gospel, then, clearly holds men responsible to believe on the basis of the signs, and, having come to some level of faith, to cling to Jesus' teaching (e.g. 8.31). But it is equally clear that external evidence, no matter how splendid, does not guarantee that someone will come to faith and persevere in that faith; and it seems it cannot even receive sole credit for engendering faith in those who do believe. If the Jews do not believe the signs because they are not of Jesus' flock (10.25f.), while those in Jesus' flock, his own sheep, hear his voice and follow him (10.27), then the question of who responds positively to the signs is pushed back to the prior question of who belongs to Jesus' flock.

None of this must be taken to mean that for John the evidence is irrelevant, the signs unimportant, the Scripture fulfilment incidental.[38] Quite the reverse: the signs, for example, in addition to whatever compelling incentive to faith they provide, *help to establish the content of that faith.* They point beyond themselves, as does so much in John's Gospel. In the miracle at Cana, the sign suggests the old religion is being turned into the new order of the gospel. The episode of the cleansing of the temple promises that a new 'temple' will arise. Chapters 3 and 4 promise new birth and new worship respectively. The miraculous healings of 4.46-5.47 reveal the power of Jesus' word both to give new life and to grant forgiveness. The feeding of the five thousand demonstrates that Jesus himself is the bread of life. Similarly for the rest of the Gospel: the 'evidential' elements in John are not designed *merely* to help people come to faith, but also to establish the factual substance in which faith is to be exercised. On reflection, any putative revelation which comes through the medium of history (as opposed to a-historical mysticism) *must* set down its roots in certain historical events and their interpretation. This is the overwhelming reason why signs, fulfilment statements and the like are important in the fourth Gospel—*not* because of some presupposition concerning the relationship between external evidence and faith.

One other piece of evidence confirms that this is the direction of John's thought. Many commentators see no necessary connection between Nicodemus's remark about signs (3.2) and Jesus' reply (3.3). Alternatively, it is suggested that a question is implied, such as 'What must I do to inherit the age to come?' (cf. Luke 18.18). It is better to see Nicodemus approaching Christ with the claim that he detects something of God's expected reign in the one who can do 'these signs' (3.2). But Jesus replies that no one can 'see' God's reign unless he is born (or begotten) from above. E. Haenchen is even prepared to translate 3.3 as 'Unless one is begotten from above, he cannot see the works (sic; not 'kingdom') of God.'[39] Nicodemus can obviously 'see' the signs in one sense; but he cannot 'see' them in another: he cannot really see the kingdom of God (cf. 11.40). Jesus' reply is not framed in terms of what Nicodemus must do to see the kingdom, but in terms of what must happen to him. The point is made both by the nature of the demanded transformation (a man neither begets nor bears himself) and by the passive mood of the verb. 'For rebirth means—and this is precisely the point made by Nicodemus' misunderstanding— something more than in improvement in man; it means that man receives a new *origin,* and this is manifestly something he cannot give himself'.[40] This approach runs counter to the suggestion that 3.3, 5 is simply a johannine version of the dominical saying recorded in Matt. 18.3. In addition to completely different contexts, both the form (*hōs* is essential in Matt. 18.3f., and absent from John 3.3, 5) and the purpose of the two logia differ. Matthew's logion is concerned with *man's* repentance, *man's* humbling of himself, *man's* conversion, while John 3.3, 5, 7 deal with God's action on man.

The answer Jesus gives to Nicodemus's claim to some knowledge is thus designed to deflate all such personal claims. This phenomenon occurs elsewhere in John (e.g. 6.70; 9.41; 16.31), and has the effect of laying an axe to the root of merit theology. Thus, the opposition to merit theology is leading back inexorably to God's sovereign election.

ELECTION

Several factors have already pointed towards some form of soteriological predestination in the fourth Gospel. God's sweeping sovereignty has entered this world and introduced the new age. This vertical step has exposed God's direct action in salvation and judgment to greater view. Man and world are presented negatively, as morally unable as in the DSS (especially *Hodayoth*) and with the same result: salvation must come from God. God's stance toward the world is salvific: but when someone raises the question who is actually saved, it becomes clear that ultimately salvation turns neither on personal merits nor on external evidence. Individuals become believers neither because they are intrinsically better and therefore able to choose aright, nor because the evidence is somehow itself more convincing in their cases. Who then is saved?

1. New birth and sonship

The consideration of Nicodemus at the end of the last section leads naturally to the broader question of new birth and sonship in the fourth Gospel. The first explicit reference is 1.12f. Accepting the plural reading 'who were born',[41] it is not immediately clear what is the precise relationship between 'all who received him', (1.12) and 'who were born ... of God' (1.13). Some see receiving Christ as the prerequisite of the new birth: 'This birth is conditional upon receiving Christ and believing on his name. The aorist is not pluperfect in tense.'[42] Others take the opposite view. Holtzmann sees this generation by God as 'the root and presupposition'[43] of faith. And Lindars says: 'Man cannot gain his end by any property of his own nature as man, nor by wishing for it with all his soul, nor by any practical steps which his own mind and reason may suggest, because man is not equal with God. Only God himself can raise man to sonship.'[44] Clearly, precisely the same people are referred to by 'all who receive him' as by 'who were born ... of God'. It is true that no one is born from God who does not receive Christ and believe on his name; but it is equally true that no one receives Christ and believes on his name, who is not born of God. Even though no causal relationship is made explicit, to read 1.12 without 1.13 is to obtain the impression that sonship is the *result* of faith. But it is possible to take 1.13 as a careful rejection of this view, and this for four reasons: (1) Even though the three negations of 1.13 appear to describe procreation in the categories of ancient times, they seem unnecessarily extravagant if their sole purpose is to contrast natural and spiritual birth without making some reference to human inability in spiritual birth. (2) There may be an implicit rejection of the sufficiency of racial descent. It is not enough to be Abraham's (racial) descendants (8.33f.; cf. Matt. 3.9). (3) The form of 1.12f.—emphasis on human responsibility, followed by an accent on divine sovereignty which lays waste human pretensions—is found elsewhere in John (e.g. 6.40-45; 6.66-70). (4) For what it is worth, the tenses and the context of 1 John 5.1 strongly argue that faith, like love (1 John 4.8) is the *evidence* of the new birth, not its cause.

The evidence for the priority of the new birth in 1.12f. is not conclusive, but it is very strong. Accepting it, however, does not mean adopting the view that the evangelist is primarily interested in the intricacies of predestination *per se*. Rather, he combats human pretensions as to who are children of God. This is confirmed by the progress of the debate between Jesus and Nicodemus. Jesus' statement (3.3) evokes a double misunderstanding on the part of Nicodemus (3.4). Nicodemus is thinking on a purely physical plane: hence his first question. But he further misses the point by making man the active agent: hence his second question. Jesus answers these objections in reverse order. In 3.5f. Jesus insists that this birth is supernatural, on the principle that like produces like. In 3.7f. Jesus answers the first objection. If Nicodemus accepts the sound and effect of the *pneuma*=wind without knowing the details of its movement and origins, why should he question the movement and origins of the *pneuma*=spirit in the generation of new life? He should not be surprised that even the rulers[45] of the Jews must be thus born from above.

A. Augustinović avoids any suggestion of predestinatory references in new birth and sonship passages by reducing them to a purely moral sphere. According to him, there is simply a correspondence *(convenientia)* between God's action and those of his sons.[46] Augustinović is largely correct as far as John 8 is concerned: there the sonship relationship is *primarily* moral (cf. especially 8.38f., 42, 44), especially so since sonship to the devil is also possible. But sonship to God and sonship to the devil are not symmetrically related. There is no suggestion that man may be 'born of the devil'. Moreover, even the moral emphasis on the sonship does not preclude something more metaphysical: after all, Jesus admits that the Jews are children of Abraham in the literal sense (8.37) while denying them the title on moral grounds (8.39). This confirms that John 8 is *primarily* concerned with the evidence which identifies paternity (cf. 1 John 3.7-10), not with the ontological status of that paternity, nor with the way that paternity may be changed. So even here, Augustinović is stretching the evidence; and he is much less believable on 1.12f. and 3.3ff. Again, the reference to 'the children of God who are scattered abroad' in 11.52 suggests that Christ's death/exaltation effects the gathering together of those destined to become the children of God (cf. 10.16). P. Benoit's criticism of Augustinović's oversimplification is just:

> The thought of St John is certainly much more profound! It is not the act of faith *per se*, nor our acts of love, which constitute us children of God; rather, if we are able to believe and to love, it is because we have received within us a seed [*un germe*] of divine life, and because the holy Spirit inhabits, lives and operates in us. The act of faith does not constitute our divine sonship; rather, it is either the occasional cause (in the philosophical sense) or the sign of sonship. Some cannot believe that God can act within us in such a fashion, while simultaneously leaving us free; but

many theologians think the two perspectives are patient of reconciliation.[47]

2. Coming to Jesus

In John 6 the coming-to-Jesus language moves unambiguously within a context of predestination. Coming to Jesus is equivalent to believing in Jesus (6.35). That Jesus' opponents have seen him and yet have not believed (6.36) is no reason for pessimism about the prospect of more conversions, for all whom[48] the Father has given to the Son will come to him (6.37). To avoid the conclusion that predestination is here assumed, J. H. Charlesworth notes the text does not say that some are *not* given to Jesus.[49] However, if *all* are given to Jesus, then *all* will surely come to him, according to this text; and the logically entailed absolute universalism contradicts both the tenor of the fourth Gospel and those explicit passages which make it clear that only some of the world is given to Jesus (cf. 17.9). The context demands that Jesus is repudiating any idea that the Father has sent the Son forth on a mission which could fail because of the unbelief of the people.

The second clause of 6.37 is frequently taken as a strong litotes meaning that Jesus will welcome and not reject the one who comes to him, often cast in a form which stresses human responsibility and thereby balances the emphasis on predestination in 6.37a. But this interpretation is excluded by two observations: (1) The verb 'cast out' *(ekballō)*, wherever it is used in John (2.15; 6.37; 9.34f.; 10.4; 12.31), implies the 'casting out' of something or someone already 'in'. The strong litotes in 6.37f., therefore, does not mean 'I will certainly receive the one who comes', but 'I will certainly preserve, keep in, the one who comes'; while the identity of the 'one who comes' is established by the preceding clause. (2) The causal *hoti* and telic *hina* in 6.38 give the reason for this keeping action by Jesus, in terms of the will of the Father, viz. that Jesus should not lose one of those given to him (6.38f.). In other words, 6.37 argues not only that the ones given to Jesus will inevitably come to him, but that Jesus will keep them individually *(ton erchomenon* as opposed to *pan ho)* once there.[50]

Comparing 6.39 and 6.40, it is obvious that 'all that he has given me' refers to the same people as 'everyone who sees the Son and believes in him', while 'that I should lose nothing of all that he has given me' parallels 'that everyone ... should have eternal life'. Those whom the Father has given to the Son may equally be described as those who see and believe the Son, even though the predestinatory 'given' precedes and enables (cf. on 6.44, 65, *infra*) the faith. These parallels militate against the expression 'irresistible grace' frequently used by theologians of the Reformed traditions. The expression is misleading, because it suggests what the theologians themselves usually seek to avoid, viz. the idea that the inevitability of the coming-to-Jesus by those given to Jesus means they do so *against* their will, squealing and kicking as it were. God's election works behind and through the 'seeing' and 'believing' of those who come to Jesus.

In response to the Jews' murmuring, Jesus puts the matter more strongly: No one can come to Jesus unless the Father draws him (6.44). 'The Father does not merely beckon or advise, he *draws!*'[51] This, indeed, is what the context demands; but those who see no soteriological predestination in John are quick to point to John's use of the same verb in 12.32: Jesus' death/exaltation *draws all* men. Many commentators try to govern the meaning of 6.44 by appeal to 12.32. But the verb alone is not determinative. John 12.32, as we have observed, occurs in a context where the arrival of the 'hour' and the request of the Greeks are evoking statements about the universal significance of Jesus' death/exaltation. Jesus draws all men, not just Jews; his stance toward the 'world' is a salvific one, one that draws. It is precarious to read more into 12.32 than that. By contrast, 6.44 occurs in a context in which (1) men have arrogantly tried to bring in the kingdom by force (6.15), and yet (2) have turned away unbelieving from the revelation given (6.36, 41f., 60, 64). The predestinatory passages in John 6 (especially vv.37-40, 44f., 64f.) speak to both of these problems: (1) Men cannot bring in the kingdom. Not only is the kingdom not political, but men must learn that salvation is by *God's* action (6.44f., 65).[52] (2) On the other hand, rejection by men does not spell defeat for God's saving purposes, but victory; for all given to Jesus will come (6.37), and Jesus himself knew from the beginning who would believe (6.64). Thus, the presentation of soteriological predestination, far from being an end in itself, is part of the framework which provides assurance concerning the inevitability of the fulfilment of God's plan of salvation, while emphasising the gratuity of grace. Both of these factors came together in 6.64f. Even Jesus' so-called disciples (6.60f., 66) were turning from him: their faith had been without hearing and learning from the Father (6.45). As in 6.44f., Jesus answers the problem of unbelief by appeal to the necessity of divine action (6.65). 'Faith in Christ is not merely difficult; apart from God it is impossible (cf. Mark 10.27). Coming to Jesus is not a matter of free human decision.'[53] But in addition to solving the enigma of unbelief, this answer, by stressing that no one comes to Jesus unless it is given to him by the Father to do so, awakens echoes of the life-imparting power of the Spirit (6.63). Human self-congratulation is thus effectively precluded.

3. Taught by God

It is surprising how often the reference to Isa. 54.13 (or perhaps Jer. 31.34) in John 6.45 is taken to mean that *all men without exception* will be taught by God, and therefore that the 'drawing' in the previous verse must also be extended to everyone. But 6.45 is adduced to explain something of the nature of the 'drawing' in 6.44. The 'all' does not mean 'all without exception' but 'all the people of God' (cf. 11.52), all those given to the Son (6.37, 39), drawn by the Father (6.44, 65). This is special 'teaching' which all believers, but only believers, enjoy (cf. 1 John 2.27). Outward evidence, like signs and testimonies, is not enough. No one can come to the Father unless the Father draws him, as the prophets themselves said: there must be 'teaching' from God. Everyone thus taught must be identified with everyone who listens to the Father and learns from him: all of these come to Jesus.

4. Given to Jesus

The idea that some men have been given by the Father to the Son is first enunciated, as has been noted, in 6.37, 39, 65. The same thought occurs again in 10.29(?); 17.2, 6, 9, 24; 18.9. Apart from the occurrences in 10.29 and 18.9, which are best considered later, there is a concentration of them in John 17.

The verb 'to give' *(didonai)* occurs in John 17 no less than seventeen times. In thirteen of these occurrences, the Father is the subject. To the Son, he gives men (17.2, 6, 9, 24), all things (17.7), words (17.8), the divine name (17.11f.), and glory (17.22, 24). In the other four occurrences, Jesus is the subject.

THE SOTERIOLOGY OF JOHN

To men, he gives eternal life (17.2), words or word (17.8, 14),
and glory (17.22).

In 17.2, the *hina* is certainly telic in force; but even so, two
meanings are possible. (1) The *hina* may be co-ordinate with
hina in 17.1. In that case the opening clause of 17.2 is
parenthetical. The granting of eternal life to those whom God
has given to the Son is part of the purpose of the Son's
glorification. (2) Alternatively, *hina* in 17.2 is not co-ordinate
with *hina* in 17.1, and depends, not on *doxason* ('glorify', 17.1)
but on *edōkas* ('thou hast given', 17.2). In this case, the
granting of eternal life to those whom God has given to the Son
is the purpose of the universal authority over 'all flesh'. Brown
thinks both meanings are true.[54] But in any case it is clear that
the giving by the Father of certain men to the Son *precedes* their
reception of eternal life, and governs the purpose of the Son's
mission. There is no way to escape the implicit election.

The same is equally true of 17.6-9. Jesus has revealed God's
name (cf. 17.26) to those God gave him out of the world, to
those who (already) *were* God's. Therefore Jesus prays for
them in distinction from the world (17.9). The words 'for they
are thine' (17.9) are merely an extension of 'thine they were'
(17.6). The priority of God's election is thus vigorously
affirmed. That these people can also be described in terms of
their receptivity and obedience to God's word (17.7f.) does not
mitigate the absoluteness of that election. Rather, they may be
described, shall we say, phenomenologically, as well as in the
terms of the prior divine possession and gift.[55]

Christ's prayer is not for the believers alone, but also for
those who will become such through their witness (17.20f.).
These too will believe in Jesus. There is an inescapable note of
certainty: Jesus is praying for the elect who are not yet
demonstrably such (cf. Acts 18.10). All believers, those presently
such and those who will become such, constitute those given by
the Father to Jesus (17.24), and will see Jesus' glory. Despite
this particularism, however, the unity among believers for
which Jesus prays has as its aim that the 'world' may believe
and know (17.21, 23; cf. 13.35; 14.30f.).[56] This is not an
instance of 'apparent universalism'[57] because in johannine
thought if the 'world' believed it would no longer be the 'world'.
Rather, it reflects God's salvific stance *through the believers*
toward the world, in the same way that passages like 1.29; 3.16

and 12.32 reflect that stance *before there are any believers* (in the full eschatological sense). To put it another way, 17.20f., 23 gives us the manner in which God's electing purposes are effected, viz., through the witness and love of the believing community. Hence in the last two verses (17.25f.), although the world has not known the Father, yet Jesus has; and now his own know him, because Jesus has revealed the Father's name to them. Jesus' continued revelation of the Father to them (17.26) will bind them in the love (and therefore implicitly the witness) for which he has prayed.

By way of final observations on John 17, it is important to note that this heavy emphasis on soteriological predestination comes within a context in which: (1) the special relationship between Jesus and his Father is stressed (first because John 17 is in the form of a prayer; second, because the crucial opening petition is that Jesus may be glorified with the glory he once had; and third, because of the repeated reference to Jesus' fulfilment of the Father's will) and therefore one might expect the divine perspective in salvation to be at the fore; and (2) there is special emphasis on encouraging the believers (cf. 16.31ff.).

5. Belonging to Jesus

Those who are given to Jesus must in some sense peculiarly belong to him. The connection is made for us in 17.9f.: those the Father gives to Jesus are God's, and all that belongs to Jesus belongs to God and vice-versa. Theoretically, belonging to Jesus could describe the believer's position *after* coming to faith. However, as with the idea of being given to Jesus, John more commonly speaks of a *prior* belonging that is unequivocally predestinatory. This idea is expressed in several different passages in the fourth Gospel, but nowhere more forcefully than in John 10.

No chapter in John (except perhaps John 6) has been the subject of such wide-ranging debate. With regret, I must overcome the temptation to discuss the secondary literature here. For the purpose of establishing the theology of the fourth Gospel, there is not sufficient reason for doing other than accepting the extended metaphor of 10.1ff. as mixed, and working with the chapter as it stands.

It is frequently insisted that the tableau of John 10 pictures several flocks, and the anarthrous *poimēn* ('shepherd') of 10.2

refers to a shepherd among many: Jesus as *the* shepherd, it is said, has not yet been introduced. That *poimēn* is anarthrous, however, in itself proves nothing. In this chapter, Jesus is the only shepherd, and all the sheep mentioned are his sheep. That he calls them by name, and they respond to his voice (10.3) is part of the parabolic colour; but the figure of speech (10.6) should not be made to run on all fours by imagining a separation of sheep from sheep. The division is rather between *aulē* ('fold') and *poimnē* ('flock'). The former is probably Judaism; the latter is made up of Jesus' sheep, which come both from the 'fold' and from outside it (10.16).

In verses 3f., the sheep are referred to as *ta idia*, 'his own', the shepherd's own sheep (contrast 10.12). In the Prologue, when Jesus comes to *ta idia* ('his own home', RSV), *hoi idioi* ('his own people', RSV) do not receive him. There (in 1.11), the reference to *ta idia* means the world which he created (or less likely, his own nation): in short, he came 'home' (cf. 19.27). But his own people (either the people he created or the people of his race) did not receive him. But this does not mean that he has no people of his own in a special sense, for his own sheep do indeed hear his voice. These will not (emphatic *ou mē*) follow anyone else (10.15). 'Those who truly are Christ's elect sheep cannot be deceived by the pretenders of v.1.'[58]

It is important to observe that in the explanation which follows, Jesus and the sheep are set over against robbers, hirelings, and wolves. Jesus is himself the gate (10.7). In the mixed metaphor, John can also say that Jesus as the shepherd enters by the gate (10.2). But whoever else enters does so through him, and will be saved (10.9). The alternative is not to stay outside, but to attempt entry as a thief (10.1, 10), bent on theft, killing and destruction. Nor is the alternative to become another shepherd, for all who came before Jesus[59] are thieves and robbers (10.8), or at best faint-hearted hirelings (10.11-13). Whatever the specific referent of the words 'all who ever came before me', the effect is to reduce all pretensions of spiritual leadership to the dust. The antithesis, therefore, is total. One either belongs to Christ and his sheep, or one is lumped together with wolves, thieves, hirelings and a rejected fold. The only desirable thing is to belong to Jesus' flock.

Already in verses 3 and 5 Jesus spells out the peculiar sensitivity his sheep have toward their shepherd's voice. It could be argued that they acquire this sensitivity *after* in some way 'becoming' his sheep. However, verses 14-16 militate against such an interpretation, and verse 26 positively excludes it. Jesus has other sheep, not of this (Jewish?) fold, and these also he must bring (10.16). They have not yet been brought to his one flock, but because they are in some sense already his sheep, they *will listen* to his voice (cf. Acts 18.10). Verse 26 is clearer still. Jesus does not say that his opponents are not among his sheep because they do not believe, but that they do not believe because they are not among his sheep. No quantity of evidence suffices to produce faith in the one who does not *already* belong to Christ's sheep (10.26), belong to God (8.47), belong to the truth (18.37).

> To tell the truth, the entire allegory *(sic)* runs like this: the sheep recognise their shepherd as soon as he presents himself to them, because even before that moment they already belong to him. Jesus recognises them, because they had been given to him by the Father to be his disciples, and they recognise Jesus because he had been sent to them by the Father to be their shepherd.[60]

What is in view is not so much an enunciated doctrine of reprobation, as an unambiguous rejection of self-sufficiency in the matter of belonging among the sheep. This is confirmed by 10.27. Where we might have expected 'and they know me', we find 'and I know them'. Christ's knowledge of the sheep, his recognition that they are his, is the determinative thing. Within this context, it is scarcely surprising to read that the shepherd lays down his life *for his sheep* (10.15; cf. 11.50-52) and gives *them* eternal life (10.28): the 'world' is no longer in view.

One other passage clearly marks this special love of Jesus for his own. John 13.1 stands at the beginning of the Gospel's second main division, which as a whole is far more interested in the authentic disciples than in the world. Some scholars take the temporal phrase 'before the feast of the Passover' (13.1) to refer not the whole sentence but to *eidōs*, 'when (Jesus) knew' (i.e. Jesus was aware before Passover), because, they say, to date Jesus' love would be absurd. But grammatically the phrase should be construed with the main verb. Far from dating Jesus' love, it points to a concrete act of love, viz. the death of Jesus

(including the footwashing which symbolizes it).[61] This special
love, 'to the end' (13.1),[62] is reserved for 'his own'.[63]

6. Chosen by Jesus

In four passages the fact that Jesus chose the disciples is
stressed. In the first (6.70), Jesus by his rhetorical question
modifies, if he does not actually contradict, Peter's confident
assertion (6.69). He, not they, did the choosing. Jesus' answer
therefore serves as a gentle put-down to over-confidence. That
Judas should be included among the Twelve whom Jesus has
chosen suggests: (1) that Jesus' choice of men is not *necessarily*
for salvation: it may be for other purposes, the way God had his
'other servants' in the Old Testament; (2) that Jesus is already
assuring his disciples (and the evangelist his readers) that the
impending betrayal, far from being outside the sphere of God's
purposes, was planned and executed under his own control.

The second occurrence (13.18) is similarly concerned to show
that the inclusion of Judas Iscariot is not a divine oversight.

The third occurrence (15.16), however, is broader in its
implications. The clause *ouch hymeis me exelexasthe* negates
the 'you': 'It was not *you* who chose me, but *I* chose you', etc.
This confirms that the nature of the 'friend'-relationship in the
preceding verses (15.14f.), previously discussed, is one which
makes Jesus supreme and the disciples responsible for
obedience. The disciples cannot even legitimately boast that they
are believers on the ground that they, unlike others, wisely
made the right choice. On the contrary: Jesus chose them. Merit
theology is thus totally savaged. On the other hand, that Jesus
chose them does not entail a robot-like stance on the part of the
disciples, but increased responsibility—responsibility to produce
enduring fruit (15.16), to pray (15.16b), to love each other
(15.17). Election entails both privilege and responsibility.

The final occurrence of an explicit mention of election
(15.19) is presented as the reason why authentic believers are
not 'of the world' any longer. The result of Jesus' election as far
as these believers is concerned, far from being undiluted bliss, is
persecution from the world out of which they have been chosen.
Election therefore functions in this passage as an incentive to
bear the brunt of opposition courageously because the one who
chose them passed this way himself (15.20f.).

7. Concluding remarks

It is not clear how Jesus' choice of some men out of the 'world' (15.19), and the Father's gift of these men out of the 'world' (17.6) fit together; but in any case, the soteriological predestination is uncompromising. Moreover, the repeated stress on the fact that the authentic disciples were once part of the 'world' has an important implication for the passages which speak of belonging to God before actual belief, viz.: this belonging pertains to the mind and purposes of God, and not to the nature of those who so belong. They are Christ's sheep in his salvific purposes before they are his sheep in obedient practice.

How then can this strong emphasis on predestination be reconciled with all the passages which speak of *man's* belief and *man's* obedience? It is difficult to better the statement of A. Vanhoye, who says that the evidence enables us to see that

> when God effects his work [of faith] in us, he does not do so without us, but by us. Certainly he does not simply give it to us to accomplish, as the Jews thought. That would be to demand the impossible. But in giving it to us to accomplish, he gives us at the same time the wherewithal to accomplish it ['Mais nous la donnant à réaliser, il nous donne en même temps de la realiser'], on the condition, naturally, that we do not claim that we ourselves are sufficient.'[64]

KEPT BY GOD, AND PERSEVERING

We have already observed that the purpose of Jesus' mission is phrased in John 6.37-40 in terms of his preservation of those given him by his Father. Does this mean that those 'given' people cannot fall away?

Whatever is meant by Jesus' keeping power, it is clear that men do not remain disciples without conscious effort. On those who had taken first steps of faith, soon to be repudiated, Jesus enjoined perseverance in holding to his teaching (8.31, 51; cf. 5.38). Only thus would they know the truth that sets men free (8.32). Elsewhere, Jesus' exhortation to 'walk in the light' (12.35f.) gains particular urgency because the light will not always be with them. The warning probably refers primarily to Jesus' departure in death/exaltation, but with overtones for

John's readers of the general danger of procrastination in the matter of coming to stable faith (not unlike Heb. 2.7ff.).

In each of these cases, it is not at all clear that Jesus is addressing the elect, i.e. those he has chosen, those whom the Father has given him. However, no such easy escape is possible in 16.1. There, Jesus assures the eleven (certainly among the elect!) that what he has told them has been with the express design of preventing them from falling away. The envisaged lapse could conceivably be temporary, but it must be a real danger or it seems a pointless warning. Before concluding that such falling away is indeed possible, however, it is important to recognise that the warning is not given to foster speculation about dark, theoretical possibilities, but functions rather so as to prevent them from occurring (cf. 16.1-4).

What then of John 15, where the need to persevere, 'to abide in the vine', is most emphatically underscored? Jesus is the true vine, and his Father is the vinedresser. The believer is the branch. Unproductive branches are removed; productive ones are pruned. The paronomasia (*airei ... kathairei ... katharoi*) is not accidental: the use of *kathairein*, which apparently was not a viticultural term at the time of composition,[65] indicates that the real interest lies in people and purity, not in vines and wine. The question is: Can true branches be cut off? Morris replies negatively: 'We should not regard this as proof that true believers may fall away. It is part of the viticultural picture, and the point could not be made without it. The emphasis is on the bearing of fruit. Pruning is resorted to ensure that this takes place.[66]

There is wisdom in refusing to make the metaphor run on all fours; but the stress on 'abiding in the vine *lest*', and perhaps the threat of 15.16 (cf. 3.36; 5.29), serve to make Morris's negation less certain.

Some points are unambiguous. First, the responsibility to abide in Christ (=Jesus' words abiding in the believer, 15.7; =abiding in Jesus' love, 15.9f.),[67] is laid squarely on the believer, however 15.4 is construed. Second, despite this responsibility, it is emphatically maintained that the 'cleanliness' of the disciples is attributed, not to their abiding in the vine, but to the word of Jesus (15.3).[68] Merit theology is excluded (cf. also 15.16). Third, as if further to disabuse the branches of residual desires for independence, Jesus insists that fruitbearing is only

possible as long as the branches abide in the vine (15.4f.).
Fourth, fruitbearing branches are contrasted with dead branches to be removed: there is total antithesis.[69] Thus, a case could
be made for authentic branches *versus* inauthentic branches. It
could be argued that only the former represent authentic
believers. These only pray successfully (15.7) and bring glory to
the Father (15.8—whichever *vario lectio* is followed).

Despite these qualifications, both 16.1 and 15.1ff. sound like
warnings of potentially real dangers. But before attempting to
draw firm conclusions about the possibility of authentic
believers falling away, it is best to survey passages which stress
how the disciples are preserved. John 6.37-40 has already been
discussed. Equally important is 17.11b-12, 14f., which
distinguishes between Jesus' action in keeping those the Father
has given him, and the action of the Father who succeeds to the
task now that Jesus' departure from the world is imminent.
Jesus' explicit petition is that the disciples be kept from the evil
one (17.15). Now they are no longer 'of the world', they must
bear the brunt of the world's hatred (17.14). But the ultimate
purpose of keeping them is 'that they may be one' (17.11).
Instead of saying that the neuter 'one' *(hen)* means the disciples
are to be kept by God not as units but as unity, it is more
accurate to say that they are to be kept individually (not one
was lost, 17.12) for the purpose of unity. That they have been
kept thus far is credited solely to Jesus' guarding activity
(17.12).

The exception is Judas Iscariot; but John always makes it
clear that Judas is not really an exception after all (cf. 6.64f.,
70; 13.18; and here). Jesus not only knew what was going to
happen, but was in control of it. Equally, at the scene of the
arrest, Jesus is portrayed fulfilling his word about not losing
one of those given him (18.8f.).

There is one other passage where the security of Christ's
sheep is unequivocally affirmed, viz. 10.27-9. No one can snatch
them from Jesus' hand, nor yet out of his Father's hand (10.29).
If from the notorious nest of variant readings in 10.29 we may
accept the reading, 'What my Father has given me is greater
than all,' there remains an ambiguity as to what the Father has
given Jesus; but whatever alternative is adopted, Christ's sheep
are secure.

How, then, is the tension between such warm assurance and

such threatening potential for apostasy to be explained? The function of both sides of the argument provides a clue. The threats without exception are designed to foster persevering endurance; the assurances are designed to remove fears, increase faith, and remove all the posturings of self-sufficiency. The pattern therefore sounds much like what is made explicit in 1 John 2.19; Heb. 3.14; Matt. 24.13; Col. 1.21-3; and elsewhere in the New Testament. Men must hold themselves responsible to persevere, but if they do so, it is God's grace upholding them; while if they fall away they demonstrate that they were not true disciples in the first place. From the perspective of a pastor, John's maintenance of this tension provides stable balance.

REPROBATION

The question to be raised is whether God's sovereignty stands behind the unrepentant in precisely the same way as it stands behind the elect. Are election and reprobation symmetrically disposed under divine sovereignty? To these questions, John 12.37ff. speaks.

Despite Jesus' signs, the people did not believe (ouk episteuon) in him (12.37), the imperfect tense being significant: 'They might give occasional evidence of a transitory belief, but that is not saving faith.'[70] But this state of affairs came about to fulfil the words of Isaiah. The first quotation (12.38), quoted verbatim from the LXX (Isa. 53.1), tells of the fact of unbelief. 'The unbelief of the Jews is not a problem; it is the precise fulfilment of prophecy (cf. Isa. xlii.19-25; Jer. v.31-9; Ezek. xii.2-16).'[71] The reason for the unbelief is given in the second quotation (John 12.40), which seems to be a modification of MT Isa. 6.10. In the MT, the verbs are imperatival: God commissions the prophet to harden the people as a punishment for their previous sin. The LXX uses the passive. John 12.39f. apparently makes God the active agent of the hardening of heart of the people.

Various efforts have been made to avoid the most obvious meaning. Among modern writers, J. Blank and J. Painter think the 'He' who blinds the eyes of the people is the devil, the god of this world (cf. 2 Cor. 4.4), to be distinguished from the 'I' who heals.[72] Others argue unconvincingly that 'they could not' (12.39) should be softened to 'they would not'.[73] Efforts to take

'lest' (*hina mē*; 12.40) as causal ('because they did not see') also
fail.[74] Brown tries to soften the passage by stigmatising it as
'primitive thought' which shows 'no theoretical awareness of
secondary causality or divine permissiveness as regards what is
related to salvation.'[75] But later thought categories are no
solution to the sovereignty-responsibility tension, as we shall
see. At best they provide helpful models around which the
diverse elements of the tension may be arrayed.

Nevertheless, it would be premature to conclude that reprobation is the symmetrical antithesis of election. John nowhere
states that Jesus chose men to be condemned; rather, he chose
some out of the 'world'. The primary mission of the Son is to
save (3.17; 12.47), and this mission springs from God's love
(3.16). This love comes to transform men who constitute the
'world' into men who do not. Jesus does not come to assign
some neutral men to life and other neutral men to condemnation. He comes rather to a world already condemned
(3.36) and proceeds to save.

How then are we to understand 12.39f? Isaiah 6.9f. is quoted
elsewhere in the New Testament (Matt. 13.14d.; Mark 4.12;
Luke 8.10; Acts 28.26f.). Acts 28.26f. makes use of the prophecy
on the plane of salvation history, to explain the mission to the
Gentiles; but this element is not made explicit in the fourth
Gospel. Closer to John's thought is Mark 4.12.[76] It is clear in
both Mark and John that those condemned are in any case
justly condemned, i.e. they are rightly accountable for their
unbelief (in John, cf. surrounding verses, especially 12.35-7,
44ff.). They are not forced into an unbelief they do not
themselves want. When it is also remembered that the 'world' to
which Jesus comes is already condemned, then the language of
12.37-43 need not be taken as reprobation on a par with
election, but as realised eschatology of condemnation. As in
2 Thessalonians 2.10f., men who do not receive the love of truth
are rewarded by God-sent delusion so that they will believe only
lies. For these men the eschatological verdict has already come.
For this reason they cannot believe. For them it is now too late.

Evangelistically, this approach functions so as to underline
the urgency of coming to faith. Moreover it assures believers
that the phenomenon of unbelief, far from arguing that God has
lost control, is rather a sign that God is active in judgment as
well as in salvation. Since they themselves were once of the

'world', they must respond with gratitude that they have been received and not condemned, and be wary of lingering unbelief in their own lives.

CONCLUDING OBSERVATIONS

All of the conclusions have emerged from or been anticipated by the exegesis. It remains to draw together a few points that might escape notice.

The sovereignty-responsibility tension in the fourth Gospel embraces two different conceptions of the scope and perhaps the objects of divine love. There is a sense in which God's love is directed toward the 'world' per se; but to absolutise the passages where this is enunciated is to fail to recognise the even more numerous passages in which the divine love is restricted to the elect, while unbelievers sit under wrath and judgment. However, granted that election is present in the fourth Gospel, the tension between the two descriptions of the scope of divine love is better than either of the other theoretically possible alternatives, viz: (1) God loves everyone without exception equally—which would make election *logically* absurd; (2) God loves *only* the elect and hates the rest—which would destroy the evangelistic thrust and the emotive incentive to believe based on God's love for the 'world', a love which sent the Son of God on his saving mission and robs the 'world' of excuse.[77] Moreover, John also relates God's special love to the obedience of men (e.g. 14.21; 16.27). Even if that obedience is not the ultimate *cause* of God's special love, the formulation of the relationship in this way designedly dispels fatalism and indolence.

The exegesis has drawn repeated attention to the function of various concepts within johannine theology. Negatively, John does not use man's responsibility to formulate a doctrine of free will (as absolute power to contrary); neither does he deduce from God's sovereignty that men are robots. The horribleness of the so-called *decretum horribile* largely disappears if men remain responsible for their sins and choices. The positive use to which John puts his teaching maximises human responsibility and God's sovereignty and grace, providing both warning and comfort. God's salvific stance toward the 'world', the piling up of evidence (including signs), the promise of final judgment (5.29), the danger of falling away, and the urgency of decision, all serve to underscore the human responsibility to believe, the heinousness of rejecting Christ and his words, the necessity for absolute obedience, and the enormity of the issues hanging in the balance. On the other hand, election serves to deflate personal claims, ensures that the saving mission cannot fail (e.g. 6.37-40), and guarantees the security of genuine believers without permitting spiritual lethargy. It thus encourages the believer to bear with tribulation and persecution (e.g. 15.18ff.). Some are already judged and rejected (12.37ff.), but the warning that this can happen makes conversion the more urgent. That faith itself is seen as a grace most clearly in those contexts which explain unbelief is one of the strongest pieces of evidence that the sovereignty of God in election functions primarily as the johannine antidote to merit theology.[78] If good works *per se* are being claimed as the means to salvation, John's answer is his description of the darkness of the world. If great claims are made, claims to be by heritage closer to God than are others (John 4 and 8) or claims to interpret Scripture in other than christocentric fashion (John 5) or even claims to have chosen Christ (6.69), John's answer is unambiguous: God's gracious sovereignty, mediated by Christ, is the exclusive ultimate ground of any man's salvation. Therefore, membership in the community of believers cannot serve as an occasion for personal boasting.

The sovereignty-responsibility tension in John serves to magnify man's sin and God's grace. The Prologue has already said it all: from the fullness of Christ we receive *charin anti charitos*, grace upon grace (1.16). 'Christian life is based at all points upon grace; as it proceeds one grace is exchanged only for another.'[79]

PART FOUR

THEOLOGICAL REFLECTIONS

CHAPTER THIRTEEN

THE FORMULATION OF
THE TENSION

DESCRIPTIVE COMPARISONS

Some time after the exile, there arises in Jewish writing the tendency to render God increasingly transcendent, in part by fostering anti-anthropomorphisms. God becomes more one-sidely sovereign; some aspects of divine personality suffer. The potter-and-clay metaphor can now function to portray a quasi-deterministic view of man. On the other hand, almost to counteract the possibility that illicit conclusions might be drawn from this emphasis, divine ultimacy is omitted in instances of evil, and the doctrine of creation is used to establish the absolute freedom of human will. God's promised blessings and curses no longer serve primarily to underline human responsibility: rather, they are historicised and serve as the basis of approaching God. In other words, it is possible now to appeal not so much to God's mercy, as to his sense of fair play. This merit theology forces theodicy in some instances to seek for solutions in the future, instead of permitting the believer to trust what is known of God and leave the rest to his 'unknownness'.

The rise of apocalypticism sharpens eschatological expectation into more clearly defined 'two ages', only the second of which witnesses God's open salvific blessing and the realisation of his judgment. The age to come is the ultimate theodicy. History until then is completely determined by God, even if it is not under his expressly beneficent rule. Merit theology develops a little further. Simultaneously the concept of being among the elect loses its connection with God's grace and forges a new link with meritorious righteousness. There is evidence of narrow exclusivism in some texts, and in others a more open form of universalism. A few apocalyptists bemoan a *cor malignum,* but most do not think in such terms.

The Dead Sea Scrolls are among the documents which lean towards the pessimistic view of man. Despite the occasional and inconsistent adoption of merit theology, there is real stress on the graciousness of God's election, which is directed toward a remnant within the Jewish people. Soteriological predestination is fairly rigid: reprobation in some passages is in close symmetry with election. Although the two-age structure is adopted, the covenanters see themselves at the very edge of the turn of the ages, a fact made clear to them by *pesher* exegesis of Old Testament texts. There is a concomitant rejection of *halakah*, a return to the pristine fount of revelation.

The targums and rabbinic literature, by contrast, represent the codification of a great deal of oral tradition. Although God is ever transcendent, free will is absolutised and fenced off from God's control. Merit theology is almost as strong as in the apocalyptic literature. Election is strongly emphasised, in staunch opposition to the church's claim to be the elect; but for the rabbis, election regularly has to do with merit: Israel was chosen because she was most worthy. The eschatological two-age structure, though less emphasised, is still present; but since salvation is more than ever dependent on man's efforts to earn it, the approach of God to man is specifically limited in the realm of soteriology.

Josephus introduces the sovereignty-responsibility tension into some passages, but affirms the freedom of the human will. He detects behind *tychē* and *heimarmenē* God's *pronoia*; but he is less than at ease with the strictest implications of monotheism. Generally, however, he fits into the pattern of the Pharisees he describes. For him, the prime lesson history teaches is the reward system of merit theology; but his treatment of the sovereignty-responsibility tension is among the most naive.

With the exception of the DSS, then, the *tendency* in all the Jewish intertestamental literature examined is toward: (1) an emphasis on God's transcendent sovereignty; (2) yet, paradoxically, a fenced-off area of formulated free will; (3) the elimination of divine ultimacy in the area of evil; (4) the elimination of gracious election (5) in favour of some form of merit theology. By contrast, the DSS not only preserve divine election, but overdo it, tending by the 'Two Spirits' doctrine to make election and reprobation symmetrical.

The fourth Gospel never presents divine sovereignty and human responsibility as mutually restrictive. Hence it feels no embarrassment at picturing God's control and purposes over events themselves evil. God is neither tainted nor thwarted by evil actions. Indeed, his purposes in salvation history are being precisely fulfilled even by such actions. Men for their part do not find their responsibility lessened by God's sovereign reign. The best paradigm of the proper relationship between divine sovereignty and human responsibility is Jesus Christ himself, who stands in stark contrast to Caiaphas who in quite a different sense fulfils God's purposes. Moreover, it is again Jesus himself who bridges the gulf between divine transcendence and human finiteness.

Men in the fourth Gospel are held accountable for their sin in general, but more particularly they are held responsible to believe in Jesus and obey his words. God's saving purposes and invitations in one sense are not restricted to the Jews, but are extended to all men without distinction, to the thoroughly lost 'world'. But on the other hand, men cannot justly boast in their spiritual attainments, for those who do not believe have been born from above, given by God to Jesus to whom they belong, taught by God, chosen by Jesus. Unbelief can be explained by the fact that the unbeliever has not been chosen, a fact which neither decreases the unbeliever's responsibility to believe, nor permits boasting by the believer. The emphasis, contrary to all merit theology, is on God's special love toward those chosen. The elect, however, demonstrate that they are such by perseverance and obedience, even while they are assured that such perseverance and obedience can testify to the fact that first Jesus, and now the Father himself, are keeping them.

Over against the general tendencies of Jewish intertestamental literature, then, the fourth Gospel (1) bridges the gulf between divine transcendence and human finiteness by Jesus himself; (2) nowhere formulates free will as absolute power to contrary, but constantly mingles ultimacy and human responsibility without mutual dilution; (3) cheerfully insists that God's hand is operating even behind evil men and events, but for his own good purposes; (4) insists repeatedly in diverse ways on the absoluteness and graciousness of God's election of some to special blessings and responsibilities, while (5) abolishing merit theology. Thus, unlike much of the apocalyptic literature (for example), John forbids pride in being among the elect, and betrays no contempt for the *massa damnata*.

It is possible to be more specific. In the areas most strongly emphasised, the fourth Gospel seems to stand over against the rabbis and their writings more than against any other group. In particular, not only are the elect chosen by God for no reason of merit, but the elect are *Jesus'* elect. The new elect community is specifically trans-racial and not *just* Jewish. Jewish ancestry itself guarantees nothing in this regard. The fourth Gospel sets its own elect over against any other claim to be elect.

There are points of contact between John and the DSS. Both share a pessimistic view of man. Both emphasise election and both hark back to the Old Testament and claim to interpret it authoritatively. But the similarities should not blind us to the differences. In the DSS, the elect constitute a smaller group than, but one which springs from, the Jewish people; in the fourth Gospel, racial barriers are crossed. In the DSS, election and reprobation tend to be symmetrically disposed; and the same is not true for John. Distinctive in the fourth Gospel is its central God-man christology, while its realised eschatology stands in contrast with the expectation of the end eagerly awaited by the covenanters.

In most of this literature some distinction is made between, on the one hand, God's sovereignty and ultimacy, and on the other, his special dealings with his people. Without some such distinction in God's activity it seems impossible to avoid drifting into denial of divine sovereignty, or into that rigid view of God's sovereignty which does not adequately distinguish between his ultimacy behind good and his ultimacy behind evil, much less between his general providence and his special activity toward his elect. However, in the later Old Testament books, there is increasing expectation of a new redemptive act to be undertaken by God in the last days. The dichotomy between what God is doing now and what he will do in the new age becomes very sharp in the apocalyptic literature. God's blessings on his elect and his judgment on the rest must await the new age. Thus the eschaton becomes the peculiar sphere of God's special dealings with his people. In the fourth Gospel, the new age has dawned, even if it is not yet consummated. John sees the coming of Christ and his revelation as the crucial dividing line, while yet reserving greater glory for the last day. God's special dealings are therefore more exposed to view, even if their final form has not yet come.

In the realm of the tension between God's sovereignty and

man's responsibility, the closest conceptual antecedents to the fourth Gospel are found in the Old Testament. In John, as in the Old Testament, God, the creator of all, is the ultimate personal cause. He is light and goodness; but in some mysterious way he stands behind dark forces of evil: he governs not only his own people, but other servants like Caiaphas. Even in salvation, an overwhelming theocentricity controls johannine theology. Moreover, as in the Old Testament, John does not seem to experience any difficulty in simultaneously adopting both divine sovereignty in the most unrestricted sense, and human responsibility that carries real significance.

The differences between John's handling of the tension, and that of the Old Testament, centre on johannine eschatology and christology. These innovations are due to the Christ-event, and John's presentation of it; and they necessarily modify the approach to such problems as theodicy.

The treatment of the sovereignty-responsibility tension by John, then, is distinctively Jewish. It stands in a direct line of descent from the Old Testament, opposed to most of the relevant developments in the intertestamental literature, but somewhat akin to the DSS. If the lines of development are not straight and neat, it must be remembered that a legitimate background can furnish something against which to react, as well as a fount from which to borrow ideas in an approving manner. Finally, I must again stress that such an analysis of conceptual antecedents is not to be confused with a search for a specific *Sitz im Leben,* nor even with neat trajectories. My approach is too methodologically limited to permit me to venture into those difficult domains.

CRUCIAL ASPECTS IN FORMULATION

It is axiomatic that any truly monotheistic religion is going to experience somewhere the tension between divine sovereignty and human responsibility, whether in the realm of philosophical speculation or in the realm of hard experience (and the two are not necessarily mutually exclusive). Some philosophers of religion hold that such tension is logically contradictory, and on this basis seek to redefine God, freedom, responsibility or some other parameter—or even to deny the existence of one or more

of these parameters. Others attempt various kinds of reconciliation, or seek to demonstrate that the tension is not
necessarily logically contradictory.

I have shown that the Old Testament, the fourth Gospel, and
some other writings juxtapose divine sovereignty and human
responsibility at every turn, manifesting little of any awareness
of the theoretical difficulties which later thinkers discover in
such a juxtaposition. If it can be demonstrated conclusively that
the tension is logically contradictory, then such contradiction
necessarily infects all those writings in which it manifests itself.
Over against such an approach, I wish now to argue that there
are enough areas of ambiguity which go into the formulation of
the tension to permit the conclusion that it is not *necessarily*
logically contradictory. I do not claim that I can demonstrate its
self-consistency. I claim only that, with a certain amount of
care, logical pitfalls may be avoided, so that belief in divine
sovereignty and in human responsibility does not *entail* logical
contradiction. Perhaps I should add that the following discussion is painfully brief, and may well fail to satisfy those of
my colleagues who are professional philosophers. Nevertheless
this is as far as my reflection on these matters has brought me so
far, and it may prove helpful to others. The notes provide more
rigorous assistance.

1. The boundaries of 'free will'

Responsibility is certainly linked to 'free will' in some
fashion; but how is 'free will' to be defined? If its essence is the
absolute power to contrary, a logical contradiction is entailed
when this absolute power to contrary is coupled with a divine
providence which in some sense foreordains all things with
certainty.

Refinements are therefore advanced. One theologian writes,
'God has decreed the free acts of men, but also that the actors
are none the less free and therefore responsible for their acts,
Genesis 50:19f.'[1] The verb 'has decreed' is used somewhat
ambiguously in this sentence; but this aside, it is important to
see how theologians of this stamp use 'free will' in a modified
sense. Usually there is heavy insistence upon man 'voluntarily
choosing'. The divine plan does not necessarily involve compulsion: 'Within the physical sphere, the Divine decree makes

certain by necessitating; within the moral sphere, the Divine decree makes certain without necessitating.'[2] For example, a man may be locked in a room, but not want to get out. He therefore cannot get out (that is certain), but equally he does not want to get out (he is not there against his will). This permits so redoubtable a Calvinist as A. A. Hodge to write: 'This matter of free-will underlies everything. If you bring it to question, it is infinitely more than Calvinism. ... Everything is gone if free-will is gone; the moral system is gone if free-will is gone; you cannot escape, except by materialism on the one hand or pantheism on the other.'[3]

Because of such distinctions, it is not uncommon to find writers denying the existence of 'free will' (in the sense of absolute power to contrary) while upholding the existence of human 'free agency', which they identify with the 'free-will' of Hodge. Hence one can find detailed arguments that certainty is not incompatible with free agency.[4] The conclusion drawn is that 'God's control is absolute in the sense that men do only that which he has ordained that they should do; yet they are truly free agents in the sense that their decisions are their own, and they are morally responsible for them.'[5] 'Free will' (free agency) is here taken pyschologically and morally, 'meaning the power of unconstrained, spontaneous, voluntary, and therefore responsible, choice.'[6] Such definitions may provide helpful working models of the problem, but no solutions, for they are less than precise on the question of the boundaries of this 'free agency', and are equally unclear on how this special control of God operates (cf. discussion, *infra*). At times they are in danger of losing the tang of the Scriptures they purport to explain.

On the other hand, to accept with Molinist theology a metaphysical definition of free will which binds it to power to contrary is to sacrifice the certainty of divine sovereignty for the contingency of human decision. This is insufficiently appreciated by many writers. For example, J. Farrelly says: 'For sin to be possible, all that is needed is that the good act which would avoid it be possible, and this is always true because man does have sufficient grace.'[7] But why must power to contrary be taken as the essence of free will? Would we not have to deduce, on this basis, that God himself is not free because his holy character precludes the possibility of his sinning? Or would sin not be sin if God did it? Again, does not free will defined in terms of absolute power to contrary generate an unavoidable logical contradiction when placed alongside divine sovereignty? Contrast the approach of John Calvin, who argues that if a sinful act is done voluntarily that is enough to establish guilt—irrespective of whether the sinner could have avoided the act.[8] In other words, for Calvin, not free will understood as power to contrary, but the voluntary character of sin, is the *ratio essendi* of human culpability. Consider also a parallel argument by R. R. Nicole:

> Just about everyone agrees that in heaven there will be no more danger of apostasy. Does this mean that in glory men will be deprived of that freedom which constitutes the distinguishing character of humanity, the gift that stands so high that even the sovereign purpose of God must be viewed as subordinate to it? Surely not. But if in glory perseverance is not inconsistent with freedom, why should it be thought incompatible on earth?[9]

If 'free will' be taken to mean that human actions are 'indeterminate' and therefore 'unpredictable', the most that could be said (if one is simultaneously to accept statements about divine sovereignty) is that such uncertainty exists solely in the human perspective, not in the divine.[10]

In most philosophical discussion, 'free will' entails what I have called 'absolute power to contrary'. It is within this framework that the perennial debate over the so-called 'free will defence' must be assessed. Many christian apologists have long supported and refined the free will defence in an effort to eliminate the possibility that God might be validly charged with evil. The detractors of the free will defence spring from two quite different camps: (1) There are some who by formulating disproofs of the free will defence seek to demonstrate the logical absurdity of the proposition that 'God is both omnipotent and good'. Their conclusion is that either God is not omnipotent, or that he is not good; and the more sceptical among them might want to urge, as a corollary, that there is therefore no God—at least, no God as conceived by traditional Christianity. Inevitably, some rejoinder is soon offered by defenders of the free will defence, who thus emerge (by design or otherwise) as christian apologists.[11] (2) On the other hand, the free will defence apologists are sometimes challenged by theists,

Christians, who do not hold that human freedom (conceived as power to contary) is logically defensible in the light of divine sovereignty, but who do not thereby feel forced to conclude that God is evil, nor that God is less than omnipotent, nor that 'human responsibility' degenerates into meaninglessness. Even to provide a summary of the arguments advanced by representatives of each side would immediately quadruple the length of this chapter; and so I must forbear, and refer interested readers to the notes.[12]

Nevertheless, I hope it is clear from what I have argued in the preceding chapters that I find myself aligned with those who remain unconvinced by apologists of the free will defence. On biblical grounds (at least, those examined), I do not think that notions of human freedom which entail absolute power to contrary can be maintained. As a result, until better formulations come along, I prefer to adopt a view of 'free will' along the lines of 'free agency' discussed earlier. This, I admit, it is less neat; but, as a Christian, I take it to be closer to the biblical perspectives than the available alternatives, and, so far as I am able to judge, not entirely lacking in solid philosophical support.

2. Time and eternity

A second area of immense difficulty in any formulation of the sovereignty-responsibility tension is the relationship between time and eternity. The significance of 'time' is obscure enough; what shall we say with certainty about eternity? Are we to accept Cullmann's model, and see linear time extrapolated *ad infinitum* in both directions? What bearing do statements about divine omniscience and omnipotence have on our understanding of these concepts? Are we required to accept the contention of Shedd—who writes: 'For the Divine mind, there is, in reality, no future event, because all events are simultaneous, owing to that peculiarity in the cognition of an eternal being whereby there is no succession in it'?[13] Or ought we accept the notion that eternity is not the opposite of time, not 'timelessness' or a negation of time, but a dimension outside the concept of time such that time and eternity are neither parallel nor contiguous?[14]

Too many apologists seek in the relationship between time and eternity the (at least partial) answer to the sovereignty-

responsibility tension.[15] In particular, the effort is made to ease
the tension by avoiding the concept of sequence inherent in
foreordination and predestination.

It must be protested that although the various time/eternity
models serve a useful purpose as bases for discussion, they are
in no sense explanatory solutions of the sovereignty-responsibility tension. That would be to explain the obscure by the
more obscure. Even if we could agree that God is 'timeless',
whatever that means, it has been shown that timelessness in
God does *not* provide humans with free will.[16] Moreover, the
biblical data are unashamedly presented in terms of sequence;[17]
and in any case, the destruction of sequence does not remove the
implications inherent in God's exhaustive *present* control. On
the other hand, the uncertainties and ambiguities surrounding
time and eternity again make it premature to insist that absolute
divine sovereignty and full human *responsibility* (if not free
will) are *necessarily* logically incompatible.

3. The nature of divine 'ultimacy'

Perhaps the greatest ambiguity surrounds the nature and
mode of operation of divine 'ultimacy'. (It is more common to
refer to 'concurrence'; but as this term has sometimes been
freighted with synergistic overtones, it must be handled with
care, and I have avoided it.) To this is related the concept of
secondary causality. Some writers make the expression 'second
causes' bear temporal significance. The schoolmen argued this
way: without God, no creation; without creation, no creatures;
without creatures, no sin; but no sin is to be charged to God, for
effectus sequitur causam proximam. This argument was picked
up by some of the reformers.[18] The resulting picture, however,
is quasi-deistic, utterly foreign to the biblical material.

Others take 'second causes' to be an a-temporal expression;
but even so, it still sounds as if God is merely *causa prima inter
pares:* the absolutely *independent* co-operation of the second
causes might be thought necessary before an action could take
place.[19] On the other hand, the concept of second causes cannot
simply be abandoned, because the resulting model must be
either pantheistic, in which case God becomes part of the causal
system; or mechanistic, with God a sovereign puppeteer.
Neither model will square with the biblical evidence; and hence
the concept of concurrence, or ultimacy, rather vaguely defined,

is appealed to. The vagueness stems from our inability to formulate precisely how God can govern with certainty without destroying some measure of significant freedom in his creatures.

Although they border on caricature, the following diagrams may help. The distance from A to B represents the action that must be taken to bring about some particular effect. The ⟍⟍⟍⟍ bar represents God's action; the ∕∕∕∕∕ bar represents man's action. I submit, then, that divine ultimacy is less like this:

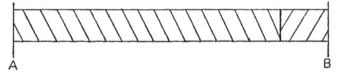

than like this:

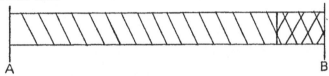

There is an unbridgeable ontological gap between the personal/transcendent God and finite men, and this gap brings about the breakdown of analogical arguments designed to picture the mode of divine causation. This has recently been well explored by J. F. Ross.[20] Calvin similarly relies on the ontological gap when he argues that in the human sphere to give one's will as the sole reason for an action is indeed tyrannical, yet insists it would be sacrilegious to apply the same principle to God.[21]

The most difficult problem confronting the theologian who wishes to formulate some unambiguous statement about ultimacy is the problem of evil.[22] No thoughtful person wishes to ascribe evil to God; but it is not easy to use the language of causation without seeming to do so. Nevertheless, the numerous instances in the Old Testament and in John, in which 'ultimacy' is ascribed to God even in evil actions, demand some such attempt; for even in the most vile human actions, man cannot break out of the sphere of divine sovereignty. But as Berkouwer points out:

It is remarkable, in this connection, that Scripture itself never presents providence in its relation to sin by way of a theoretical argument, but always in the historical actuality of the invincible power of God and our continued responsibility. ... We cannot explain the sequences of history with an all-devouring system of causation, nor by a theory of divine flux. The Scriptures show us God's work.[23]

Moreover, I have earlier argued that the mode of divine 'ultimacy' has a built in asymmetry to it. The manner in which God stands behind evil and the manner in which he stands behind good are not precisely identical; for he is to be praised for the good, but not blamed for the evil. Failure to recognise this essential asymmetry mars the work of J. F. Ross, to which I have just referred: he does not see that grace makes men differ. The negative side of divine ultimacy guarantees (1) that even my sinful deeds cannot escape God's sovereignty, and (2) that I cannot rightly shift my blame to God. The positive side of divine ultimacy is that little bit more immediate, so that I must recognise God's grace behind whatever good I may do; yet God's action remains sufficiently indirect to preserve my genuine responsibility. It is this sort of model which, however difficult it is to formulate, best conforms to the biblical data. From John's perspective (not to say the perspective of the New Testament), if I withstand the seductive music of the world and come at last safely to the port of salvation, it is not because Jesus is to me as the mast and ropes were to Ulysses, but because Jesus is to me as Orpheus was to his sailors.

The mysterious nature of God's 'ultimacy' is thus related to the problem of defining free agency. If divine causation is immediate and mechanical, belief both in God's goodness and in man's responsibility must be abandoned. However, there are in fact enough unknown features in the mode of God's rule to *necessitate* the abandonment of neither.

4. The 'will(s)' of God

A fourth area of ambiguity lies in the nature of the divine will. An example or two will bring the heart of the problem into focus. On several occasions God is said 'to repent' of something, e.g. of the creation of man (Gen. 6.6), of his decision to wipe out his rebellious calf-worshipping people (Exod. 32.7-14). Similarly, the decree that Hezekiah should die is revoked (2 Kgs. 20.1-6). Cf. also 1 Samuel 15.11; 2 Samuel 24.16; Jonah 3.10; Ecclesiastes 2.13f. On the other hand, God repeatedly insists that he, unlike man, does not repent (Num. 23.19f.; 1 Sam. 15.29; Jer. 4.28; cf. Ps. 89.34f.). Again, in the account in Genesis 22, Abraham is told to sacrifice his son; yet as the narrative develops, it appears that God never really intended him to do so. Yet again, God is presented as waiting and longing to be gracious (Isa. 30.18f.; 65.2; Hos. 11.7-9), as one who extracts no pleasure from the death of the wicked (Ezek. 33.11), as the one who punishes with extreme reluctance (Lam. 3.33-6); yet at other times, as we have seen, he is said to control the thoughts of men, keep his people, and bring nations to the point where he may punish them severely.

Such phenomena as these have evoked theological distinctions concerning the 'will' of God. Some distinguish between God's revealed will and his hidden or secret will (cf. Deut. 29.29); others, between God's prescriptive will and his determinative will; others, between his permissive will and his decretive will; still others, between his antecedent will and his consequent will. All of these paired 'wills' suffer from serious shortcomings. For example, although the greatest part of the divine will must surely remain 'hidden' (i.e. unknown to men), and although any increase in the knowledge of that will is due to revelation of that hidden but already operative will,[24] nevertheless this model is inadequate as a total explanation of the relation between the divine will and reality, because in too many instances the hidden will appears to make a mockery of the revealed will. Since the hidden will is always effective, it appears to be the actual will of God; while the revealed will is little more than precept. In that case, man does not know anything of God's actual will, except by what actually happens; and conversely, everything that happens is exactly what God really wills to happen. This problem is related to the tension between the *deus absconditus* and the *deus revelatus*.[25]

Similarly, distinctions between permissive will and decretive will appear desperately artificial when applied to an omniscient and omnipotent being; for if this God 'permits' sin, it cannot be unknowingly and unwillingly, and therefore his 'permission' must be granted knowingly and willingly. Wherein then does this permission differ from decree?

Indeed, any combination of these 'wills' leads inexorably to curious situations. For example, Yahweh foresees that the people will go astray, and that his wrath will be kindled (Deut. 31.15-22). This surely suggests something more than consequent wrath—perhaps something more akin to willed wrath. In the same way, Micaiah can warn the king of impending doom and be assured that the king will fail to heed the warning: God has decreed it so. This puts Micaiah in the invidious position of Cassandra.

At the same time, we cannot do without *some* distinctions concerning the 'will(s)' of God. Both in the Old Testament and in the fourth Gospel, not to say elsewhere, God is sometimes presented as the one who seeks men out, loves a lost world, declares his yearning for their repentance, and the like. This 'will' of God is his disposition; it is not necessarily his decree. But precisely how both operate in one sovereign God is extremely difficult to understand.

5. Anthropomorphism, anthropopathism, and personality

Each of the areas of ambiguity so far discussed can be traced back to the biblical presentation of God in both transcendent and personal categories. If God transcends both space and time and enjoys the exercise of all authority, there are aspects of his nature and activity necessarily unknown to finite creatures, bound as we are by space and time. But this infinite God is also presented as a personal being;[26] and the way transcendence and personality combine is also obscure to finite personal beings. When stress is laid upon God's sovereignty and transcendence, it is clear that nothing comes to pass outside the sphere of his will. When God is pictured in intercourse with men, it is his personality which is presupposed. No doubt much of the language of divine personality is anthropomorphic, pure and simple; but to relegate all such anthropomorphisms to the dustbin of antiquated ideas would be to strip God of his personality. The result may satisfy the deists; but the God of the Bible would no longer be in view.[27] The combination of the transcendent and the personal in one being, God, lies at the heart of the sovereignty-responsibility tension in all forms of monotheism, not least in the Bible.

Just as it is possible to treat the sovereignty-responsibility tension in a reductionistic fashion by limiting God's sovereignty and transcendence while simultaneously magnifying man's freedom of will, so also is it possible to treat it in a reductionistic fashion by disproportionately magnifying divine transcendence at the expense of divine personality. There are two common ways of doing this. The first is of long standing: it is the appeal to the alleged impassibility of God. Defended by the early fathers, adopted into the mainstream of christian tradition, and encoded in various confessions,[28] the doctrine of divine impassibility nevertheless depends on the dogmatic assertion that all contrary biblical evidence (e.g. Jer. 31.20; Hos. 11.8) is nothing but anthropopathism.

But on what basis is this dogmatic assertion predicated? In the final analysis, we have to do with the influence of certain strands of Greek metaphysical thought, strands which insist that emotion is dangerous, treacherous, and often evil. Reason must be set against emotion; and vulnerability is a sign of weakness. One may trace this line from Aristotle's 'unmoved mover' through platonic and neo-platonic writings to the Stoics. The conclusion must be that 'God is sensible, omnipotent, compassionate, *passionless;* for it is better to be these than not to be' (so Anselm, in *Proslogium,* chapter 6).[29] Even if we allow that anthropopathisms are to be found in the Bible, however, it does not follow that their presence is so extensive that God is impassible. One must not only ask what the anthropopathisms signify, but also observe the tenor of the Scriptures in this regard, viz. that God takes both a rational *and an emotional* part in his relationships with his creatures. As a result of these reflections, I find it extremely difficult to decide, in many cases, if an apparent anthropopathism is a real one; and I fear reductionism, even if at first glance it appears to ease the sovereignty-responsibility tension.[30]

The second form of reductionism which makes some sort of appeal to divine transcendence is much more recent. It is Karl Barth's treatment of election. Perhaps Barth has proved to be more influential in this area than in any other.[31] The kernel of his argument rests on his interpretation of Ephesians 1.4: God chose us in Christ before the foundation of the world. Because Christ is both God and man, he is simultaneously the subject and the object of election. Thus election is self-election, interpreted as self-determination, on the part of God. God has chosen *for* men: all men are chosen in Christ, and therefore tremendous issues hinge on their belief. This either means absolute universalism, or the hesitant admission that some may opt out. But Barth's theological *tour de force* will not withstand close scrutiny. For a start, it is not at all clear that the 'us' of Ephesians 1.4 refers to all men: the epistle is, after all, addressed 'to the saints who are also faithful in Christ Jesus' (1.1), not to the world at large (cf. also 2.3ff.; 4.7, 17). Nor does the New Testament conceive of judgment *only* in the way of which Barth writes: there is over and above the judgment which Christ received the judgment of all individuals not in Christ. Moreover, both Paul and John (and other New Testament writers for that matter) speak of *individuals* being elected to salvation (e.g. John 17.9; Acts 13.48; Rom. 9; Col. 1.26f.). That such election is 'in Christ' (Eph. 1.4) does not affect its individuality. Still other criticisms have been offered.[32]

Yet after rejecting both the doctrine of the impassibility of God and Barth's understanding of election, it must none the less be acknowledged that most of the elements which make up the tension between God's sovereignty and man's responsibility can be traced to the further tension between God's sovereignty/transcendence and his personality/responses.

6. *Experience and theory*

The biblical characters, as we have seen, never face the sovereignty-responsibility tension as an abstract theological conundrum; but there is a profound experiential awareness of it among those who are faced with personally painful and perplexing predicaments (e.g. Habakkuk; Asaph, Ps. 73; Job; Qoheleth). This is what G. I. Mavrodes calls an 'epistemic dilemma'.[33] Consider any set S of propositions. Either S is consistent, or it is not. If not, no 'solution' is possible; but if S is consistent, no solution is necessary. The most that would be desirable would be a demonstration that nothing in S renders the set inconsistent. But it is possible to attach to set S a rider R, which states that S is inconsistent. Suppose someone believes both S and R. He then faces an 'epistemic dilemma', and for his own peace of mind he must either see that S is consistent and abandon belief in R; or discover that R is true (and therefore S is inconsistent) and abandon belief in S as a consistent system (or at least abandon belief in those elements of S which make S inconsistent). In the present study, S includes propositions about evil, human responsibility, and about God and his goodness and absolute sovereignty. Clearly, there is no 'epistemic dilemma' when someone believes S (irrespective of whether or not S is consistent); he must believe R as well. And this may well come about only when he faces circumstances which make him question the elements of S. The epistemic dilemma is thus person-variable. In itself it says nothing about the truth or falsehood of the propositions in S. From this perspective it is clear why only some of the biblical writers grapple with the problem of evil or with the tension between divine sovereignty and human responsibility, and why their wrestling stems from personal anguish.

The example of Job is particularly instructive. Job and his friends stress equally that God is all-powerful and perfectly good; but the message of the book as a whole is that their conception of God is not high enough. God's ways are unfathomable; his knowledge, limitless; his power, effectual; who can tell him he is wrong? What man has the arrogance to deny divine providence by ignorant words? (Cf. Job 26.14; 37.5, 15, 23; 36.22-6; 38.2; 40.8-10; 41.10f.; etc.) No simple solution is possible, for men with their limited knowledge cannot judge God's government. Man's peace must come from knowing and trusting this God.[34] 'It is significant that Job cries out in the end, not "I understand!" but "I repent." '[35]

In point of fact, God's transcendence (and hence his 'unknownness' except for what he chooses to reveal) emerges throughout the Old Testament (Deut. 10.10ff.; 1 Kgs. 8.12; Isa. 40.25-28; 55.8f.; Ps. 77.19; 92.4f.; 97.2; etc.), indeed much more than his immanence.[36] The same perspective is presupposed in the New Testament. Since it is this transcendent God who directs man's goings, how can man comprehend his own way (Prov. 20.24; cf. 3.16; 16.1-4; Jer. 10.23; Job 38.2; 42.3)?

Whatever other answers to the problem of theodicy the biblical writers proffer, it is clear that the transcendence of God figures most prominently as the 'solution' *par excellence.* Hence, in a strict sense, there is no ultimate theodicy in the Scriptures: there is no attempt to vindicate God by beginning with human observations, perspectives, and reasonings. Theodicy makes God's power and goodness a deduction of human reason; and this the biblical writers will not allow. Their closest approach to theodicy comes in the recognition of their inability to comprehend many aspects of God; and even this divine 'unknownness' is known to be such only because it has been revealed. Thus it attacks man's arrogance, defines the limits of his knowledge, and makes the only 'solution' one of faith.

For us mortals there are no rational, logical *solutions* to the sovereignty-responsibility tension: it should be clear from the foregoing that neatly packaged harmonisations are impossible. But on the other hand, it is difficult to see why *logical* inconsistency is *necessitated*,[37] especially in view of the many ambiguous parameters and numerous unknown quantities. The whole tension remains restless in our hands; but it is the restlessness of having a few randomly-selected pieces of a jigsaw puzzle when thousands more are needed to complete the design.[38]

How then shall the tension be characterised? C. K. Barrett, in a seminal essay called 'The Dialectical Theology of St John',[39] fits both the christological tension and the problem of soteriological predestination into the category of 'dialectical theology'. As long as this expression suggests that the evangelist, without attempting total rational synthesis, looks at each aspect of the tension first from this perspective, then from that, and so on, it is helpful. However, because for some readers the expression may be connected with the (logically) irrational, it is potentially misleading. Moreover, the other examples of 'dialectical theology' which Barrett offers are not at all of the same character. They include (with special reference to John 6): (1) faith is, and is not, sight; (2) faith is, and is not, work; (3) the Old Testament is, and is not, to be searched. But each of these dialectical statements can be unpacked to make a rationally whole and coherent formulation, while such does not seem possible with the problem of divine sovereignty and human responsibility. It seems best therefore to retreat to the nebulous expression 'tension theology'.

This conclusion does not mean that all expressions of monotheism deal with the tension in precisely the same way. Not only may different points be accented (different parts of the puzzle, as it were), but a single motif, or a particular model (e.g. the potter-and-clay), may be used by an individual writer for distinctive purposes. That is why so much attention was paid in the last chapter to the *function* of various theological motifs. God is sovereign: but what conclusions are drawn from this? That men are robots? That God stands behind sin in the same way he stands behind evil? When does divine sovereignty function in its context to inspire comfort, or humility? Men are responsible: but does this mean they are so free that God becomes contingent? To ask these questions, and answer them, does not constitute an attempt to find a 'solution' to the sovereignty-responsibility tension, but is part of the effort to make the theological conclusions as precise as possible.

To see with what distinctives the tension emerges out of a particular text requires the examination of the total tension within that text, not just some part of it, such as election. In addition, there must be some observation of how the individual aspects of the tension function within the theology of the text. The fourth Gospel maximises human responsibility while simultaneously abolishing merit theology. It maximises God's sovereignty in salvation history and in election while simultaneously demanding that men believe. And it presents Jesus as the final demonstration of the way divine predestination and human freedom under God are joined, not set antithetically against each other.

HISTORICAL AND PRACTICAL OBSERVATIONS

Perhaps no area of doctrine has been more consistently debated throughout the twenty centuries of Christianity's life than that of God's sovereignty and man's responsibility. This debate has waxed warmer since the Reformation. Some of the polemic is little more than ignorant name-calling; but not a little is immensely erudite and, because of the language barrier, still unavailable to the person who is unversed in ecclesiastical Latin.[40] Even to begin to comment on this rich heritage would immediately double the length of this book. However, in addition to the treatments found in the standard dictionaries and encyclopedias of philosophy and theology, there are a few scattered historical studies which repay careful reading.[41] Moreover, the biographies of theologians who exercised major influence in these debates also provide much useful information to inquisitive readers. I cannot forbear to mention two of the most recent: A. Dallimore's *George Whitefield* (the second and final volume is due out shortly), and C. Bangs's *Arminius.*

It seems to me that most (although not all) of the debate can be analysed in terms of the tendency toward reductionism. I have argued at length that a fair treatment of the biblical data leaves the sovereignty-responsibility tension restless in our hands. If a person disagrees with this conclusion and seeks final solutions to the problem, we will enjoy little common ground in the debate. Suppose, for example, that my opponent is so impressed with God's sovereignty that he constructs his theological system out of all the texts and arguments which support this important truth, and then with this grid filters out evidence which could be taken to call some of his theological system into question. My instant response is that his procedure is methologically indistinguishable from the person who first constructs his theological system out of those texts and theorems which seem to support some form of human freedom, and who then filters out election and predestination passages until he can safely defuse them by re-defining them. The name of the game is reductionism.

In fact, reductionism doesn't *really* work. Even if we discount the fact that it plays with the evidence selectively, reductionism never solves or eliminates the sovereignty-responsibility tension, but only changes its shape. For example, believers of more Arminian persuasion tend to argue that a man has a free will (i.e. including absolute power to contrary) at the point of deciding to become a Christian.[42] But only very rarely have I seen such believers tackle the much larger question of God's relation to the countless thousands of decisions each person makes every day. If God in some sense controls such decisions, why not the decision to become a Christian? If he does not, in what precise sense does his sovereignty control history? Or must we retreat to God the master chess player? Even in that case, it is difficult to see how the divine permission to play the game differs from the divine decree, if it be acknowledged that God is omnipotent and omniscient. In other words, for the monotheist there is no escape from the sovereignty-responsibility tension, except by moving so far from the biblical data that either the picture of God or the picture of man bears little resemblance to their portraits as assembled from the scriptural texts themselves. It is no answer to me to tell me that my presentation of the sovereignty-responsibility tension still embraces certain unresolved tensions. Of course it does. But to correct me you must not claim to resolve all the tensions, for such delusion is easily exposed. Rather, if you wish to convince me that your theology in this matter is more essentially christian than my own, you must show me how your shaping of the tension better conforms to the biblical data than mine does.

In terms of the literature studied in this book, it is essential to recognise that the shape of the tension changes dramatically when one moves from, say, the Dead Sea Scrolls to Judith, or from Josephus to the apocalyptic literature, or from the rabbis to John. But never is the tension resolved so that there is divine sovereignty and human responsibility but no tension.

A more subtle form of polemic in the historical debate springs out of fears that the deductions that may derive from the other person's position could prove disastrous to one's own position. For example, a preacher may encourage his congregation to believe, repent, choose—and he is doing nothing but what Scripture sanctions by its example and precept. A believer with strong Calvinistic convictions may fear that such exhortations will encourage people to think that they enjoy a power to contrary which limits God, and therefore argue against the theological legitimacy of such exhortations. Conversely, an Arminian (let alone a Pelagian or semi-Pelagian) might hear a preacher insist on the primacy of God's elective action in salvation, and conclude that such a doctrine must prevent the preacher from being an evangelist. History shows the assessment to be false.

In other words, it is essential to recognise that the *functions* of each side of the sovereignty-responsibility tension are subject to abuse of a sort which might illegitimately eliminate some other aspect of truth; that the particular aspect of the tension appealed to in this biblical passage or that often springs from the circumstances which the writer was confronting; and that pastoral attempts to resolve the tension may only serve to distort the balance which the Bible preserves in its treatment of the tension.

Biblical balance is difficult to maintain in any area of doctrine; but perhaps it is particularly difficult here. Two little booklets in my library come to mind. Each is titled, *Why I am a Christian.* The first gives an answer in terms of divine, gracious, sovereignty; but its evangelistic appeal is virtually nil. The other gives a large number of standard reasons: the person of Christ, fulfilled prophecy, personal experience of forgiveness, the evidence for the resurrection, and the like; but it absolutises free will, and fences God off from the important decisions. The unfortunate aspect of the first book is that in providing the true *ultimate* reason, it seems to suggest that no further apologetic is needed, or even permitted. The unfortunate aspect of the second is that it treats its answers as if they were ultimate, and thereby ends up limiting God. The evangelistic practices reflected in the New Testament forbid both of these approaches.

I would be prepared to argue that any christian leader's handling of the tension between divine sovereignty and human responsibility will affect large areas of his theological understanding, evangelistic practices, and ecclesiastical methods. This is not to say that the tension *by itself* is determinative, still less that genuinely devout men and women can be found only within the camp of one ecclesiastical or theological tradition. Nevertheless, the sovereignty-responsibility tension certainly affects the outlook of the individual. More significantly, the local church, or some larger identifiable group such as a denomination or a segment of a denomination, is massively influenced by the shape of the sovereignty-responsibility tension which is promulgated (implicitly or explicitly) within its borders and believed to be true. Obvious examples would make up a long chapter, a chapter sometimes painful, sometimes humorous. But the benefit which could accrue to the Church as Christians ruefully saw such reflections of themselves might well repay the person who carefully set out the record. Perhaps some theologically minded Church historian will take up his pen where I put mine down.

NOTES

CHAPTER ONE (pp. 1-6)

1. Cf. F. Nötscher, 'Schicksal und Freiheit', *Biblica*, Vol. xl (1959), pp. 446-62.

2. This is a fairly standard distinction: cf. A. Flew, 'Divine Omnipotence and Human Freedom', *New Essays in Philosophical Theology* (London, 1955), pp. 160-1. See R. Young, *Freedom, Responsibility and God* (London, 1975), pp. 39 41, for a more sophisticated, philosophical definition of determinism.

3. On the one side, cf. H. Hoeksema, *Reformed Dogmatics* (Grand Rapids, 1966), and, less rigid, G. H. Clark, *Biblical Predestination* (Nutley, 1969). From the opposing camp, examples include S. Fisk, *Divine Sovereignty and Human Freedom* (Neptune, 1973), and many essays in a book edited by C. H. Pinnock, *Grace Unlimited* (Minneapolis, 1975).

4. I. T. Ramsey, *Freedom and Immortality* (London, 1960); W. S. Towner, *How God Deals With Evil* (Philadelphia, 1976); J. Farrelly, *Predestination, Grace and Free Will* (London, 1964). Other contemporary systematicians use biblical terminology to convey modern philosophical/theological conceptions. They include, *inter alios*, P. Tillich, *Systematic Theology* (London, 1953-64), Vol. i, pp. 158-9, 300, 316; J. Macquarrie, *Principles of Christian Theology* (London, 1966), pp. 302-4, who argues that predestination means God chooses everyone equally to the 'letting-be' of 'authentic existence'. Karl Barth is a special case, and is treated separately in Part Four.

5. A splendid example of abuse is the work of R. T. Forster and V. Marston, *God's Strategy in Human History* (Kent, 1973). Far better work is found, *inter alia*, in B. B. Warfield, 'Predestination', *Biblical and Theological Studies* (Philadelphia, repr. 1968), pp. 271-333; G. Quell and G. Schrenk, *TDNT*, Vol. iv, pp. 144-92.

6. E.g. Th. C. Vriezen, *Die Erwählung Israels nach dem Alten Testament* (Zürich, 1953); K. Galling, *Die Erwählungstraditionen Israels* (Giessen, 1928); H. H. Rowley, *The Biblical Doctrine of Election* (London, 1950); P. Altmann, *Erwählungstheologie und Universalismus im Alten Testament* (Berlin, 1964).

7. For example, Th. C. Vriezen, op. cit., and H. H. Rowley, op. cit., focus so narrowly on the *purpose* of election in the Old Testament, construed in terms of service, that they end up by reducing election to an entirely contingent divine choice.

CHAPTER TWO (pp. 9-17)

1. Cf. G. von Rad, *Genesis: A Commentary* (London, 1961), p. 427.

2. *Pace* many commentators and systematicians who say that God here turns evil into good: e.g. G. C. Berkouwer, *The Providence of God* (Grand Rapids, 1952), p. 91, who writes of God's 'deflection' of the evil. There are, of course, Old Testament passages in which God is portrayed as the one who 'deflects' human evil; but this is not one of them.

3. G. von Rad, *Old Testament Theology* (London, 1962-5), Vol. i, pp. 172f.

4. *Pace* K. Elliger, *Leviticus* (Tübingen, 1966), p. 301, who says that all of these clauses signify that God is sanctified by the Israelites' observance of the ritual laws he himself has bestowed.

5. Cf. K. Budde, *Das Buch der Richter* (Tübingen, 1897), p. 99; and G. F. Moore, *A Critical and Exegetical Commentary on Judges* (Edinburgh, 1895), p. 328.

6. A few scholars have argued that the 'he' of 14.4 refers to Samson, not Yahweh. But it is unlikely the writer means that *Samson* was out to provoke the enemy: Samson was interested in winning a woman, not punishing a people. Cf. Judg. 15.6, where, in a similar construction, the closest noun to the verb serves as that verb's subject: 'Samson, the son-in-law of the Timnite, because he (the Timnite) has taken his wife ...'

7. R. A. Carlson, *David, the Chosen King* (Uppsala, 1964), pp. 203f., thinks that to say God's wrath here has no known reason is 'a complete misunderstanding' of the structure of chapters 10-24. He takes the words 'Uriah the Hittite' at the end of the bridge 21.15—23.39 to be an important associative link, providing 'an adequate reason for the new outburst of the wrath of Yahweh in 24.1.' K. Budde, *Die Bücher Samuel* (Tübingen, 1902), pp. 327-8, resorts to the desperate expedient of placing all of 2 Sam. 24 before 2 Sam. 21.1-14.

8. NASB says '*it* incited David against them'—'it' presumably finding its antecedent in Yahweh's anger. But to personify this anger not only provides no solution (it is still Yahweh's anger), but is needless in the light of 1 Sam.26.19. P. Dhorme, *Les livres de Samuel* (Paris, 1910), p. 441, long ago rightly insisted, 'The subject of *wyst* can only be Yahweh.'

9. H. P. Smith, *A Critical and Exegetical Commentary on the Books of Samuel* (Edinburgh, 1899), p. 388.

10. G. von Rad, *Theology*, op. cit., Vol. i, p. 318; similarly, H. H. Rowley, *The Faith of Israel* (London, 1956), p. 67.

11. Cf. T. Willi, *Die Chronik als Auslegung* (Göttingen, 1972), pp. 155-6.

12. This *hapax* (*sibbāh mēʿim yhwh* in 1 Kgs. 12.15; *nᵉsibbāh mēʿim haʾᵉlōhîm* in 2 Chr. 10.15) is usually taken to mean a 'turning', and hence a 'development', from Yahweh (cf. the verb *sbb* in 1 Kgs. 2.15b).

13. The point is overstressed by many scholars. See, *inter alios*, G. B. Gray and A. S. Peake, *A Critical and Exegetical Commentary on the Book of Isaiah* (Edinburgh, 1912), pp. 196f.; H. Wildberger, *Jesaja 1-12* (Neukirchen-Vluyn, 1972), p. 396; and especially F. Huber, *Jahwe, Juda und die anderen Völker beim Propheten Jesaja* (Berlin, 1976), for whom this is a major conclusion from his research.

14. H. H. Rowley, *The Biblical Doctrine of Election* (London, 1950), pp. 124-8.

15. *Commentary on the Book of the Prophet Isaiah* (Edinburgh, 1850-4), Vol. i, p. 352.

16. R. K. Harrison, *Jeremiah and Lamentations* (London, 1973), p. 190. Precisely the same concept is found in 1 Sam. 2.22-5, where the sons of Eli 'would not listen to the voice of their father; for it was the will of the LORD to slay them.' See M. Tsevat, 'The Death of the Sons of Levi', *Journal of Bible and Religion*, Vol. xxxii (1964), pp. 355-8.

17. G. Baldwin, *Haggai, Zechariah, Malachi* (London, 1972), pp. 42-3.

18. The subject of this and the ensuing verses is Yahweh (cf. verse 7). The suggestion of M. Dahood, *Psalms* (New York, 1970), Vol. iii, p. 59—that $m^{e'}\bar{o}d$ here be taken as a stative adjective, 'the Great One', to provide an explicit subject—is neither helpful nor convincing in the light of the long list of verses in which Yahweh is subject. Dahood's alleged parallel (Ps. 109.30) falls under the same condemnation. See the useful discussion in H.-J. Kraus, *Psalmen* (Neukirchen, 1961), Vol. ii, p. 721.

19. E.g. C. F. Keil and F. Delitzsch, op. cit., Vol. iv, p. 153. S. R. Hirsch, *The Psalms* (New York, 1966), Vol. ii, p. 240, is among those who prefer to take the verb intransitively (cf. 2 Kgs. 5.26); but he goes so far to avoid the obvious as to say that if the verb is active, the subject is 'This' or 'It'; i.e. the growth of the people turned the hearts of the Egyptians.

20. See especially E. Robertson, 'Samuel and Saul', *Bulletin of the John Rylands Library*, Vol. xxviii (1944), pp. 175-206.

CHAPTER THREE (pp. 18-38)

1. H. H. Rowley, *Faith*, op. cit., p. 63; and cf. his *Election*, op. cit., pp. 45ff.

2. Cf. G. von Rad, *Wisdom in Israel* (London, 1972), pp. 62f.; W. Eichrodt, *Man in the Old Testament* (London, 1951), p. 23; F. D. Kidner, 'Wisdom Literature of the Old Testament', *New Perspectives on the Old Testament* (Waco, 1970), p. 118.

3. See especially Th. C. Vriezen, *An Outline of Old Testament Theology* (Oxford, 1970), pp. 176ff.

4. J. Lindblom, op. cit., p.324.

5. G. C. Berkouwer, *Providence*, op. cit., p. 92.

6. B. B. Warfield, 'Predestination', op. cit., pp. 48f.

7. G. C. Berkouwer, *Providence*, op. cit., p. 92. Cf. G. Von Rad, *Theology*, op. cit., Vol. i, pp. 51f., who points out that the purpose of a number of these narratives hinges on a theological phrase or clause revealing Yahweh's governing hand.

8. J. Lindblom, op. cit., p. 325; cf. pp. 323-6. See also K. Galling, op. cit., pp. 92f.; U. Cassuto, 'The Beginning of Historiography among the Israelites', *Biblical and Oriental Studies* (Jerusalem, 1973), Vol. i, pp. 7-16; and especially J. L. McKenzie, *A Theology of the Old Testament* (Garden City, 1976), pp. 135-44, who sees in Israel's historiography the first perception of intelligible unity in a series of events. This approach must be sharply distinguished from that which claims for Israel's historiography a supposedly

linear view of time as opposed to a cyclical view, an approach rightly criticised by J. Barr, *Biblical Words for Time* (London, 1969), pp. 143-51.

9. F. D. Kidner, *The Proverbs* (London, 1964), p. 118.

10. A. Cohen, *Proverbs* (Hindhead, 1945), p. 103.

11. J. A. Motyer, *The Day of the Lion* (London, 1974), p. 97. See the important observations of J. Pedersen, *Israel: Its Life and Culture* (London, 1940), Vols. iii-iv, pp. 486-91.

12. R. K. Harrison, *Introduction to the Old Testament* (London, 1970), p. 1099. Similarly, it has been argued convincingly that one of the main themes of Ruth is the election and birth of David: e.g. O. Loretz, 'The Theme of the Ruth Story', *CBQ*, Vol. xxii (1960), pp. 391-9.

13. J. K. S. Reid, 'Determinate, etc.', *A Theological Word Book of the Bible* (London, 1950), p. 65.

14. *Pace* G. Quell, *TDNT* Vol. iv, p. 159, who argues that the concept of election-of-king preceded that of election-of-people. This view is no longer very popular, although P. Altmann, *Erwählungstheologie*, op. cit., resurrects it in modified form by arguing that Israel's consciousness of her election sprang up during the glorious reigns of David and Solomon. Many Old *Testament Against Its Environment* (London, 1950), pp. 54-60), he is accurately describing some strands of Old Testament thought; but whenever the remnant motif becomes dominant, the simple equation between the elect J. Lindblom, op. cit., pp. 330f. Others, more careful, point out that the exodus does not constitute the genesis of the election traditions because all aspects of this tradition are already present: cf. H. J. Zobel, 'Ursprung und Verwurzelung des Erwählungsglaubens Israels', *Theologische Literaturzeitung*, Vol. xciii (1968), cols. 1-12, especially col. 8; G. Hasel, *The Remnant* (Barrien Springs, 1972), pp. 153f.

15. This use of *yada'* clearly means choose: cf. Amos 3.2; Hos. 13.5; G. Quell, *TDNT*, Vol. iv, pp. 147f.

16. P. Altmann, op. cit., *passim*, wrongly rejects any idea of mission in Israel's election, by preserving a rigid distinction between election and universalism. His work is thus marred by inadequate consideration of the semantic range of 'universalism'. Election does not necessarily exclude mission, and mission does not necessarily entail universalism. Nevertheless, it must be remembered that nowhere in the Old Testament is Israel's 'mission' spelled out in categories of systematic foreign proselytising: cf. A. Martin-Achard, *A Light to the Nations* (London, 1962), *passim*.

17. G. Vos, *Biblical Theology* (Grand Rapids, 1948), p. 90. This particular purpose of Israel's election is sadly exaggerated by, *inter alios*, H. H. Rowley, *Election*, op. cit., and Th. C. Vriezen, *Erwählung*, op. cit., *passim*, to the virtual exclusion of all else. They stress the fact that election involves commission in order to minimise any suggestion of privileged exclusivism. But this distiction is artificial. To be chosen by God means both privilege and commission.

18. G. E. Mendenhall, 'Ancient Oriental and Biblical Law', and 'Covenantal Forms in Israelite Tradition', both in *Biblical Archaeologist*, Vol. xvii (1954), pp. 26-46 and pp. 50-76 respectively.

19. Of course, this perspective differs from the Sinai covenant: cf. H. Ringgren, *Israelite Religion* (London, 1966), p. 117. When G. E. Wright,

God Who Acts (London, 1952), p. 21, says that 'God has bound his elect to himself, on the one hand, by great acts of love and grace, and, on the other hand, by a covenant in which his will is expressed' (cf. also his *The Old Testament Against Its Environment* (London, 1950), pp. 54-60), he is accurately describing some strands of Old Testament thought; but whenever the remnant motif becomes dominant, the simple equation between the elect and the people of the covenant cannot be made. On the whole question, see G. Hasel, op. cit., pp. 256ff.; and W. E. Müller and H. D. Preuss, *Die Vorstellung vom Rest im Alten Testament* (Neukirchen-Vluyn, 1973), *passim*.

20. G. Vos, op. cit., p. 93. This gave grounds for the later Pauline differentiation between election to privilege and election to life: 'For not all who are descended from Israel belong to Israel' (Rom. 9.6; cf. 11.28). Cf. J. I. Packer, *NBD*, p. 359.

21. J. Bright, *Covenant and Promise: The Prophetic Understanding of the Future in Pre-Exilic Israel* (Philadelphia, 1976), comes to similar conclusions by ascribing to the prophets a creative role as they wrestle with the tension between the Mosaic-Sinaitic tradition, with its emphasis upon Israel's obligation to covenant law, and the Davidic-Zion tradition, with its unconditional promises of blessing. My approach is essentially a modified form of the argument presented by J. Lindblom, op. cit., pp. 315-21.

22. *Theology*, op. cit., Vol. i, p. 286. Cf. also L. L. Walker, ' "Love" in the Old Testament: Some Lexical Observations', *Current Issues in Biblical and Patristic Interpretation*, (Grand Rapids, 1975), pp. 277-88.

23. Cf. F. J. Helfmeyer, 'Segen und Erwählung', *BZ*, Vol. xviii (1947), pp. 208-33, who draws attention to the discriminating significance of divine blessing in the Old Testament: 'The blessing selects, seizes, chooses, commissions, produces a position of superiority and evokes resignation' (p. 222). Cf. also N. H. Snaith, *The Distinctive Ideas of the Old Testament* (London, 1944), p. 139: 'Either we must accept this idea of choice on the part of God with its necessary accompaniment of exclusiveness, or we have to hold a doctrine of the love of God other than that which is biblical.'

24. V. Herntrich, *TDNT*, Vol. iv, p. 203.

25. F. Hesse, *Das Verstockungsproblem im Alten Testament* (Berlin, 1955), provides a helpful analysis, especially of the terms and metaphors involved (pp. 7-30).

26. *Election*, op. cit., chap. 5.

27. J. I. Packer, *NBD*, pp. 358f.

28. Cf J. I. Packer, *NBD*, pp. 1050f.

29. Jorg Jeremias, *Die Reue Gottes: Aspekte Alttestamentlicher Gottesvorstellung* (Neukirchen-Vluyn, 1975).

30. J. A. Motyer, op. cit., pp. 156f.

31. (Tübingen, 1924).

32. Th. C. Vriezen, *Erwählung*, op. cit., pp. 115f., rightly attacks the confusion between the pretentiousness of 'being elect' and the fact of being the object of 'election': he distinguishes between *Erwähltheit* and *Erwählung*. F. M. Th. de Liagre Bohl, 'Missions- und Erwählungsgedanke in Alt-Israel',

Opera Minora (Groningen, 1953), especially p. 88, points out that other nations enjoy the conviction of being elected: e.g. Egyptians, Greeks, Romans. But in these cases, quite unlike Israel's prophets, the idea of election is based on some note of superiority.

33. See the important article by I. A. Seeligmann, 'Menschliches Heldentum und göttliche Hilfe. Die doppelte Kausalität im altestamentlichen Geschichtsdenken', *Theologische Zeitschrift,* Vol. xix (1963), p. 401.

CHAPTER FOUR (pp. 41-44)

1. That is how the Greek should be taken: Joseph says he belongs to God, not that he is God's servant. It is true that in 50.18 the brothers tell Joseph they are his servants, and some have taken Joseph's reply in 50.19, *tou gar theou eimi egō,* to mean 'for I am God's (servant)'. But the structure in 50.18 is dative; in 50.19, genitival. The thought in 50.19 is closer to *ego de Christou* (1 Cor. 1.12), 'I am of Christ('s party)', i.e. 'I follow Christ'. Similarly Joseph belongs to God's party: he follows God.

2. 'God's "Repentance" and the LXX', *Ex. T,* Vol. lxxv (1964), p. 367.

3. *The Exegetical Method of the Greek Translator of the Book of Job* (Philadelphia, 1952).

4. *The Anti-Anthropomorphisms of the Greek Pentateuch* (Princeton, 1943).

5. T. W. Manson, 'Miscellanea Apocalyptica', *JTS,* Vol. xlvi (1945), pp. 78-80; P. Katz (Walters), 'Septuagintal Studies in the Mid-Century', *The Background of the New Testament and Its Eschatology* (Cambridge, 1956), pp. 176-208; S. Jellicoe, *The Septuagint and Modern Study* (Oxford, 1968), pp. 270f.; T. Wittstruck, 'The So-Called Anti-Anthropomorphisms in the Greek Text of Deuteronomy', *CBQ,* Vol. xxxviii (1976), pp. 29-34. For similar conclusions in another part of the LXX, cf. A. Soffer, 'The Treatment of Anthropomorphisms and Anthropopathisms in the Septuagint of Psalms', *Hebrew Union College Annual,* Vol. xxxviii (1957), pp. 85-107, now reprinted in *Studies in the Septuagint: Origins, Recensions, and Interpretations* (New York, 1974), pp. 395-417.

6. Cf. H. M. Orlinsky's review of Fritsch in *Crozer Quarterly,* Vol. xxi (1944), pp. 156-60. He has also written a number of articles on Job: in particular, 'Studies in the Septuagint of the Book of Job: On the Matter of Anthropomorphisms, Anthropopathisms, and Euphemisms', *Hebrew Union College Annual,* Vol. xxx (1959), pp. 153-67, and Vol. xxxii (1961), pp. 239-68.

7. D. H. Gard, op. cit., pp. 67ff.; G. Gerleman, *Studies in the Septuagint I. The Book of Job* (Lund, 1946). A major weakness of Gard's book is that it does not use Gerleman, published six years earlier.

8. 'Problems of Text and Midrash in the Third Book of Reigns', *Textus,* Vol. vii (1969), pp. 1-29.

9. R. Loewe, 'Divine Frustration Exegetically Frustrated', *Words and Meanings* (Cambridge, 1968), pp. 137-58.

CHAPTER FIVE (pp. 45-54)

1. D. S. Russell, *The Method and Message of Jewish Apocalyptic* (London, 1964), pp. 37f.; K. Koch, *The Rediscovery of Apocalyptic* (London, 1970), pp. 18-35.

2. W. Schmithals, *The Apocalyptic Movement* (Nashville, 1975).

3. J. Bright, *A History of Israel* (London, 1972), p. 449.

4. R. H. Pfeiffer, *History of New Testament Times* (London, 1949), p. 378.

5. So also 42.24 in Greek, but not in Hebrew. The translator has apparently read *šnym* for *šwnym* and consequently reintroduced the theme of opposed pairs.

6. It is quite common to exaggerate the importance of those few texts which could be understood as universalistic in tendency: e.g. Tobit 13.3f., 11; 14.6f.; Ecclus. 10.19-22. For example, J. Bright, op. cit., p. 448, takes Tobit 13.3f. to reflect a sensed obligation to witness before the nations. But this witness does not apparently have conversion in view as the goal: cf. 3.5. True, many nations shall come bearing rich gifts to the Lord (13.11); but the result is an opulent Jerusalem (13.16ff.). Although all nations shall turn to the Lord and bury their idols (14.6f.), the comforting aspect lies in the fact that they will then show mercy to the Jewish people (14.7b). And, *pace* Bright, Ecclus. 10.19-22, far from widening the boundaries of God's people by removing racial criteria, narrows the boundaries to those who keep the law within the race, while the pagans are rather summarily dismissed (10.14-17). There are some few brighter spots; but the tendency is not toward universalism: cf. H. J. Wicks, *The Doctrine of God in the Jewish Apocryphal and Apocalyptic Literature* (New York, repr. 1971), pp. 255f.

7. Cf. E. P. Sanders, *Paul and Palestinian Judaism* (London, 1977), pp. 329-32.

8. Where 'chosen' is omitted (Aleph) it is due to haplography of *ek*.

9. M. S. Enslin and S. Zeitlin, *The Book of Judith* (Leiden, 1972), p. 33.

10. Ibid., pp. 83f., 90.

11. Of course, the emphasis changes somewhat from book to book. For example, the martyrs whose death is said to be a propitiatory death in behalf of the nation, a death brought about by the divine providence (4 Macc. 17.22), elsewhere claim they are dying because of their own sins (2 Macc. 7.18).

12. I use the expression advisedly. Nevertheless I hasten to add that my use of 'merit theology' is not meant to conjure up visions of supererogation, a divine judgment based exclusively on human merits and demerits, and so forth. It carries only the freight of the surrounding discussion. This caveat becomes the more important in discussing the rabbis (chap. 8, *infra*), not least because of the recent and important book by E. P. Sanders, op. cit., which I discuss at length a little farther on.

13. See especially G. L. Prato, *Il problema della teodicea in Ben Sira* (Rome, 1975). Prato especially stresses the historical background which calls forth such arguments. Similarly B. L. Mack, both in his article, 'Wisdom Myth and Myth-ology', *Interpretation*, Vol. xxiv (1970), pp. 46-60, and in his book, *Logos und Sophia: Untersuchungen zur Weisheits Theologie im hellenistischen Judentums* (Göttingen, 1973), makes a great deal of the

problems of theodicy arising out of the trauma of this exile, as the background to wisdom speculation. How is Yahweh sovereign over history when history seems to contradict such a belief? Mack develops a 'near' wisdom present with God at creation and sustaining all that is good, and a 'hidden' wisdom associated with God's transcendence. The latter later gives rise to the need for revelation; but due to human sinfulness it must become 'disappeared' (*entschwunden*) wisdom. By contrast, apocalyptic, instead of bringing wisdom 'down', brings men 'up'.

14. There is somewhat more among the apocalyptists, but then it is primarily offered by celestial beings: cf. N. B. Johnson, *Prayer in the Apocrypha and Pseudepigrapha* (Philadelphia, 1948), pp. 36f. Praises are also offered for particular victories, especially after the numerous Maccabean successes.

15. Ibid., p. 39.

16. *APOT*, Vol. i, p. 61.

CHAPTER SIX (pp. 55-74)

1. A. Nissen, 'Tora und Geschichte in Spätjudentum', *Novum Testamentum*, Vol. ix (1967), pp. 241-77.

2. K. Koch, *The Rediscovery of Apocalyptic* (London, 1970), p. 137, n. 43.

3. Op. cit., p. 54.

4. *NBD*, p. 42.

5. M. R. James, *The Testament of Abraham* (Cambridge, 1892), pp. 23-9. See M. Delcor, *Le Testament d'Abraham* (Leiden, 1973), pp. 63-73; and several essays in G. W. E. Nickelsburger, Jr., ed., *Studies on the Testament of Abraham* (Missoula, 1976).

6. Op. cit., p. 61.

7. M. de Jonge, *The Testaments of the Twelve Patriarchs* (Assen, 1953). He modifies his view somewhat in 'The Testaments of the Twelve Patriarchs and the New Testament', *St. Ev.*, Vol. i (1959), pp. 546-56, to allow more room for oral tradition in both Jewish and Christian circles; and his most recent statement of his position is found in several essays in a book edited by him, *Studies on the Testaments of the Twelve Patriarchs* (Leiden, 1975). Constrast H. C. Kee, 'The Ethical Dimensions of the Testaments of the XII as a Clue to Provenance', *NTS*, Vol. xxiv (1978), pp. 259-70. The recent work by H. D. Slingerland, *The Testament of the Twelve Patriarchs: A Critical History of Research* (Missoula, 1977), provides a more balanced statement of the problem; cf. also J. H. Charlesworth, 'Reflections on the SNTS Pseudepigrapha Seminar', *NTS*, Vol. xxiii (1976-7), p. 304, for a succint statement of the present consensus.

8. D. W. Bousset, *Die Religion des Judentums im neutestamentlichen Zeitalter* (Berlin, 1906), pp. 571ff.; followed by, *inter alios*, W. R. Murdock, 'History and Revelation in Jewish Apocalypticism', *Interpretation*, Vol. xxi (1967), p. 173; and H. Conzelmann, *An Outline of the Theology of the New Testament* (London, 1969), p. 23.

9. E.g. H. D. Betz, 'On the Problem of the Religio-Historical Understanding of Apocalypticism', *Journal of Theology and Church*, Vol. vi (1969), pp. 134-56, sees Jewish apocalyptic as part of a world-wide and essentially

hellenistic movement. W. A. Beardslee, 'New Testament Apocalyptic in Recent Interpretation', *Interpretation,* Vol. xxv (1971), p. 435, objects that his sampling of the data is too limited.

10. F. M. Cross, *Canaanite Myth and Hebrew Epic* (Cambridge, Mass., 1973), pp. 90, 144, 170, 343-6; *idem,* 'New Directions in the Study of Apocalyptic', *Journal of Theology and Church,* Vol. vi (1969), p. 165, n. 23.

11. *Wisdom in Israel,* op. cit., pp. 263-82. His argument has been refined by H. P. Müller, 'Mantische Weisheit und Apokalyptik', *VT Suppl.* Vol. xx (Uppsala, 1971), pp. 268-93.

12. P. D. Hanson, 'Jewish Apocalyptic against its Near Eastern Environment', *RB,* Vol. lxxviii (1971), pp. 31-58. For a complete statement of his views, especially focusing on the way apocalyptic is said to emerge in post-exilic prophecy, see his *The Dawn of Apocalyptic* (Fortress, 1975).

13. Cf. M. Hengel, *Judaism and Hellenism* (London, 1974), Vol. i, pp. 175ff.; and R. J. Bauckham, *Themelios,* Vol. iii (1978), 10-18.

14. *Apocalyptic* (Grand Rapids, 1972), p. 32.

15. There is some uncertainty as to the meaning of the text. Cf. H. M. Hughes, *The Ethics of Jewish Apocryphal Literature* (London, n.d.), pp. 276f. The text either means that our works are in both the divine choice and in our own power, or that they are in our own choice and power. Both *APOT,* Vol. ii, p. 642, and *APAT,* Vol. ii, p. 140, opt for the latter translation.

16. C. G. Montefiore, *Lectures on the Origin and Growth of Religion as Illustrated by the Religion of the Ancient Hebrews* (London, 1897), p. 518.

17. *Torah in the Messianic Age and/or the Age to Come* (Philadelphia, 1952), p. 3, n. 4; cf. also D. S. Russell, op. cit., pp. 100-103.

18. Op. cit., p. 59.

19. H. M. Hughes, op. cit., p. 243.

20. Ibid., p. 240; cited also by G. H. Box, *APOT,* Vol. ii, p. 557.

21. Op. cit., p. 51.

22. S. B. Frost, *Old Testament Apocalyptic* (London, 1952), p. 230. Cf. also R. H. Charles, *Eschatology* (London, 1913), p. 206.

23. Such examples render somewhat premature the contention of K. Koch, op. cit., p. 29, that only epochs, not individuals, are determined. He goes so far as to say that 'the behaviour of the individual is never (*sic*) accounted in these writings as being predestined toward good or evil ...'

24. 'Jüdische Apokalyptik', *RGG³,* Vol. i, col. 465. On the development of eschatological dualism within Jewish apocalyptic, and the historical reasons for it, cf. M. Hengel, op. cit., Vol. i, pp. 190-96.

25. Op. cit., p. 202.

26. Op. cit., p. 186.

27. Op. cit., p. 271f.

28. 'Apocalyptic and New Testament Theology', *Reconciliation and Hope* (London, 1974), p. 292.

29. Op. cit., p. 88.

30. *A History of Israel,* op. cit., p. 460.

31. 'Some Reflections on Apocalyptic', *Aux sources de la tradition chrétienne* (Neuchâtel, 1950), p. 142. The 'other side' is the 'scribal treatment of the Law leading to the codification in the Mishnah'.

32. *Eschatology*, op. cit., p. 183.

33. Op. cit., pp. 218ff.

34. *The Relevance of Apocalyptic* (London, 1947), pp. 151-5.

35. 'Why Not Prophetic-Apocalyptic?', *JBL*, Vol. lxxvi (1957), pp. 192-200. Along similar lines and apparently without consulting Ladd, is B. Vawter, 'Apocalyptic: Its Relation to Prophecy', *CBQ*, Vol. xxii (1960), pp. 33-46.

36. W. A. Beardslee, op. cit., p. 424. This is one point on which there is solid agreement among many scholars who have written recently on the subject of apocalyptic, even when they agree on little else. As representative sampling, cf. R. J. Bauckham, op. cit., pp. 18-23; C. F. D. Moule, *The Birth of the New Testament* (London, 1962), p. 103; D. S. Russell, op. cit., p. 106; L. Hartman, 'The Functions of Some So-Called Apocalyptic Timetables', *NTS*, Vol. xxii (1975-6), pp. 1-14; G. W. E. Nickelsburger, 'The Apocalyptic Message of I Enoch 92-105', *CBQ*, Vol. xxxix (1977), pp. 302-28; G. I. Davies, 'Apocalyptic and Historiography', *Journal for the Study of the Old Testament*, No. 5 (1978), pp. 15-28; J. Priest, 'Some Reflections on the Assumption of Moses', *Perspective in Religious Studies*, Vol. iv (1977), pp. 92-111; and, on early apocalyptic, W. R. Millar, *Isaiah 24-27 and the Origin of Apocalyptic* (Missoula, 1976).

37. 'Apocalyptic Eschatology as the Transcendence of Death', *CBQ*, Vol. xxxvi (1974), pp. 21-43.

38. Cf. especially P. Bogaert, *Apocalypse de Baruch* (Paris, 1969), 2 vols. The date is late (Bogaert pinpoints AD 96), and so no doubt the fall of the Temple constitutes a large part of the crisis.

39. For further discussion, cf. G. H. Box, both in *Apot* and also in his *The Ezra-Apocalypse* (London, 1912), *passim;* and especially A. L. Thompson, *Responsibility for Evil in the Theodicy of IV Ezra* (Missoula, 1974). Some conclude that 2 Esdras is extremely pessimistic, and the notes of hope are necessarily interpolations: cf. E. P. Sanders, op. cit., 409-18, who takes the book to be the sole intertestamental exemplar of 'covenantal nomism' collapsing into legalistic perfectionism.

40. *Die Eschatologie der jüdischen Gemeinde im neutestamentlichen Zeitalter* (Tübingen, repr. 1966), p. 352.

41. *TDNT*, Vol. iv, p. 170.

42. Y. Kaufmann, *The Religion of Israel from Its Beginnings to the Babylonian Exile* (London, 1961), pp. 127f.

43. The question of a human role for Israel within the framework of eschatological universalism is much contested: cf. J. Blauw, *The Missionary Nature of the Church* (London, 1962), pp. 55-64.

44. Op. cit., p. 299; cf. pp. 297-303.

.45. P. Volz, *Die Eschatologie*, op. cit., p. 356.

46. *Le Judaïsme avant Jesus-Christ* (Paris, 1931), p. 84.

47. *APOT*, Vol. ii, pp. 411f.

48. *APOT*, Vol. ii, pp. 424.

49. His emendations seem reasonable. In verse 7, for example, behind 'strength' he reads *firmitatem* for ms. *infirmitatem*.

50. *TDNT*, Vol. ii, p. 197.

51. The same stance is apparently adopted by Test. Ab. (B). Like (A), (B)

records the dilemma of the soul with equal merits and sins; but unlike (A), (B) does not record the prayers of Michael and Abraham in behalf of that soul. This is one of several ways in which (B) seems to be more severe than (A). M. R. James, *The Testament of Abraham* (Cambridge, 1892), pp. 64-70, notes that (B) expunges much of Abraham's unwillingness to die, probably because such an attitude might appear unmanly. Noteworthy, too, is the fact that (B) places Abraham's cursing of earth's sinners (12) *after* his observation of judgment. This is much harsher than (A). For less significant theological differences between the two recensions, cf. M. Delcor, op. cit., pp. 11-14.

CHAPTER SEVEN (pp. 75-83)

1. Cf. A. Fitzgerald, '*MTNDBYM* in IQS', *CBQ*, Vol. xxxvi (1974), pp. 495-502.

2. To this may be added 4QDb, which appears to fill in the lacuna at the end of column 15 of the Qumran CD (15.15-17)—i.e. *APOT*, Vol. ii, following 19.12.

3. J. T. Milik, *Ten Years of Discovery in the Wilderness of Judaea* (London, 1959), p. 114. Philo, *Hyp.* 11.2, notes that the Essene community was a voluntary association.

4. J. P. Hyatt, 'The View of Man in the Qumran "Hodayot"', *NTS*, Vol. ii (1955-6), pp. 276-84.

5. Cf. M. Burrows, *The Dead Sea Scrolls* (London, 1956), pp. 263f.; G. Vermes, *The Dead Sea Scrolls in English* (Harmondsworth, 1968) pp. 39-41.

6. This is not really a horribly mixed metaphor, since, as E. Lohse, *Die Texte aus Qumran* (Darmstadt, 1971), p. 239, n. 34, points out, the community=the holy *mţ'* (plantation?) in 6.15.

7. *TDNT*, Vol. iv, p. 171. For further discussion, cf. W. Günther in *Theologische Begriffslexikon zum Neuen Testament* (Wuppertal, 1967-71), Vol. iii, p. 1044a.

8. The best work in this area is now that of E. H. Merrill, *Qumran and Predestination: A Theological Study of the Thanksgiving Hymns* (Leiden, 1975). By 'predestination', however, Merrill usually means what I would call '*soteriological* predestination', or election; yet he draws sweeping conclusions about (what I would call) predestination from his treatment of election. Too often, too, he draws deductions from the texts which the covenanters of *Hodayoth* would not draw, and here and there tries to resolve the sovereignty-responsibility tension for them.

9. One passage, 1QH 16.10, though probably highly predestinarian, is semantically ambiguous, because of the doubtful meaning of the verb *ršm*, which occurs only here in the DSS and only once in the Old Testament as a participle (at Dan. 10.21). T. Gaster, *The Scriptures of the Dead Sea Sect* (London, 1957), p. 191, translates, 'Thou dost *keep a record* of every righteous spirit. ...' This suggests that the psalmist's choice to keep his hands clean is due to the prospect of coming judgment. But others think the verb in its context means that God *has written down* (sc. the destiny) of the spirit of the just (e.g. S. Holm-Nielsen, *Hodayot; Psalms from Qumran* (Aarhus, 1960), p. 238, n. 10), i.e. because God has determined the spirit of the just, the just man will choose to be pure. The latter interpretation better suits the

context, since 16.11 goes on to insist that man is not righteous except through God. This understanding of the text, which makes man's choice the result of the divine determining, is rigorously predestinarian; but admittedly the evidence is ambiguous. E. H. Merrill, op. cit., p. 31, does not decide.

10. Cf. W. D. Davies, 'The Dead Sea Scrolls and Christian Origins', *Christian Origins and Judaism* (London, 1962), p. 117: 'We miss in the Sect the concern for the lost, for the "world"; the land for which it offers propitiation is the "land of Israel". The Sect remains a Jewish community ...' E. P. Sanders, op. cit., pp. 245ff., insists there is strong indication that the covenanters do not restrict the elect to their own community; but the evidence he adduces is of mixed value. Certainly their vision does not really extend beyond Israel, even when it barely extends beyond the community.

11. Cf. J. M. Allegro, 'An Astrological Cryptic Document from Qumran', *Journal of Semitic Studies*, Vol. ix (1964), pp. 291-4; published as 4Q186 in *DJD*, Vol. v, pp. 88-91. Cf. further M. Hengel, op. cit., Vol. i, pp. 236ff.

12. So H.-W. Kuhn, *Enderwartung und gegenwärtiges Heil* (Göttingen, 1966), especially pp. 44ff.

13. Op. cit., p. 75.

14. *The Dead Sea Scrolls*, op. cit., p. 374.

15. A. R. C. Leaney, *The Rule of Qumran and its Meaning* (London, 1966), *in loc.*

16. M. Burrows, *More Light*, op. cit., p. 292..

17. 1QS 4.16, 25 may be taken to support this interpretation. In these verses, A. A. Anderson, 'The Use of "Ruah" in 1QS, 1QH and 1QM', *Journal of Semitic Studies*, Vol. vii (1962), pp. 293-303, takes *bd bbd* to mean 'in certain quantities or parts', i.e. 'proportionately', not 'in equal quantities'.

18. Cf. *inter alia* M. Treves, 'The Two Spirits of the Rule of the Community', *Revue de Qumran*, Vol. iii (1961-2), p. 451; A. Marx,'Y a-t-il une prédestination à Qumran?', *Revue de Qumran*, Vol. vi (1967-9), pp. 163-81; F. Nötscher, *Zur theologischen Terminologie*, op. cit., pp. 79f.

19. See M. Treves, op. cit., and especially P. Wernberg-Moller, 'A Reconsideration of the Two Spirits in the Rule of the Community (1Q Serek iii.13—iv.26)', *Revue de Qumran*, Vol. iii (1961-2), pp. 413-41, who has changed his mind since writing *The Manual of Discipline* (Leiden, 1957).

20. On the meaning of *yēṣer* ('inclination') in the Qumran corpus, see R. E. Murphy, '*Yēṣer* in the Qumran Literature', *Biblica*, Vol. xxxix (1958), pp. 334-44. Often in *Hodayoth* it is found in the expression 'creature (*yṣr*) of clay'; but even there, as J. P. Hyatt, op. ct., pp. 280f., has pointed out, it can mean 'impulse' or 'inclination': cf. 1QH 39.6, 31f., 41.3f.; and possibly also 40.32; 41.16; 45.20; 54.3, 9f.

21. M. Treves, op. cit., p. 451, n. 9.

22. G. Maier, *Mensch und freier Wille* (Tübingen, 1971), pp. 222-63; and J. H. Charlesworth, 'A Critical Comparison of the Dualism in 1QS 3:13-4:26 and the "Dualism" Contained in the Gospel of John', *NTS*, Vol. xv (1968-9), pp. 389-418; reprinted in *John and Qumran* (London, 1972), pp. 72-106, especially pp. 76-89.

23. Ibid., p. 89.

24. H. W. Huppenbauer, *Der Mensche zwischen zwei Welten* (Zürich, 1959), p. 113.

25. Op. cit., pp. 53-5.

26. Op. cit., p. 261.

27. Op. cit. In fact, a number of scholars have not been content to let the sovereignty-responsibility tension emerge naturally from the DSS, but feel compelled to polarise it or explain it by appeal to diverse sources or the like. For example, P. von der Osten-Sacken, *Gott und Belial* (Göttingen, 1969), has attempted a total reconstruction of the development of dualism at Qumran. He thinks dualism is linked inseparably with eschatology in 1QM 1, which he takes to be the oldest stratum of that scroll. In the rest of 1QM this link is weakened, and more ethical dualism is introduced. 1QS 3.13-4.14 is the next stage: light and darkness are de-eschatologised and linked to God's creation, while the elect are narrowed from Israel to the community. Late developments are found in CD and other pseudepigraphical writings, while the original eschatological dualism is carried on and remains discernible in 11QMel, as in Rev. 12.7-12. But if this 'early' strand is so clear in 'late' material must we not question whether the entire reconstruction is not 'all too pat and logical' (review by J. Fitzmeyer, *CBQ*, Vol. xxxii (1970), p. 469)? In particular, the dating of 1QM is much disputed: for example, Y. Yadin, *The Scroll of the War of the Sons of Light against the Sons of Darkness* (Oxford, 1962), pp. 243ff., argues for a date in the second half of the *first* century BC—not to mention the extreme views of the G. R. Driver, *The Judaean Scrolls* (Oxford, 1965), pp. 168-225, who advocates end of the first century AD. Yet this is one of the crucial, and debatable, points on which the thesis of von der Osten-Sacken rests. Unfortunately, H. Räisänen's work, *The Idea of Divine Hardening* (Helsinki, 1972), pp. 73ff., is severely marred by following von der Osten-Sacken rather closely and uncritically. For other examples, cf. E. P. Sanders, op. cit., pp. 265f.

28. J. P. Hyatt, op. cit., p. 283, n. 1. Cf. A. R. C. Leaney, op. cit., pp. 44f.

29. Cf. R. H. Charles, *APOT*, Vol. ii, p. 785; M. Burrows, *The Dead Sea Scrolls*, op. cit., pp. 250f.; and especially L. H. Schiffman, *The Halakah at Qumran* (Leiden, 1975).

30. Cf. S. B. Thiering, 'The Biblical Source of Qumran Asceticism', *JBL.* Vol. xciii (1974), pp. 429-44. She also points out (p. 439) that Zoroastrianism is distinctly *anti*-ascetic.

31. J. T. Milik, op. cit., p. 113. This interpretation therefore differs quite radically from that of R. E. Brown, 'The Qumran Scrolls and John', *A Companion to John* (New York, 1977), p. 76, who overestimates the force of predestination in the DSS, and underestimates it in the Old Testament. E. H. Merrill, op. cit., commits the latter error also.

32. F. Nötscher, 'Schicksalsglaube in Qumran und Umwelt', *Biblische Zeitschrift*, Vol. iii (1959), p. 218. Later in the article, Vol. iv (1960), pp. 98ff., he points out that the tension between predestination and freedom finds in Qumran only a practical, ascetic solution, not a theoretical, theological one.

CHAPTER EIGHT (pp. 84-109)

1. (London, 1977).

2. In particular, J. Neusner, *The Rabbinic Traditions about the Pharisees*

before 70 (Leiden, 1971), 3 vols.; but also E. Rivkin, 'Defining the Pharisees: the Tannaitic Sources', *Hebrew Union College Annual,* Vols. xl-xli, pp. 234-8, and other of his essays he there cites; and J. Bowker, *Jesus and the Pharisees* (Cambridge, 1973), pp. 1-37.

3. Cf. H. H. Ben-Sasson, *A History of the Jewish People* (Cambridge, Mass., 1976), pp. 307-13.

4. P. Wernberg-Møller, 'An Inquiry into the Validity of the Text-Critical Argument for an Early Dating of the Recently Discovered Palestinian, Targum', *VT,* vol. xii (1962), pp. 312-330.

5. Cf. A. D. York, 'The Dating of Targumic Literature', *Journal for the Study of Judaism,* Vol. v (1974), pp. 49-62; and E. P. Sanders, op. cit., p. 26, n. 5, and the literature there cited.

6. C. J. Cowling, 'New Light on the New Testament? The Significance of the Palestinian Targum', *TSF Bulletin,* Vol. li (1968), pp. 6-15.

7. (Jerusalem, 1975), 2 Vols.

8. The English translation is in this instance by M. McNamara in A. Diez Macho, *Nesphyti 1: Targum Palestinense MS de la Biblioteca Vaticana* (Madrid, 1968-), Vol. i, p. 641. Where there· are established English translations of the targums available, I have used them; otherwise the English renderings are my own.

9. Ibid., Vol. iii, p. 384.

10. For example, Lev. 22.32 is found in the Babylonia Talmud at B. Ber. 2lb; B. Meg. 23b; B. Sanh. 74a; B.A.Z. 27b, 54a. However, the last clause of Lev. 22-32 is included in none of these quotations.

11. Cf. M. McNamara, *Targum and Testament* (Shannon, 1972), pp. 93-95.

12. P. Ber. 9.8 suggests also that David's sin consisted in not asking for the ransom money of Exod. 30.12.

13. A. Sperber, *The Bible in Aramaic* (Leiden, 1959-73), Vol. iv/в, p. 37.

14. J. Bowker, *The Targums and Rabbinic Literature* (Cambridge, 1969), p. 212.

15. Cf. the choice passages culled by C. G. Montefiore and H. Loewe, *A Rabbinic Anthology* (New York, repr. 1974), pp. 1-57.

16. Op. cit., pp. 37-41.

17. Cf. M. McNamara, op. cit., pp. 73f.; E. Schürer, *The History of the Jewish People in the Age of Jesus Christ* (revised edn; Edinburgh, 1973-), Vol. i, p. 100. See also the important studies of M. Ginsburger, *Die Anthropomorphismen in den Targumim* (Braunschweig, 1891), pp. 12f.; J. Schunary, 'Avoidance of Anthropomorphism in the Targum of Psalms', *Textus,* Vol. v (1966), pp. 133-44.

18. This perspective should not be confused with that in 3 Enoch, where Enoch=Metatron=*yhwh hqṭn* ('little Yahweh'). The rabbis opposed the attempt to promote Metatron to divine status: cf. B. Sanh. 38*b*; B. Hag. 15a (cf. Deut. R.2.13, which may be anti-christian). On the origin of the name Metatron, cf. H. Odeberg, *3 Enoch* (New York, repr. 1973), pp. 79ff.; and M. Black, 'The Origin of the Name Metatron', *VT,* Vol. i (1951), pp. 217-19. There is another strand of rabbinic thought which results in the extreme literalism of the Kabbalist period (which went so far as to estimate God's

physical dimensions): cf. E. M. Yamauchi, 'Anthropomorphism in Hellenism and in Judaism', *Bibliotheca Sacra*, Vol. cxxvii (1970), pp. 212-22, and the literature there cited. The earlier traditions are pre-eminently the other way. This does not mean that God became a mere metaphysical object: the rabbis preserved warmth and deep worship: cf. S. Schechter, *Some Aspects of Rabbinic Theology* (London, 1909), pp. 21ff.; and G. F. Moore, *Judaism in the First Centuries of the Christian Era* (New York, repr. 1971), Vol. i, pp. 439-42.

19. See *inter alia* G. F. Moore, ibid., vol. ii, pp. 377-95; J. Bonsirven, *Le judaîsme palestinien au temps de Jésus-Christ* (Paris, 1934-35), Vol. i, pp. 307-21; M. McNamara, op. cit., pp. 133-41; and also A. J. Saldarini, 'Apocalyptic and Rabbinic Literature', *CBQ*, Vol. xxxvii (1975), pp. 348-58.

20. *The Targums and Rabbinic Literature,* op. cit., p. 158.

21. Cf. G. F. Moore, op. cit., Vol. i, pp. 479-93; S. Schechter, op. cit., pp. 242-92; C. G. Montefiore and H. Loewe, op. cit., pp. 295-314; E. E. Urbach, op. cit., pp. 471-83. In particular, cf. B. Sukk. 52*a-b*.

22. J. M. Price, *JE*, Vol. v, p. 505a.

23. E. E. Urbach, op. cit., pp. 257f. See his entire section on providence, pp. 255-85.

24. Cf. J. Abelson, *The Immanence of God in Rabbinical Literature* (London, 1912), pp. 292-4.

25. B. W. Helfgott, *The Doctrine of Election in the Tannaitic Literature* (New York, 1954), p. 4; with helpful discussion pp. 32-6.

26. Cf. H. J. Schoeps, 'Die Tempelzerstörung des Jahres 70 in der judischen Religionsgeschichte', *Aus Frühchristlicher Zeit* (Tübingen, 1950), pp. 144-83.

27. For an excellent discussion, cf. E. E. Urbach, op. cit., pp. 525-54.

28. E.g. R. Joshua, *contra* R. Eliezer, argued that Messiah's coming is independent of Israel's repentance (B. Sanh. 97*b*-98*a*). So also R. Meir (B. Kidd, 36*a*). See further B. W. Helfgott, op. cit., pp. 105ff., 147ff. R. Judah b. Ilai, however, believed that the filial bond between God and Israel was conditioned by good behaviour (B. Kidd, 36*a*; *Sifre* on Deut. 4.1).

29. H. J. Schoeps, 'Haggadisches zur Auserwählung Israels', *Aus frühschristlicher Zeit* (Tübingen, 1950), pp. 184-200, argues convincingly that this sort of *Haggadah* was the rabbinic answer to christian polemic on election.

30. Cf. references in SB, Vol. iv, p. 35.

31. So taught a Tanna in the name of R. Meir. The Epstein English translation wrongly translates '*zyn* by 'impetuous'; but, as B. W. Helfgott, op. cit., p. 155, n. 5, points out, the word means 'energetic' as in Gen. 49.7; Exod. 14.21; Num. 13.28. Note the parallel in the same passage, attributed to R. Simeon b. Rakish: 'There are three distinguished in (fierce) strength ('*zyn*): Israel among the nations, the dog among animals, (and) the cock among birds.'

32. (New York, 1939).

33. On the whole question of merits, see C. G. Montefiore and H. Loewe, op. cit., pp. 202-32; A. Marmorstein, *The Doctrine of Merits in Old Rabbinical Literature* (London, 1920); W. D. Davies, *Paul and Rabbinic*

Judaism (London, 1970), pp. 270-72; S. Schechter, op. cit., pp. 170-98; E. P. Sanders, op. cit., *passim;* E. E. Urbach, op. cit., especially chapters 13, 15, and 16.

34. A modern and not altogether surprising parallel comes from Solomon Zeitlin in the preface of his book, *The Rise and Fall of the Jewish State* (Philadelphia, 1962-), Vol. i, p. xii; 'I consider myself fortunate and assigned to great merit to have lived to see the establishment of the Third Commonwealth ...'

35. Cf. J. Abelson, op. cit., pp. 248ff.

36. G. F. Moore, op. cit., Vol. ii, pp. 273-5, especially p. 275.

37. Cf. H. J. Schoeps, 'Weiteres zur Auserwählung Israels', *Aus frühchristlicher Zeit* (Tübingen, 1950), pp. 201-11.

38. For an excellent discussion, cf. E. E. Urbach, op. cit., pp. 511-23.

CHAPTER NINE (pp. 110-119)

1. See the important work by H. W. Attridge, *The Interpretation of Biblical History in the Antiquitates Judaicae of Flavius Josephus* (Cambridge, Mass., 1976).

2. G. Stählin, 'Das Schicksal im Neuen Testament und bie Josephus', *Josephus-Studien* (Göttingen, 1974), p. 342, argues plausibly that Josephus' bragging is in part a function of his syncretism. However, sometimes it is probably an understandable reaction to his double agony: he is frequently distrusted both by the Romans and by his own people. A more telling measure of hellenistic influence on Josephus is his 'eschatology': cf. A. Schlatter, *Die Theologie des Judentums nach dem Bericht des Josefus* (Gütersloh, 1932), p. 259.

3. Some manuscripts omit all but the last three words.

4. Likely emendation: cf. the Loeb edition, *in loc.*, footnote.

5. 'Fate and Free Will in the Jewish Philosophies according to Josephus', *Havard Theological Review*, Vol. xxii (1929), p. 388.

6. For other solutions to the question of why Josephus used such terminology, cf. G. Stählin, op. cit., pp. 338ff.; and H. W. Attridge, op. cit., chap. 5.

7. Cf. G. Maier, 'Die jüdischen Lehrer bei Josephus', *Josephus-Studien* (Göttingen, 1974), pp. 268f.

8. L. Wächter, 'Die unterschiedliche Haltung der Pharisäer, Sadduzäer und Essener zur Heimarmene nach dem Bericht des Josefus', *Zeitschrift für Religions und Geistesgeschichte*, Vol. xxi (1961), pp. 97-114, argues that Josephus has been influenced by Stoic versus Epicurean debates, among whom predestination (*Vorherbestimmung*) and free will (*Willensfreiheit*) were live issues. He says that *no* Jewish sect believed in a will quite as free as the Sadducees are made out to believe, but that Josephus needed this polarity in his argument and therefore attributed Epicurean beliefs to them. Against this line of argument, G. Maier, *Mensch und freier Wille*, op. cit., p. 158, sees Ben Sira as 'the teacher who serves as fore-runner (*der frühen Zeit Lehrmeister*) of the later Sadducees, who are pictured for us by Josephus'. He rightly points out that the literature of Judaism *is* concerned with these problems.

CHAPTER TEN (pp. 120-121)

1. *Theology in Reconstruction* (London, 1965), pp. 169-91.
2. Op. cit.

CHAPTER ELEVEN (pp. 125-162)

1. So the verb *katelaben* should here be translated: cf. 12.35, its only other occurrence in this Gospel.
2. R. E. Brown, *The Gospel according to John* (New York, 1966), p. 155.
3. 'L'ami de l'époux (Jo., III, 29)', *A la rencontre de Dieu* (Le Puy, 1961), pp. 289-95.
4. B. Lindars, *The Gospel of John* (London, 1972), pp. 166f.
5. M.-J. Lagrange, *Evangile selon Saint Jean* (Paris, 1936), pp. 94f.
6. So rightly R. Schnackenburg, *Das Johannesevangelium* (Freiburg, 1965-76), Vol. i, pp. 452f. The German reads: '*Es ist ihm verliehen, etwas zu tun*'—precisely the meaning also of 6.65. The English translation, available only for Vol. i, is possible, but probably misleading: 'being empowered to do something'.
7. R. Bultmann, *The Gospel of John: A Commentary* (Oxford, 1971), p. 172.
8. Ibid.
9. E.g. C. K. Barrett, *The Gospel according to St John* (London, 1955), p. 213, who draws attention to Luke 13.1-5. Bultmann, p. 243, says that 5.14 is surprising; but it is only surprising if 9.1-3 is arbitrarily adopted as normative for the fourth Gospel.
10. Barrett, p. 295.
11. Brown, p. 371.
12. So Bultmann, p. 410, n. 10. Cf. W. F. Howard, *The Fourth Gospel in Recent Criticism* (revised by C. K. Barrett; London, 1955), p. 187; Bernard, Vol. ii, p. 404; Brown, pp. 439f. BDF §186(2) shows the genitive can be construed as temporal, an approach to this verse which goes back as far as Origen.
13. So Barrett, p. 339. Prophecy is not infrequently associated with the office of the High Priest: cf. Num. 27.21; 2 Sam. 15.27; Philo, *Spec. Leg.* iv.192; Josephus, *Ant.* xi.326f.; xiii.300; and SB, Vol. ii, p. 546. E. Bammel, 'ARCHIEREUS PROPHĒTŌN', *Theologische Literaturzeitung*, Vol. lxxix (1954), pp. 351-6, has shown that in rabbinic thought the prophetic character of the high-priestly office is still a living tradition.
14. L. Morris, *The Gospel according to John* (London, 1971), p. 797.
15. Reading *eiches* (with B W Θ f.1 *pm*) rather than *echeis* (with ℵ A f.13 *al.*). Possibly the latter variant developed because *an* is omitted (as in 8.39).
16. The 'authority' or 'power' to which Pilate makes appeal is the authority of the state. However, Jesus' rejoinder does not argue that state authority has been granted the Procurator by God, since the participle is *dedemenon* (*dedemenē* would be required, to agree with *exousia*). What is in view is God's determining of the *event* of the betrayal: so rightly T. Zahn, *Das Evangelium des Johannes* (Leipzig, 1908), p. 633; E. Hoskyns, *The Fourth Gospel* (London, 1947), p. 524; Lagrange, p. 483; Schnackenburg, Vol. iii,

p. 301; and the later editions of Bultmann, *in loc.* The handing over of Jesus to Pilate was determined by God, and therefore if Pilate now finds himself in a position of authority it is by God's doing: it is in this sense that Pilate's authority is circumscribed, not by an argument that all human authority finds its source and limitation in the divine will, as W. Bauer, *Das Johannesevangelium* (Tübingen, 1933), p. 219, maintains.

17. Morris, p. 797.

18. So we may deduce from 6.68f., by observing the emphatic 'we', in contrast to those who withdrew (6.66), and the two perfects, *pepisteukamen* and *egnōkamen*, which, in the present context, are virtually synonymous and mutually emphatic.

19. The ones most commonly cited are *Corpus Hermeticum* 6.4 and Rev. 17.17 (the former displacing 'heart', *kardia*, with the less biblical 'mind', *nous*).

20. Barrett, pp. 365f.

21. Lindars, p. 449.

22. Bauer, p. 168.

23. Brown, p. 578. Barrett, p. 373, notes that *meta*, 'after' (13.27) is temporal, not causal, and therefore argues that 'receiving the morsel does not make Judas Satan's tool'. However, the *tote*, 'then', joins Satan's entry into Judas so closely with the receiving of the morsel that it is difficult to resist the conclusion that this was the decisive step.

24. Barrett, p. 370; similarly Brown, pp. 553f.

25. J. H. Moulton, *A Grammar of New Testament Greek* (Edinburgh, 1906-1976), Vol. i, pp. 178f., 248; BDF §387(3).

26. Morris, p. 728.

27. J. H. Bernard, *A Critical and Exegetical Commentary on the Gospel according to St John* (Edinburgh, 1928), Vol. ii, p. 325.

28. Cf. W. D. Davies, *The Gospel and The Land* (Berkeley, 1974), pp. 289ff., who argues persuasively that Jesus replaces all the 'holy space' in the fourth Gospel. For example, in John 4 he comes to Jacob's well, but he himself is the 'living water'. On the temple replacement, cf. also L. Gaston, *No Stone on Another* (Leiden, 1970), pp. 205-7. Cf. also S. Pancaro, *The Law in the Fourth Gospel* (Leiden, 1975), pp. 367-487, and E. J. Epp, 'Wisdom, Torah, Word: The Johannine Prologue and the Purpose of the Fourth Gospel', *Current Issues in Biblical and Patristic Interpretation* (Grand Rapids, 1975), pp. 128-46, for the idea that Jesus replaces the law.

29. Cf. the works by T. F. Glasson, *Moses in the Fourth Gospel* (London, 1963); W. A. Meeks, *The Prophet-King: Moses Traditions and the Johannine Christology* (Leiden, 1967); and K. Haacker, *Die Stiftung des Heils* (Stuttgart, 1972).

30. Cf. R. N. Longenecker, *Biblical Exegesis in the Apostolic Period* (Grand Rapids, 1975), pp. 152f.

31. Ibid., pp. 70ff., 152-7, 218.

32. Cf. S. Amsler, *L'Ancien Testament dans l'église* (Paris, 1960), pp. 39f.; and especially A. Dauer, *Die Passionsgeschichte im Johannesevangelium* (München, 1972), pp. 295-306.

33. *An Introduction to the Theology of the New Testament* (London, 1958), pp. 186f.

34. The verb *plēroun* occurs at 12.38; 13.18; 17.12; 19.24, 36, as well as here, and virtually ensures in each case that *hina* is telic in force: cf. Bernard, Vol. i, pp. clii-clvi, especially p. cliii.

35. *New Testament Apologetic* (London, 1961), p. 267.

36. *Studien zum alttestamentlichen Hintergrund des Johannesevangeliums* (Cambridge, 1974), p. 261. The precise significance of these 'Ego Eimi' statements in John's Gospel is much disputed. For a convenient survey of the most important literature, cf. G. H. Parke-Taylor, *Yahweh: The Divine Name in the Bible* (Waterloo, Ont., 1975), pp. 73ff.

37. R. N. Longenecker, op. cit., p. 155.

38. J. K. S. Reid, op. cit., p. 67.

39. D. A. Carson, 'Current Source-Criticism of the Fourth Gospel: Some Methodological Questions', *JBL*, Vol. xcvii (1978), pp. 411-29. Although this paper glances at the theories of R. Bultmann, J. Becker, R. Schnackenburg, R. Nicol, R. Fortna, H. Teeple, and S. Temple, it focuses on the work of R. T. Fortna.

40. *The Apostolic Preaching and its Developments* (London, 1936), pp. 155ff.; *The Interpretation of the Fourth Gospel* (Cambridge, 1953), pp. 144ff. Cf. E. F. Scott, *The Fourth Gospel: Its Purpose and Theology* (Edinburgh, 1908), pp. 295-319.

41. 'Agnostos Christos: Joh. 2.24 und die Eschatologie des vierten Evangeliums', *The Background of the New Testament and its Eschatology* (Cambridge, 1956), pp. 281-99.

42. *Jesus and His Coming* (London, 1957).

43. Viz. G. E. Ladd, *A Theology of the New Testament* (Grand Rapids, 1974). Moreover, the use of a christian document's eschatology as an index of its date is a highly doubtful procedure: cf. S. S. Smalley, 'The Delay of the Parousia', *JBL*, Vol. lxxxiii (1964), pp. 41-54.

44. *Die Eschatologie des Johannesevangeliums* (Assen, 1962).

45. Ibid., pp. 60ff., 74-80. Cf. T. Preiss, *Life in Christ* (London, 1954), p. 27, who describes eternal life in John as a possession *in spe nondum in re*.

46. *Salvation in History* (London, 1967), pp. 289f.

47. *Die Eschatologie des vierten Evangeliums* (Zürich, 1966).

48. *Krisis: Untersuchungen zur johanneischen Christologie und Eschatologie* (Freiburg, 1964).

49. *Consummatum Est. Eschatology and Church in the Gospel of St John* (London, 1958), pp. 85-112.

50. C. F. D. Moule, 'The Individualism of the Fourth Gospel', *Nov. T* Vol. v (1962), pp. 171-90; *idem*, 'A Neglected Factor in the Interpretation of Johannine Eschatology', *Studies in John* (Leiden, 1970), pp. 155-60.

51. E. Grässer, 'Jesus und das Heil Gottes: Bemerkungen zur sog. "Individualisierung des Heils" ', *Jesus Christus in Historie und Theologie* (Tübingen, 1975), pp. 167-84, points out how often the 'individualising of salvation' occurs not only in Paul and John but in the synoptic Gospels as well.

52. *The Cultic Setting of Realized Eschatology in Early Christianity* (Leiden, 1972), pp. 65-102.

53. Cf. especially D. Hill, 'On the Evidence for the Creative Role of

Christian Prophets', *NTS*, Vol. xx (1974), pp. 262-74; R. Bauckham, 'Synoptic Parousia Parables and the Apocalypse', *NTS*, Vol. xxiii (1977), pp. 162-76; J. D. G. Dunn, 'Prophetic "I"—Sayings and the Jesus Tradition: The Importance of Testing Prophetic Utterances within Early Christianity', *NTS*, Vol. xxiv (1978), pp. 175-98.

54. *Cultic Setting*, op. cit., pp. 89-102.

55. The structure of Bultmann's eschatology can most conveniently be examined in his *Theology of the New Testament* (London, 1952-55); but, as it emerges in his study of John, it must be gleaned piecemeal from his commentary, op. cit. For a rigorous critique, cf. D. E. Holwerda, *The Holy Spirit and Eschatology in the Gospel of John* (Kampen, 1959), pp. 113-33.

56. This spatial dualism itself encourages the rendering 'from above', rather than 'again' or 'anew'. Further, cf. F. Büchsel, *TDNT*, Vol. i, p. 378.

57. Brown, p. cxv.

58. For a succinct summary of the arguments in favour of this point, cf. J. D. G. Dunn, *Baptism in the Holy Spirit* (London, 1970), pp. 173-6; and *contra*, pp.176-8.

59. Cited by J. D. G. Dunn, *Baptism*, op. cit., p. 176, from a private communication.

60. Otherwise, as W. Thüsing, *Die Erhöhung und Verherrlichung Jesu im Johannesevangelium* (Münster, 1970), pp. 265f., notes, the appearances to Mary and to the disciples must have been of vastly different types.

61. Op. cit., p. 176.

62. L. Morris, *Studies in the Fourth Gospel* (Grand Rapids, 1969), pp. 65-138.

63. Lindars, p. 612 (italics mine).

64. J. D. G. Dunn, *Baptism*, op. cit., p. 178.

65. To use the choice expression of C. K. Barrett, 'The Place of Eschatology in the Fourth Gospel', *Ex. T*, Vol. lix (1947-48), p. 305.

66. J. D. G. Dunn, *Baptism*, op. cit., p. 181.

67. Cf. J. Painter, 'Eschatological Faith in the Gospel of John', *Reconciliation and Hope* (Exeter, 1974), pp. 49-51.

68. D. Hill, *Greek Words with Hebrew Meanings* (Cambridge, 1967), p. 196.

69. *The Fourth Gospel* (Amsterdam, 1929, repr. 1968), pp. 293f.

70. Cf. C. F. D. Moule, 'The Influence of Circumstances on the Use of Eschatological Terms', *JTS*, Vol. xv (1964), p. 8, who says that 'apocalyptic has its value in emphasising the transcendent and "vertical", as against the "horizontal" and merely human.' C. K. Barrett, *The Fourth Gospel and Judaism* (London, 1975), in tracing parallel developments between late first century Judaism and Christianity, points out that 'apocalyptic is not characteristic of the [fourth] gospel' (p. 44; cf. pp. 66f). However, the basic two-age structure (with christian modification) *is* characteristic of it. Moreover, the major New Testament Apocalypse has many points of contact with the fourth Gospel. Nor is it, *pace* Barrett (p. 66) an exception: he himself later notes (p. 89, n. 24) that the hope of the parousia is alive and well in the second century, which, of course, also witnesses the flourishing of *christian* apocalyptic.

71. S. S. Smalley, *John—Evangelist and Interpreter* (Exeter, 1978),

pp. 210ff., sees the divine/human tension in Jesus as the *Mitte* of the fourth Gospel's use of christological titles; but I must forbear to discuss the matter here. However, because this monograph concerns John and *Jewish* background, therefore one question I cannot evade, even if I do not have space to treat it at length, is this: How truly Jewish is John's ascription of divine status to Jesus? The actual ascription of *theos* to Jesus is not common in the New Testament, but it is scattered widely even if thinly: cf. Heb. 1.8f.; 2 Pet. 1.1 (on which see R. E. Brown, *Jesus, God and Man* (Milwaukee, 1967), p. 25); 2 Thess. 1.12; Titus 2.13; almost certainly Rom. 9.5 (cf. B. M. Metzger, 'The Punctuation of Rom. 9:5', *Christ and Spirit in the New Testament* (Cambridge, 1973), pp. 95-112); and the three references in the fourth Gospel discussed in this section. Of course, Jesus' deity does not turn exclusively on the word *theos*. But much, perhaps most, current New Testament scholarship holds that the ascription of deity to Jesus reflects the change in the Church's christology occasioned by the Church's penetration of one form or another of hellenistic culture. The Church, it is held, affected by the pressures of syncretism, presented Jesus, for the first time, in divine categories. See, for example, F. Hahn, *The Titles of Jesus in Christology* (London, 1969), pp. 108-14. The attempt to understand John's *logos* in philonic terms has largely passed away. More recently, however, a strong case for Jewish roots to johannine christology has sprung up from several quarters. R. N. Longenecker, *The Christology of Early Jewish Christianity* (London, 1970), pp. 136ff., has demonstrated that the explicit ascription of the title *theos* to Jesus arose in *Jewish* Christian circles. C. H. Talbert, 'The Myth of a Descending-Ascending Redeemer in Mediterranean Antiquity', *NTS*, Vol. xxii (1975-6), pp. 418-40, has shown that it is unnecessary to resort to Gnosticism to find descent/ascent themes; indeed, there are numerous parallels within Judaism. Similarly, cf. J. P. Miranda, *Der Vater, der mich gesandt hat* (Bern, 1972). Other works of importance which support the essential Jewishness of 'God' and 'Son of God' christology, the position taken in this monograph, include: J. A. Fitzmyer, 'Der semitische Hintergrund des neutestamentlichen Kyriostitels', *Jesus Christus in Historie und Theologie* (Tübingen, 1975), pp. 267-98; C. F. D. Moule, *The Origin of Christology* (Cambridge, 1967); I. H. Marshall, *The Origins of New Testament Christology* (Leicester, 1967); M. Hengel, 'Christologie und neutestamentliche Chronologie', *Neues Testament und Geschichte* (Zürich, 1972), pp. 43-67; idem, *The Son of God* (London, 1976).

72. Viz., the UBS text, the Nestle-Kilpatrick text, and the Nestle-Aland text. The first and third are in the process of getting together.

73. Barrett, p. 160.

74. Cf. P. B. Harner, *The 'I Am' of the Fourth Gospel* (Philadelphia, 1970), pp. 39ff., 51ff. He points out that the 'I Am' sayings are often found in a subordinationist context; but in 8.58, the deity of Christ is in view: cf. Brown, p. 367. W. D. Davies, *The Gospel and the Land*, op. cit., pp. 294f., not only recognises this point, but sees 8.58f. in terms of the Feast of Tabernacles background (especially Sukk. 4.5) and argues that the divine Presence is here abandoning the 'holy space' of the Temple: 'The Shekinah is no longer *there*, but is now found wherever Christ is' (p. 295).

75. C. F. D. Moule has repeatedly suggested that the anarthrous *huios*

244   SOVEREIGNTY AND RESPONSIBILITY

anthrōpou (5.27) most likely means simply 'man': cf. his 'Neglected features in the Problem of "the Son of Man"', *Neues Testament und Kirche* (Freiburg, 1974), p. 420; *idem, The Origin of Christology,* op. cit., pp. 16f., n. 15.

76. Cf. R. Longenecker, *Christology,* op. cit., p. 102.

77. Cf. Schnackenburg, Vol. iii, pp. 294-6; *idem,* 'Die Ecce-homo-Szene und der Menschensohn', *Jesus und der Menschensohn* (Freiburg, 1975), pp. 371-86; F. J. Moloney, *The Johannine Son of Man* (Rome, 1976), pp. 202-7.

78. Whatever possible symbolic meaning there may be, the evangelist saw the event first of all as historical fact: cf. Barrett, p. 461; J. Wilkinson, 'The Incident of the Blood and Water in John 19.34', *Scottish Journal of Theology,* Vol. xxviii (1975), pp. 149-72.

79. *The Jesus of St. John* (London, 1958), pp. 90-157.

80. This is true even of John 10.34-6. I think the argument is *ad hominem;* but its *a minori ad maius* form also indicates the *minimum* that Jesus expects the Jews to believe about him, the purpose being to show Jesus' superiority (10.36) in a context that has already made Jesus out to be God (10.33). Of course, the precise meaning of the passage turns in part on the background envisaged: cf. J. A. Emerton, 'Some New Testament Notes', *JTS,* Vol. xi (1960), pp. 329-36; *idem,* 'Melchizedek and the Gods: Fresh Evidence for the Jewish Background of John x.34-36', *JTS,* Vol. xvii (1966), pp. 394-401; J. S. Ackermann, 'The Rabbinic Interpretation of Psalm 82 and the Gospel of John: John 10:34', *Harvard Theological Review,* Vol. lix (1966), pp. 186-91; and especially A. T. Hanson, 'John's Citation of Psalm lxxxii Reconsidered', *NTS,* (Vol. xiii (1966-7)), pp. 363-7.

81. Accepting the minority reading (but the *lectio difficilior*) of the Western text, along with most commentators since Harnack.

82. O. Cullmann, *The Christology of the New Testament* (London, 1963), pp. 306ff; Bultmann, *passim,* perhaps especially pp. 248-54.

83. *Introducing the New Testament* (London, 1972), p. 65; idem, *According to John* (London, 1968), p. 115.

84. *The Oneness Motif in the Fourth Gospel* (Tübingen, 1976).

85. 'The Use of the Fourth Gospel for Christology Today', *Christ and Spirit in the New Testament* (Cambridge, 1973), p. 73.

86. *The Fourth Evangelist and His Gospel* op. cit., pp. 200-6.

87. Cf. the questions raised by R. H. Fuller, *The Foundations of New Testament Christology* (London, 1965), pp. 247ff., who, although he thinks the restatement of the gospel for the hellenistic world contributed largely to ontological categories, nevertheless acknowledges: 'For it is not just a quirk of the Greek mind, but a universal apperception, that action implies prior being—even if, as is also true, being is only apprehended in action. Such ontic reflection about Yahweh is found even in the OT, e.g. "I AM" (Exodus and Deutero-Isaiah)', (pp. 248f.). Cf. especially the careful statement of Longenecker, *Christology,* op. cit., pp. 154-6.

88. *Johannine Christology and the Early Church* (Cambridge, 1970), p. 17.

89. *Johannine Christology,* loc. cit.

90. Lindars, p. 615.

91. 'A Neglected Feature of the Christology of the Fourth Gospel', *NTS*, Vol. xxii (1975-6), p. 45.

92. Cf. *Christology*, op. cit., pp. 139ff.; adapted by Mastin, art. cit.

93. B. A. Mastin, 'The Imperial Cult and the Ascription of the Title *Theos* to Jesus (John xx.28)', *St. Ev.*, Vol. vi (1973), pp. 352-65.

94. *Jesus, God and Man*, op. cit.

95. *The New Testament Christological Hymns* (Cambridge, 1971), pp. 20ff.

96. 'The Prologue of St John's Gospel', *New Testament Essays* (London, 1972), pp. 27-48.

97. Ibid., pp. 32-51.

98. R. Leistner, *Antijudaismus im Johannesevangelium?* (Bern, 1974).

99. *History and Theology in the Fourth Gospel* (New York, 1968).

100. *New Testament Essays*, op. cit., pp. 65f.; idem, ' "The Father is greater than I" (Jo. 14, 28): Subordinationist Christology in the New Testament', *Neues Testament und Kirche* (Freiburg, 1974), pp. 144-59.

101. *Die Stiftung des Heils*, op. cit., pp. 25-7.

102. Ibid., pp. 90ff.

103. Ibid., p. 116.

104. *The Testament of Jesus* (London, 1968).

105. Cf. *inter alia* G. M. Davis, 'The Humanity of Jesus in John', *JBL*, Vol. lxx (1951), pp. 105-12; J. Knox, *The Humanity and Divinity of Christ* (Cambridge, 1967), pp. 25ff.

106. E. Käsemann, 'Aufbau und Anliegen des johanneischen Prologs', *Libertas Christiana* (München, 1957), p. 94.

107. *Testament*, op. cit., p. 10.

108. In particular, cf. G. Bornkamm, 'Zur Interpretation des Johannesevangeliums', *Geschichte und Glaube* (München, 1968), Vol. i, pp. 104-21; R. E. Brown, 'The Kerygma of the Gospel according to St John', *NTS* (London, 1970), pp. 218ff.; S. S. Smalley, 'The Testament of Jesus: Another Look', *St. Ev.*, Vol. vi (1973), pp. 495-501; H. Hegermann, 'Er kam in sein Eigentum: Zur Bedeutung des Erdenwirkens Jesu im vierten Evangeliums', *Der Ruf Jesu und die Antwort der Gemeinde* (Göttingen, 1970), pp. 112-31.

109. E. Malatesta, 'The Spirit/Paraclete in the Fourth Gospel', *Biblica*, Vol. liv (1973), pp. 539-50.

110. G. Richter, 'Die Fleischwerdung des Logos im Johannesevangelium', *Nov. T*, Vol. xiii (1971), pp. 81-126.

111. K. Berger, 'Zu "Das Wort ward Fleisch" Joh. I 14a', *Nov. T*, Vol. vxi (1974), pp. 161-6.

112. Cf. the carefully qualified corroboration by W. D. Davies, *Paul and Rabbinic Judaism* (London, 1970), pp. 164f. and notes. On pp. 166f., he argues that the development of Wisdom was in part an attempt to reconcile transcendence and immanence in the realm of creation and elsewhere. It is not surprising therefore that a growing number of recent scholars have connected John's *Logos* doctrine with Wisdom motifs: e.g. Lindars, *passim;* F. M. Braun, *Jean le théologien*, op. cit., especially Vol. iii.

113. *The Central Message of the New Testament* (London, 1965), pp. 89f.

Cf. B. F. Westcott, *The Revelation of the Father* (London/Cambridge, 1884), pp. 7-10.

114. W. Kümmel, *Theology,* op. cit., p. 273.

115. Barrett, p. 62.

116. E. Haenchen, ' "Der Vater ..." ', *NTS,* Vol. ix (1962-3), p. 210. Quite a number of scholars recognise the revelatory function of Jesus Christ in John's Gospel, yet keep it in proportion. Among the most useful recent articles are: P. J. Cahill, 'The Johannine *Logos* as Center', *CBQ,* Vol. xxxviii (1976), pp. 54-72; E. Ruckstuhl, 'Abstieg und Erhöhung des johanneischen Menschensohn', *Jesus und der Menschensohn* (Frieburg, 1975), pp. 314-41; H. Vorländer, ' "Mein Herr und Mein Gott." Christus als "personlicher Gott" im Neuen Testament', *Kerygma und Dogma,* Vol. xxi (1975), pp. 120-46; T. W. Manson, 'The Johannine Jesus as Logos', reprinted in *A Companion to John* (New York, 1977), pp. 33-58.

117. F. Amiot, '*Deum Nemo Vidit Unquam:* Jo. I, 18', *Mélanges Bibliques* (Paris, n.d.), pp. 470-77.

118. E. Haenchen, ' "Der Vater ..." ', op. cit., p. 211.

119. A. Loisy, *Le Quatrième Evangile* (Paris, 1921), p. 415.

120. F.-M. Braun, *Jean le théologien,* op. cit., Vol. iv, p. 93.

121. A. Dauer, *Die Passionsgeschichte,* op. cit., p. 286.

122. A. Richardson, *An Introduction to the Theology of the New Testament* (London, 1958), pp. 187f. The use of 'solved' is perhaps infortunate. Cf. also the extended discussion by D. M. Baillie, *God Was in Christ* (London, 1948), pp. 106-32.

123. 'The Manhood of Jesus in the New Testament', *Christ, Faith and History* (Cambridge, 1972), pp. 95-110. One must nevertheless be careful with this sort of statement, lest it descend once more into mere functionalism. The same caution pertains especially to the work of A. T. Hanson, *Grace and Truth: A Study in the Doctrine of the Incarnation* (London, 1975); for when he speaks of divinity revealing itself in humanity, I am never entirely sure if he is referring to character *as opposed to* essence.

124. J. D. G. Dunn, 'The Washing of the Disciples' Feet in John 13:1-20', *Zeitschrift für die neutestamentliche Wissenschaft,* Vol. lxi (1970), pp. 247-52, is surely correct in refusing to split off 13.12ff from 13.1-11. Cf. also A. Weiser, 'Joh. 13, 12-20—Zufügung eines späteren Herausgebers?', *Biblische Zeitschrift,* Vol. xii (1968), pp. 252-7.

CHAPTER TWELVE (163-198)

1. *Pace* R. Bultmann, *Faith and Understanding* (London, 1969), p. 169; P. Benoit, 'Paulinisme et Johanisme', *NTS,* Vol. ix (1963), pp. 193-207; and many others.

2. W. D. Davies, *The Setting of the Sermon on the Mount* (Cambridge, 1966), p. 410. Cf. the discussion in G. Stemberger, *La symbolique du bien et du mal salon saint Jean* (Paris, 1970).

3. 'A Grammatical and Contextual Inventory of the Use of *kosmos* in the Johannine Corpus with some Implications for a Johannine Cosmic Theology', *NTS,* Vol. xix (1972-3), pp. 81-91.

4. In the case of 2.23-5, the *de* in 3.1 probably bears adversative force.

5. Cf. Lagrange, p. 411: 'The meaning, therefore, is: If, having come, I had not spoken to them ...'

6. C. F. D. Moule, *The Birth of the New Testament* (London, 1962), p. 94.

7. Morris, p. 481.

8. Barrett, p. 289.

9. J. A. Bengel, *Gnomon of the New Testament* (Edinburgh, 1874), Vol. ii, p. 437.

10. In one sense, of course, they had come to Jesus (6.2, 4), but their present coming 'has not been a true coming, their present seeing has not been a true seeing' (C. J. Wright, *Jesus the Revelation of God* (London, 1950), p. 174).

11. D. Mollat, 'La conversion chez saint Jean', *Lumière et Vie,* Vol. xlvii (1960), p. 101.

12. C. K. Barrett, *New Testament Essays,* op. cit., p. 64.

13. Cf. Morris, p. 406: 'His hearers had raised the question of his competence as a teacher. He raises the question of their competence as hearers.'

14. This is even more emphatically the case in 5.6, where commentators regularly misinterpret Jesus' question, 'Do you want to be healed?' E.g. Morris, p. 303: 'He begins by inquiring as to his willingness to be cured'; W. Barclay, *The Gospel of John* (Edinburgh, 1955-6), Vol. i, p. 175: 'The first essential towards receiving the power of Jesus is the intense desire for it.' Similarly Zahn, pp. 282f. But Jesus' question, far from evoking any faith and hope, seems only to reveal the man's bankruptcy. Moreover, faith required in 4.46-54 is not required in 5.1ff.; so it cannot be a *necessary* precursor of a display of Christ's power in the fourth Gospel.

15. The *hoti* clauses following *pisteuein* are in 6.69; 8.24; 11.27, 42; 13.19; 14.10f.; 16.27 (cf. 8.42; 17.8); 16.30; 17.8, 21; those following *ginōskein,* in 6.69; 8.28; 10.38; 14.20, 31; 17.7f., 23; cf. also 7.26, in the words of the crowd; and those following *eidenai,* in 3.2; 4.42; 16.30; cf. also 7.28; 14.5. Cf. J. T. Forestell, *The Word of the Cross* (Rome, 1974), pp. 45f., n. 119; and discussion in J. M. Boice, *Witness and Revelation in the Gospel of John* (Exeter, 1970), pp. 53-61.

16. The example of John the Baptist most likely stands behind the 'others' of 4.38, as well. Cf. J. A. T. Robinson, 'The New Look at the Fourth Gospel', *St. Ev.,* Vol. i (1959), pp. 510-15; *contra* O. Cullmann, in several of his writings, perhaps especially 'Samaria and the Origins of the Christian Mission', *The Early Church* (London, 1956), pp. 183-92; and most recently, in *The Johannine Circle* (London, 1976).

17. Actually, Jesus never expressly calls his followers 'slaves' (*douloi*) in the fourth Gospel, although in 13.13, 16 he comes close to it.

18. *Pace* the idea that *philos,* 'friend', here suggests 'a mutual intimacy and confidence on equal terms' (Lindars, pp. 491f.).

19. In the case of John 14.15, there is textual ambiguity. The reading *tērēsēte* (p 66 ℵ al.) makes the protasis include all of verse 15: cf. Brown, pp. 637f.: 'If you love me and keep my commandments, then at my request etc.' But Brown has to read in a *kai* to remove the awkwardness. The

imperative *tērēsate* claims support of A D K W X Λ: (·) Π fl f13 *al.*, but this ill accords with the *erōtēsō* clause in 14.16. Of course this objection has no weight if there is a break in thought between 14.15 and 14.16; but in that case 14.15 appears to be a terribly isolated logion. The future *tērēsete* (B L Ψ *al.*) best fits the context and is paralleled in thought by 14.21 (cf. also 1 John 5.3), and in grammar by 14.23f.

20. Barrett, p. 414.

21. Most commentators give *krisis* a neutral significance here. Morris, p. 223, distinguishes between *krima* and *krisis* and argues that the latter here means 'the *process* of judging, not the *sentence* of condemnation'. Similarly Bultmann, p. 157, sees a great division in the world. He is followed enthusiastically on this point by J. Blank, op. cit., pp. 95ff. Lindars, p. 160, and Brown, p. 134, agree. But the rest of the verse surely shows that *krisis*, like *krinein* in 3.17, here has the sense of condemnation: cf. Barrett, pp. 181f.; Hendriksen, *Exposition of the Gospel according to John* (Grand Rapids, 1966), Vol. i, p. 143; and especially Schnackenburg, Vol. i, pp. 403ff.

22. A number of scholars take the verb *elenchein* only in the neutral sense of 'to expose': e.g. Schnackenburg, Vol. i, p. 406, n. 160; Lindars, p. 161. The verb may have this neutral sense in Eph. 5.13. In the LXX, however, it usually translates *ykḥ*, retaining a forensic meaning. *Pace* Schnackenburg, *elenchthē* (3.20) is not strictly parallel with *phanerōthē* (3.21). Rather, the removal of the common elements of the last clause in each verse shows that *elenchthē* is structurally parallel with, and thematically set over against, *phanerōthē ... hoti en theō estin eirgasmena.* Moreover, it is hard to see how mere exposure would keep the one who does evil away from the light, unless that exposure shamed him, rebuked him, or convicted him. Cf. also F. Büchsel, *TDNT*, Vol. ii, p. 437-5.

23. Barrett, p. 182.

24. Vol. i, pp. 406f.

25. Westcott, p. 57. Cf. NIV: '... so that it may be plainly seen that what he has done has been done through God.'

26. Lindars, p. 161.

27. Vol. i, p. 399.

28. Cf. B. B. Warfield, *Biblical and Theological Studies* (Nutley, repr. 1952), pp. 505-22; Bultmann, p. 153, n. 3.

29. The choice of tense is significant. The believer is *ou krinetai*, the unbeliever *ēdē kekritai*. The world is already condemned and perishing; but it is a new thing when someone from the world believes and is *ou krinetai*.

30. B. B. Warfield, 'Predestination', op. cit., p. 55.

31. The failure to observe this point mars Schnackenburg's generally excellent excursus, 'Selbstentscheidung und -verantwortung, Prädestination und Verstockung', Vol. ii, pp. 328-46. He argues, p. 330, that the possibility of coming to faith is 'not seen as unfulfillable', because Jesus demands faith from everyone, not just from an esoteric circle of disciples. But the demand, the obligation, does not entail the independent ability. A demand that we fly like birds would be unjust because we are constitutionally unable to do so; but a demand to be holy is not unjust if the only inability is a moral one, i.e. a set determination to choose not to be holy. So it is, in John's view, with Christ's demand for belief.

32. Cf. P. S. Minear, 'The Audience of the Fourth Evangelist', *Interpretation*, Vol. xxxi (1977), p. 347: 'In fact, the author presents his book as a substitute for the signs, thus recognising that his readers will have access to faith through reading rather than through seeing.' That the entire Gospel is to be seen in this sort of light, cf. *inter alia* A. E. Harvey, *Jesus on Trial* (London, 1976); S. S. Smalley, *John—Evangelist and Interpreter* (Exeter, 1978), pp. 138ff.; A. A. Trites, *The New Testament Concept of Witness* (Cambridge, 1977), pp. 78ff.

33. As in Mark 8.11-33, no gratifying miracle is given because no miracle will suffice; 'the request is unanswered because it is unanswerable; no sign can prove (though many signs suggest) that Jesus is the messenger of God' (Barrett, p. 239). Cf. G. H. C. MacGregor, *The Gospel of John* (London, 1928), p. 143: 'In the days of his flesh, as in the Evangelist's own day, Christ could produce no credential so conclusive but that the Jews would demand one more conclusive still.'

34. There is a well-known textual difficulty here. John 6.30 presents the people asking for a sign, that they may see (*sc.* 'it') and believe. In 6.36, all manuscripts read *hoti kai heōrakate me*, except אA it^{a,b,e,q} syr^{c,s} which omit *me*. Many commentators, seeing in 6.36 a reference to 6.26, 30, favour the omission of the word against the textual evidence: e.g. Bauer, p. 97; Bernard, Vol. i, p. 199; Bultmann, p. 232, nn. 5f.; Barrett, p. 243; J. N. Sanders and B. A. Mastin, *A Commentary on the Gospel according to St John* (London, 1968), p. 189, n. 1; Lindars, p. 260; J. Marsh, *The Gospel of St John* (Harmondsworth, 1968), p. 301. Schnackenburg, Vol. ii, p. 71, is noncommittal. Westcott and Hort, before the discovery of p$^{66, 75}$ (which corroborate the majority reading), included it only in brackets. The UBS text includes it with rating {C} : cf. B. M. Metzger, *Textual Commentary*, op. cit., p. 213. It is possible to understand the words to mean 'have seen me (*sc.* performing signs)'; but that is unnecessary. More likely the ambiguity is intentional. *Really* to see the signs is to see Jesus. To see Jesus and not believe means to see the signs only superficially—in which case more signs won't help. In the immediate context, moreover, the Jews ask for bread (6.35)—and Jesus says they have seen him, but not believed. By this form of expression, the evangelist has tied together 6.26, 30, 35f. (*contra* Schulz, p. 105).

35. R. V. G. Tasker, *The Gospel according to John* (London, 1960), p. 149.

36. Cf. E. Bammel, 'John Did No Miracle', *Miracles* (London, 1965), pp. 179-202.

37. Because of the parallel instances cited, there is no need to take the evasive action advocated by many, to avoid identifying the believers in 8.30 with these in 8.31ff.: (1) Some (e.g. W. F. Howard, 'The Gospel According to John', *Interpreter's Bible*, Vol. viii (New York, 1952), p. 600) suggest that *pisteuein* plus dative (8.31) refers to a different, or at least smaller, group than that referred to by *pisteuein eis* plus accusative (8.30). This is contextually improbable, the more so since the latter expression is used for defective faith in 2.23f.; 12.42 (cf. Bultmann, p. 252, n. 2). (2) E. A. Abbott, *Johannine Grammar* (London, 1906), 2506, suggests that because Greek has no pluperfect active participle, the perfect participle (*pepisteukotas*) has that sense in 8.31. But nowhere else in the fourth Gospel does the perfect of

pisteuein have that sense. (3) Schnackenburg, Vol. ii, p. 259, n. 1, says the occurrences of the perfect of *pisteuein* 'always express an established faith (or non-faith): 3.18; 6.69; 11.27; 16.27; 20.29; compare 1 John 4.16; 5.10.' But 16.27 needs to be seen beside 16.31, and 3.18 and 1 John 5.10 are prescriptive. (4) Brown, pp. 354f., Lindars, p. 323, and others, prefer to omit the words *pepisteukotas autō*. But if the alleged gloss were redactional, the problem is only pushed back to the redactor; if accidental, it must have been very early, for there is no manuscript evidence to support it. (5) Some scholars follow Augustine in taking the 'they' of 8.33 to refer to 'the Jews', not to 'the Jews who had believed in him'. This is convenient, but artificial. (6) C. H. Dodd, *More New Testament Studies* (Manchester, 1968), pp. 41ff., sees an anachronistic reference to Jewish-Christians of the judaising type. But would even Paul have charged the Judaisers with 8.43f.?

38. Cf. F. Hahn, 'Sehen und Glauben im Johannesevangelium', *Neues Testament und Geschichte* (Zürich, 1972), pp. 125-41.

39. ' "Der Vater, der mich gesandt hat" ', op. cit., p. 208.

40. Bultmann, pp. 137f.

41. Considering the fact that not one Greek manuscript supports the singular *hos ouk ... egennēthē* (constituting a reference to the virgin birth), it is astonishing how many scholars have accepted this reconstruction. External evidence is versional and patristic, a dubious basis for emendation when it stands alone. The Latin witness *b* is further weakened by the fact that *qui* is both singular and plural: the difference between *qui natus est* and *qui nati sunt* is only in the verb. The unambiguous patristic evidence most frequently cited is Irenaeus, *Ad. Haer.* iii.xvi.2; xix.2; and Tertullian, *De carne Christi* xix, who says the plural was an invention of the Valentians. Both Bodmer papyri (ii and xiv—i.e. p[66.75]) have the plural. Those who nevertheless opt for the singular include F. Blass, *Euangelium Secundum Joannem* (Leipzig, 1902), p. 2; Zahn, pp. 73; C. F. Burney, *Aramaic Origin*, op. cit., pp. 43ff.; Loisy, pp. 101ff.; C. C. Torrey, *Our Translated Gospels* (London, n.d.), pp. 151-3; F.-M. Braun, 'Qui ex Deo natus est', *Aux sources de la tradition chrétienne* (Paris, 1950), pp. 11-31; R. C. H. Lenski, *The Interpretation of St John's Gospel* (Minneapolis, 1943), pp. 62-8; M.-E. Boismard, *St John's Prologue* (London, 1957), pp. 35-9; idem, 'Critique textuelle et citations bibliques', *RB*, Vol. lvii (1950), pp. 401-8; L. Sabourin, ' "Who Was Begotten ... of God" (Jn. 1:13)', *Biblical Theology Bulletin*, Vol. vi (1976), pp. 86-90; J. McHugh, *The Mother of Jesus in the New Testament* (Garden City, 1975), pp. 255-68; M. Vellanickal, *The Divine Sonship of Christians in the Johannine Writings* (Rome, 1977), pp. 112-32; and especially the extended treatment by J. Galot, *Etre né de Dieu* (Rome, 1969). MacGregor, pp. 14f., is sympathetic, but following Loisy doubts that the singular by itself would imply a virgin birth, 'for the words in question would exclude the idea of human mother no less than human father.' It is easy to imagine an *a fortiori* argument whereby the text was corrupted from plural to singular: if Christians are begotten by God, how much more so Jesus Christ? Indeed, Hoskyns, p. 166, Barrett, pp. 137f., and Morris, p. 100, see just such an allusion in the plural text. It is difficult to imagine so thorough a corruption of the text the other way.

42. Barrett, p. 137. See *inter alia* Howard, p. 471; Bultmann, p. 59, n. 4.

43. H. J. Holtzmann, *Lehrbuch der neutestamentlichen Theologie* (Tübingen, 1911), Vol. ii, p. 534.; cf. also his commentary, pp. 41f.

44. 'The Fourth Gospel an Act of Contemplation', *Studies in the Fourth Gospel* (London, 1957), p. 27. Cf. Morris, p. 101: 'The new birth is always sheer miracle. All human initiative is ruled out.'

45. The plural *hymas* (3.7) is puzzling (as are other shifts in pronoun and number in this pericope), but a general reference to Nicodemus's class (cf. 3.1) seems best to explain the text at this point.

46. A. Augustinović, *Critica 'determinismi' Joannei* (Jerusalem, 1947), pp. 53, 118.

47. Review of Augustinović, op. cit., in *RB*, Vol. lv (1948), p. 472.

48. 'The neuter (*pan ho*) is sometimes used with reference to persons if it is not the individuals but a general quality that is emphasised' (BDF §138(1). MacGregor, p. 146, sees here 'a comprehensive neuter, the thought of the believer's individuality being thus subordinated to that of the Father's grace.' Cf. the important discussion by F.- M. Braun, 'La réduction du pluriel au singulier dans l'Evangile et la Première Lettre de Jean', *NTS*, Vol. xxiv (1977), pp. 40-67.

49. 'A Critical Comparison of the Dualism in 1QS 3.13-4.26 and the "Dualism" Contained in the Gospel of John', *John and Qumran* (London, 1972), p. 95.

50. Cf. the excellent summary of 6.37-40 by Barrett, p. 243; and now also O. Hofius, 'Erwählung und Bewahrung. Zur Auslegung von Joh. 6, 37', *Theologische Beiträge*, Vol. viii (1977), pp. 24-9.

51. Hendriksen, Vol. i, p. 238.

52. Cf. W. Eborowicz, 'L'exégèse augustinienne de Jean vi, 44', *Studia Evangelica*, Vol. vi (1973), pp. 95-9; G. Berkouwer, *Divine Election* (Grand Rapids, 1960), p. 47.

53. Barrett, p. 252; cf. Morris, p. 387. Cf. also the so-called 'johannine logion', Matt. 11.27.

54. Brown, p. 741.

55. *Pace* Lindars, p. 521, who says, 'There is no rigid doctrine of predestination here, though the tendency of Semitic to see the whole contained in the beginning gives the impression of such a doctrine.' But that is just the point: if the whole is indeed contained in the beginning, it is difficult to avoid predestination.

56. Against this interpretation, J. C. Earwaker, 'John xvii21', *Ex. T*, Vol. lxxv (1963-4), pp. 316f., sees all the *hina* clauses in 17.21 as co-ordinate. This not only makes the prayer extremely disjointed, but it is excluded by the fact that the main clause (17.20) designates the people specifically prayed for as believers-to-be. Cf. Bultmann and Morris, *in loc.* E. A. Abbott, op. cit., §§2511, 2524-6, 2528, tries to preserve a rigid distinction between aorist and present subjunctives in *hina*-clauses. Hence in §2554 he contrasts 17.21d ('that the world may grow in belief') with the parallel clause in 17.23c ('that knowledge may dawn on the world'). If Abbott were right, 17.21d would imply that the world already believes, and Jesus is praying that this belief may continue and deepen. That would contradict, for instance, 16:33; 17.9, 25. But the dilemma is a false one. Abbott seems to think *ginōskē* in

17.23c is an aorist; but it is not, and there is no significant textual evidence for *gnō*.

57. *Pace* Barrett, p. 428.

58. Barrett, p. 306.

59. It is difficult to decide if *pro emou* is original. The words are omitted by $p^{45(vid.).75}$ ℵ* E F G M S U Γ Δ 28 892, most minuscules, and by manuscripts of OL, OS, and Coptic versions; but the probability seems to be with inclusion.

60. A. Vanhoye, 'Notre foi, oeuvre divine, d'après le quatrième évangile', *Nouvelle Revue Theologique*, Vol. lxxxvi (1964), p. 343. Cf. also E. K. Lee, *The Religious Thought of St John* (London, 1950), pp. 169f.

61. Cf. C. Spicq, 'La charité est amour manifeste', *Revue Biblique*, Vol. lxv (1958), pp. 360-62; BDF §207(3); A. M. Hunter, *According to John*, op. cit., pp. 87f.; Morris, pp. 612f.

62. The expression may mean: (1) To the death: note the cognate verb *tetelestai* in 19.30. Brown, p. 555, draws attention to LXX Deut. 31.24. (2) To the uttermost: cf. NEB. (3) To the last moment of life: cf. Barrett, p. 365. In any case, in 13.1 'the piling up of participial clauses is unusual for John, and gives a most solemn effect' (Lindars, p. 448).

63. This nuanced approach is vastly to be preferred to the work of M. Lattke, *Einheit im Wort* (Münich, 1975), who attempts to force all love references into a single mould. Love, in John, he says, has no psychological or mystical element, but means simply to exist in the unity of the word, and can therefore refer only to believers and their Lord. Needless to say, he has enormous difficulties with John 3.16; 10.17f.; 13.1; 15.13.

64. As in n. 60, *supra*, p. 350.

65. Cf. the references in Morris, pp. 669f., n. 10. R. Borig, *Der wahre Weinstock* (München, 1967), says that *katharos* does not mean free from sin, but from everything that would hinder fruitbearing. However, in the context of johannine thought, there is no distinction between the two. Cf. John's only other use of the word, in 13.10f.

66. Morris, p. 669.

67. This simple interpretation gets rid of the strained exegesis which sees Jesus' love as the motivating power for Christians, or which takes *kathōs* in 15.9 to be causative (BDF §453(2); Brown, p. 663). Barrett, p. 397, thinks 14.15, 21 are parallels which, taken with this passage (15.10), indicate 'that love and obedience are mutually dependent. Love arises out of obedience, obedience out of love.' But the relationship is not so symmetrical. John 14.15, 21 speaks of the love of believers for Christ, resulting in obedience to him; while 15.10 speaks of the obedience of believers to him, which results, not explicitly in love *for* Christ, but in an enduring love *from* Christ for them (cf. 16.27).

68. Cf. the translation of Brown, p. 658: 'You are clean already, thanks to the word I have spoken to you.' This takes *dia* plus the accusative in its ordinary sense: so also Bernard, Vol. ii, p. 480, and many others. Cf. Schlatter, p. 305, who says that Jesus' word declares (*heissen*) the disciples to be clean.

69. Cf. Brown, p. 675; and Augustine's oft-quoted remark, '*Aut vitis, aut*

ignis' (*In Jo.* 81.3). *Contra* cf. F. W. Grosheide, *Het Heilig Evangelie Volgens Johannes* (Amsterdam, 1950), Vol. ii, p. 335, who construes *en emoi* in 15.2 not with branch but with fruit. The idea would then be that in addition to the branches in the vine (=Christ), there are branches in *other* vines, and these branches do not bear fruit in Christ. In that case, the urgency of abiding in Christ (15.4) seems rather forced. I. H. Marshall, *Kept by the Power of God* (Minneapolis, 1975), p. 184, argues that since the branches thrown away were once in the vine (=in Christ), they must have been authentic believers. That may be pushing the metaphor too hard, in a book in which being a 'disciple' does not itself guarantee anything.

70. Morris, p. 603.

71. Hoskyns, p. 428.

72. *Krisis* (Freiburg, 1964), pp. 304f.; 'Eschatological Faith', art. cit., pp. 46f. The change from third person to first is probably due to the evangelist's appended identification of Jesus as the one whom Isaiah saw (12.41): cf. R. Schnackenburg, 'John 12, 39-41', art. cit., pp. 174-6.

73. So, for example, A. Augustinović, op. cit., pp. 188-90.

74. M. Zerwick, *Biblical Greek* (Rome, 1963), §§412-14, notes that the very existence of causal *hina* in New Testament Greek is still disputed (although it is attested in the second and third centuries). In any case, 'to posit it here does not seem to do justice to the passage' (Brown, p. 484).

75. Brown, p. 485.

76. Cf. Schnackenburg, Vol. ii, pp. 345f.; and J. Gnilka, *Die Verstockung Israels* (München, 1961), especially pp. 23ff. *Contra*, cf. C. F. D. Moule, 'Mark 4:1-20: Yet Once More', *Neotestamentica et Semitica* (Edinburgh, 1969), pp. 95-113. Cf. also R. P. Maye, 'Mark 4, 10: "Those about Him with the Twelve",' *St. Ev.*, Vol. ii (1964), pp. 211-18; W. L. Lane, *The Gospel according to Mark* (Grand Rapids, 1974), pp. 156-9.

77. Cf. Calvin's wrestlings with this problem in connection with Rom. 9, in *Concerning the Eternal Predestination of God* (London, 1961), p. 76ff.

78. Cf. G. E. Ladd, *Theology*, op. cit., p. 277, who says that the 'decision of faith is not a human meritorious achievement like the Jewish works of the Law, but simply the fitting answer, made possible by the grace of God, to the revelation given by Jesus.'

79. Barrett, pp. 140f. The emphasis on grace is but little changed if we follow I. de la Patterie, '*Charis* paulinienne et *charis* johannique,' *Jesus und Paulus* (Göttingen, 1975), pp. 256-82, who sees the grace of Christ's truth replacing the earlier (and lesser) grace of law. Cf. also idem, *La vérité dans Saint Jean* (Rome, 1977), Vol. i, pp. 129ff.

CHAPTER THIRTEEN (PP. 201-222)

1. L. Berkhof, *Systematic Theology* (Grand Rapids, 1941), p. 106.

2. W. G. T. Shedd, *Dogmatic Theology* (Edinburgh, 1889), Vol. i, p. 403. Cf. J. H. Thornwell, *Election and Reprobation* (Philadelphia, repr. 1961), p. 73, who argues that God's saving decree does not force men to act contrary to their wills. But it does renew their wills, and so they choose aright.

3. A. A. Hodge, *Evangelical Theology* (London, 1890), p. 157.

4. E.g. C. Hodge, *Systematic Theology* (New York, 1872), vol. ii, pp.289ff.

5. J. I. Packer, *NBD*, p. 1052.

6. Ibid., p. 734.

7. Op. cit., p. 16.

8. *Concerning the Eternal Predestination of God*, op. cit., p. 123.

9. 'Some Comments on Hebrews 6:4-6 and the Doctrine of the Perseverance of God with the Saints', *Current Issues in Biblical and Patristic Interpretation* (Grand Rapids, 1975), p. 357.

10. K. Rahner, *Theological Investigations* (London, 1961-), Vol. ii, p. 246, wisely admits that 'freedom of choice ... can be defined only with difficulty.' Then he goes on to state that the 'causality of free action ... can ... be possible only when faced with the finite, or the infinite conceived as merely finite, and hence can have meaning only in the face of the finite.' In general he accepts the Roman Catholic view which relates responsibility to human freedom: see, for example, his *Grace in Freedom* (London, 1970), *passim;* and his *Theological Investigations*, op. cit., Vol. vi, pp. 197ff. In the latter instance he purposely skirts the question of whether some other concept of responsibility is possible in the very nature of things—e.g. one which operates under the presuppositions of a psychological or theological determinism.

11. For example, A. Flew, 'Divine Omnipotence and Human Freedom', *New Essays in Philosophical Theology* (London, 1955), pp. 144-69, and J. L. Mackie, 'Evil and Omnipotence', *God and Evil* (Englewood Cliffs, 1964), chap. 6, have advanced a new disproof of the free will defence; and they are in turn answered by the joint arguments of S. T. Davies, 'A Defense of the Free Will Defense', *Religious Studies*, Vol. viii (1972), pp. 325-43, and A. D. Steven, 'Once More on the Free Will Defense', *Religious Studies*, Vol. x (1974), pp. 301-11.

12. Among those who have recently attempted to ease the sovereignty-responsibility tension by in some way limiting God's omnipotence while everywhere positing that human free will entails power to contrary, are B. Hebblethwaite, *Evil, Suffering and Religion* (London, 1976), especially pp. 55ff.; A. Plantinga, *God, Freedom and Evil* (London, 1975), who, among other things, argues that the crucial factor in the free will defence is that the proposition 'God is omnipotent, and it was not within his power to create a world containing moral good but not moral evil' is true (which prompts me to wonder what the new heaven and new earth will be like); J. R. Lucas, *Freedom and Grace* (London, 1976), who strongly defends human freedom and reduces God to a super chess player who is able by his superior playing ability to defeat his opponents; P. Geach, *Providence and Evil* (Cambridge, 1977), whose work is highly individualistic, introducing a fundamental distinction between God's 'almightiness' and his 'omnipotence'. On Geach, see especially P. Helm, 'Omnipotence and Change', *Philosophy*, Vol. li (1976), pp. 454-61. On Lucas, I am indebted to the review by O. O'Donovan in *Churchman*, Vol. xci (1977), pp. 74-6, and especially to the first draft of a paper by P. Helm, 'Grace and the Logic of Causality', read in Oxford in 1977 (I have not seen the final draft in print.) On the whole question of the nature of human freedom, cf. R. Young, 'Human Freedom and Christian Theism',

Interchange, No. 16 (1974), pp. 241-8; and especially his *magnum opus, Freedom, Responsibility, and God* (London, 1975). From a theological perspective, cf. J. Murray, *The Collected Writings of John Murray* (Edinburgh, 1977), Vol. ii, pp. 60-67. For further discussion, not always in agreement with what I here defend, cf. also A. Farrar, *The Freedom of the Will* (London, 1963); and K. Lehrer, ed., *Freedom and Determinism* (New York, 1966), especially the last chapter.

13. Op. cit., p. 402.

14. E. G. J. Jocz, *A Theology of Election* (London, 1958), pp. 166-71; alternatively, in the manner of the existential theologians, e.g. P. Tillich, *Systematic Theology* (London, 1953-64), Vol. iii, pp. 421-7.

15. The proposed solutions have varied widely, despite N. Pike, *God and Timelessness* (London, 1970), pp. 53-86, who analyses the solutions of Boethius and Augustine and thinks both are possible—and that they exhaust the possibilities. Thomists say that God's foreknowledge is causative, and yet, because all things are 'present' to God, he can know all 'future' acts without destroying their freedom. Cf. K. Rahner, *SM*, Vol. v, pp. 89f. Molina proposed a complex three-fold knowledge in God, in order to deny that divine foreknowledge is in any sense deterministic (for convenient discussion, cf. J. Farrelly, op. cit., pp. 23f.). E. Brunner, *The Christian Doctrine of God* (London, repr. 1966), pp. 317f., tries not only to divorce time and eternity, but to associate time with decision rather than with sequence. In the past it has also been common to set chronological time over against allegedly distinctive Hebrew concepts of 'psychic time', 'realistic time', or the 'quality of time'— e.g. H. W. Robinson, *Inspiration and Revelation in the Old Testament* (Oxford, 1946), pp. 106ff.; J. A. T. Robinson, *In the End, God ...* (London. 1950), pp. 44ff.; T. Boman, *Hebrew Thought Compared with Greek* (London, 1960), pp. 137ff.; J. Manek, 'The Biblical Concept of Time and Our Gospels', *NTS*, Vol. vi (1959-60), pp. 45-51. These approaches will, by and large, no longer stand: cf. especially J. Barr, *Biblical Words for Time,* op. cit. Some approaches are more drastic: W. Pannenberg, *Basic Questions in Theology* (Philadelphia, 1973), Vol. iii, pp. 80-98, argues that all conceptions of divine foreknowledge and predestination exclude any meaningful idea of human freedom, and again presents God as the 'power of the future'. Cf. also his article in *RGG* (third edition), Vol. ii, pp. 614-22. He is criticised in the last few pages of R. G. Hamerton-Kelly, *Pre-Existence,* op. cit. More recently Pannenberg has built on his earlier work in *Human Nature, Election, and History* (Philadelphia, 1977); but despite the many valuable insights in everything he writes, this book does not escape the weaknesses of the presuppositions he expressed earlier.

16. Cf. especially P. Helm, 'Divine Foreknowledge and Facts', *Canadian Journal of Philosophy,* Vol. iv (1974), pp. 305-15; idem, 'Timelessness and Foreknowledge', *Mind,* Vol. lxxxiv (1975), pp. 516-27.

17. C. S. Lewis, *Mere Christianity* (London, 1955), pp. 144f., is one of the few who appeals to the distinction between time and eternity, but who also admits that this distinction is not a *biblical* insight.

19. E.g. Jerome Zanchius, *Absolute Predestination* (Grand Rapids, repr. 1971), p. 76.

18. This is a very common approach. For example, it is adopted by J. R.

Lucas in his study, 'Pelagius and St. Augustine', *JTS*, Vol. xxii (1971), pp. 73-85.

20. *Philosophical Theology* (Indianapolis, 1969).

21. *Concerning the Eternal Predestination of God*, op. cit., pp. 117f.

22. For a recent outline of the structure of the argument, cf. M. L. Peterson, 'Christian Theism and the Problem of Evil', *Journal of the Evangelical Theological Society*, Vol. xxi (1978), pp. 35-46.

23. *The Providence of God* (Grand Rapids, 1952), pp. 153f. It is customary at this point in some theological discussion to distinguish between the *materia* and the *forma* of the sinful act: e.g. L. Berkhof, op. cit., pp. 174.; and especially H. Bavinck, *Gereformeerde Dogmatiek* (Kampen, 1906-11), Vol. ii, pp. 595ff. On the artificiality of such distinctions, cf. G. C. Berkouwer, *Providence*, op. cit., pp. 131ff.

24. Often do biblical characters, especially in the Old Testament, assume that God is leading in the approaching events, even though the direction of that leading may be revealed only in the events themselves: e.g. Gen. 24.7f.; Exod. 32.30-35; 2 Sam. 5.12; Joel 2.11-14; Amos 5.15; Jonah 3.9f.; Zeph. 2.3; Esther 4.14; Dan. 3.17f.

25. There is an excellent if brief discussion in G. C. Berkouwer, *Divine Election*, op. cit., pp. 115-30.

26. The personality of God in the Old Testament is vehemently defended by, *inter alios*, C. R. North, *The Old Testament Interpretation of History* (London, 1946), pp. 143ff.; W. Eichrodt, *Theology*, op. cit., Vol. i, pp. 206-10; J. Lindblom, *Prophecy*, op. cit., pp. 315, 322f.; E. Brunner, *The Christian Doctrine of God*, op. cit., pp. 121-3; J. Daane, *The Freedom of God* (Grand Rapids, 1973), pp. 63f., 68, *passim*. Cf. also the perceptive analysis by H. Thielicke, *Gotteslehre und Christologie* (Tübingen, 1973), pp. 123-39, in particular p. 138: 'When we speak of God as a person, we do not mean this in some anthropomorphic sense. On the contrary: when we speak of the human person, we mean this in a theomorphic sense.' On the models used to discuss God's personality, and the course of the debate in church history, cf. H. C. Wolf, 'An Introduction to the Idea of God as Person', *Journal of Bible and Religion*, Vol. xxxii (1964), pp. 26-33.

27. Cf. W. Vischer, 'Words and the Word: the Anthropomorphisms of the Biblical Revelation', *Interpretation*, Vol. iii (1949), pp. 1ff.; E. M. Yamauchi, 'Anthropomorphism in Hellenism and in Judaism', *Bibliotheca Sacra*, Vol. cxxvii (1970), pp. 220-22.

28. E.g. in the *Thirty-Nine Articles*, Art. ı; the *Westminster Confession of Faith*, ii.1.

29. I am indebted to Dr Paul D. Feinberg for stimulating discussion on this whole question of the impassibility of God, and for showing me a rough draft of one of his papers, which, I hope, will not be long in appearing in print.

30. For some elegant discussion of the problems surrounding anthropomorphism and anthropopathism, cf. G. D. Kaufman, *An Essay on Theological Method* (Missoula, 1975), *passim*, especially pp. 52, 67.

31. Cf. his *Church Dogmatics* (Edinburgh, 1857), Vol. ii/2, pp. 3-506. For briefer expositions of Barth's thought, cf. *inter alia* P. Maury, 'Predestination', *Predestination and Other Papers* (London, 1960), pp. 19-71,

T. H. L. Parker, 'Predestination', *A Dictionary of Christian Theology* (London, 1969), pp. 264-72; J. K. S. Reid, in his introduction (especially pp. 40-4) to a new translation of Calvin's *Concerning the Eternal Predestination of God*, op. cit.; C. Gunton, 'Karl Barth's Doctrine of Election as Part of His Doctrine of God', *JTS*, Vol. xxv (1974), pp. 381-92; M. Barth, *Ephesians* (New York, 1974), Vol. i, pp. 105-9.

32. For further critique, cf. K. Standahl, 'The Called and the Chosen. An Essay on Election', *The Root of the Vine* (London, 1953), pp. 67ff.; G. C. Berkouwer, *Divine Election*, op. cit., pp. 154-62; C. Brown, *Karl Barth and the Christian Message* (London, 1967), pp. 134-9.

33. *Belief in God* (New York, 1970), pp. 97ff.

34. Cf. A. S. Peake, *The Problem of Suffering in the Old Testament* (London, 1904), p. 102. Th. C. Vriezen's discussion, in *Outline*, op. cit., pp. 316f., is excellent. This point is quite missed by those who overlook God's speeches and seek the solution to Job's suffering only in the prologue (suffering tests faithfulness, 1.6-12), or in the epilogue (suffering can be made redemptive by the right attitude, 42.10): cf. J. Bowker, *Problems of Suffering in Religions of the World* (Cambridge, 1975), pp. 19f.

35. F. D. Kidner, 'Wisdom Literature', op. cit., p. 125.

36. Cf. J. Abelson, *The Immanence of God*, op. cit., p. 52. Yet R. Otto, *The Idea of the Holy* (Oxford, 1929), is quite wrong to emphasise the transcendence of God by associating it with non-rationality. Election and predestination he then dismisses as numinous experiences of utter dependence upon the transcendence God (pp. 116f.).

37. Cf. C. F. D. Moule, 'The Influence of Circumstances on the Use of Eschatological Terms', *JTS*, Vol. xv (1964), pp. 5f.: 'so vast are the purposes of God that the human mind can only adumbrate lists of them as thesis and antithesis, never, in this life, reaching synthesis; and, consequently, it is not surprising if a single thinker is found using antithetic formulations at one and the same period of his own development.' Similarly, cf. J. I. Packer, 'What Did the Cross Achieve?', *Tyndale Bulletin*, Vol. xxv (1974), pp. 35f.: 'The way to stand against naturalistic theology is to keep in view its reductionist method which makes man the standard for God; to stress that according to Scripture the Creator and his work are of necessity mysterious to us, even as revealed (to make this point is the proper task of the word "supernatural" in theology); and to remember that what is *above* reason is not necessarily *against* it.'

38. It is not uncommon to find the word 'antinomy' applied to the sovereignty-responsibility tension. Unfortunately, the term is ambiguous. Following the development of Kantian usage, it is generally defined as a 'logical contradiction between two accepted principles or between conclusions drawn from premises which have equal claim to objective validity' (so *DPP*, Vol. i, p. 56; also D. E. Runes, ed., *Dictionary of Philosophy* (Totowa, N. J., 1966), p. 14; *OED, in loc.*). With this meaning the term is applied by Th. C. Vriezen, *Outline*, op. cit., pp. 87f., to various theological tensions, including the sovereignty-responsibility tension (Dutch 'antinomiën'). Other writers assign a modified definition to the word, so that it refers to an *apparent* contradiction between two true principles or conclusions: So J. I. Packer, *Evangelism and the Sovereignty of God* (London, 1961), pp. 18ff.;

H. Dunelm, *ISBE*, Vol. ii, p. 926. Because of this ambiguity, I have avoided the term in this book.

39. *New Testament Essays* (London, 1972), pp. 49-69.

40. E.g. most of the writings of Voetius, Turretin, and many others.

41. In particular, cf. H. D. McDonald, 'The Changing Emphasis in the Doctrine of Providence', *Vox Evangelica*, Vol. iii (1964), pp. 58-75; and now especially G. Kraus, *Vorherbestimmung: Traditionelle Predestinationslehre im Licht gegenwärtiger Theologie* (Freiburg, 1977), who critically assesses the positions of Augustine, Aquinas, Luther, Calvin, and Barth, and then opts for a modified Barthian position.

42. More refined statements are possible. Some who claim to be of Arminian persuasion would not say that man has a free will in the sense that he, all by himself, can make a decision for Christ. Rather, like all other men, he will choose to reject Christ, unless the grace of God prompts him to choose aright. However, these 'Arminians' would go on to say that this divine grace operates in all men; so that if a man chooses the good, he cannot say he has done so apart from the grace of God. Nevertheless, they would say that the man retains the absolute freedom to reject the wooing of this universal grace. This theological perspective can be traced to John Wesley himself, prompting critics to label him, not an Arminian, but an inconsistent Calvinist; cf. I. W. Reist, 'John Wesley and George Whitefield: A Study in the Integrity of Two Theologies of Grace', *Evangelical Quarterly*, Vol. xlvii (1975), pp. 26-40. Epithets aside, it remains obvious that even this so-called 'inconsistent Calvinism' involves a concept of human freedom which includes power to contrary. The *ultimate* distinguishing feature between the man who chooses for Christ and the man who chooses against Christ turns, not on divine elective grace, but on the choices of the men themselves apart from any distinguishing grace.

INDEX OF BIBLICAL REFERENCES

OLD TESTAMENT

HABAKKUK						
1ff.	30	3.5	36	2.22	43	7.12–14	20
2.8	78	3.9–13	29	2.23	37	11.16	43
2.19f.	76	3.12f.	33			13.8f.	33

HAGGAI		ZECHARIAH		MALACHI	
1.9–11	20	1.14–17	31	1.2	30
1.12–14	15f., 98	2.11f.	30	3.6	32

ZEPHANIAH
1.2ff.   28
2.3   18, 256

1.14   37   3.2   30   3.10   18
2.4ff.   16   6.15   21   3.10f. 21
                     7.11   33

NEW TESTAMENT

MATTHEW		1.29–31	174	3.27ff.	149	5.29	163, 193, 197
3.9	182	1.30	147, 149	3.28–30	127	5.29f.	168
11.27	251	1.31–4	169	3.29	239	5.30	148, 157, 160
13.14f.	196	1.34	149	3.30	127	5.35	178
16.1	176	1.41	168	3.31	140, 149, 172	5.36	157
18.3f.	181	1.45	133, 169	3.32	164	5.37–40	177
24.13	195	1.48	148	3.32f.	177	5.38	192
		1.49	149	3.33ff.	156	5.39f.	133, 169, 177
MARK		1.49f.	168	3.34	147, 156, 157	5.40	165
4.12	196, 253	1.51	139	3.34f.	156, 157	5.42	148, 165
8.11–33	249	2.4	135	3.36	161, 163, 167,	5.43	147, 165
8.11f.	176	2.11	168, 178		171, 193, 196	5.44	163, 165, 169
10.27	186	2.13	133	4	180, 198, 240	5.45–7	169
14.36	158	2.13ff.	133, 163	4.1	148	5.45–57	177
		2.15	184	4.6f.	148	5.46f.	133, 177
LUKE		2.16	147	4.10	169	6	177, 184, 185, 188,
8.10	196	2.18	176	4.13f.	167		218
11.16	176	2.22	144, 168, 178	4.16–18	163	6.2	177, 247
13.1–5	128, 239	2.23	133, 178	4.19f.	179	6.4	133, 247
16.30f.	177	2.23–5	164, 247, 250	4.21–23	140	6.6	148
18.18	180	2.24	241	4.22	148	6.14	147, 178
22.37	133	2.24f.	178	4.23	136	6.15	148, 178, 185
24.45–9	143	2.25	148	4.29	147	6.26	163, 177, 249
		3	180	4.34	147, 148, 157,	6.26f.	164
JOHN		3.1	247		158, 159	6.27	169
1–12	164	3.2	180, 247	4.35–8	169	6.28	157, 169
1.1	146, 147, 151,	3.3	140, 180, 181,	4.38	247	6.29	169
	155		182	4.39	168, 169, 178,	6.30	176, 177, 249
1.1–18	153	3.3ff.	183		179	6.31	133, 148
1.3	140, 146, 155	3.4	182	4.41f.	168, 178, 179	6.32f.	157
1.4	125	3.5	140, 181	4.42	173, 247	6.33	173
1.6f.	169	3.5f.	182f.	4.46–5.47	180	6.35	184, 249
1.7	167, 174, 176	3.6	140	4.46–54	247	6.35f.	167, 249
1.9	125, 164, 174	3.7	181, 251	4.48	164, 176, 177	6.36	177, 178, 184,
1.10	163, 164	3.7f.	183	4.53	178, 179		185, 249
1.10f.	155, 164, 174	3.10	167	5	198	6.37	125, 126, 184f.,
1.11	189	3.11	177	5.1	133		186, 251
1.12	167, 168, 181f.	3.13	139, 172	5.1–47	153, 247	6.37f.	184
1.12f.	156, 181f., 183	3.14	135	5.6	148, 247	6.37–40	159, 184f.,
1.13	181f., 250f.	3.15	172	5.14	127–8, 161, 163		192, 194,
1.14	140, 146, 148,	3.15–18	167	5.17	157		198, 251
	153, 154, 155,	3.16	128, 129, 140,	5.17f.	147, 152, 157	6.38	148, 157, 184
	245		157, 170, 173,	5.19	147, 148, 160	6.38f.	184
1.14f.	155		187, 196, 252	5.19f.	157	6.39	138f., 184, 186
1.15	147, 149, 155	3.17	147, 164, 173,	5.19–30	157	6.39f.	136, 138, 140,
1.16	198		175, 196, 248	5.19ff.	157		147
1.17	146, 147, 153,	3.18	163, 173, 250	5.20	160, 176	6.40	139, 184
	155	3.18f.	171	5.21–30	133, 140	6.40–45	182
1.18	147, 151, 155,	3.19	166	5.23	147, 149	6.41f.	185
	156, 162, 246	3.19f.	163, 164	5.23f.	147	6.44	136, 138f., 140,
1.20	169	3.19–21	171, 248	5.24	156, 160, 167		167, 174, 184,
1.23	133	3.20	164, 173, 248	5.25	136		186, 251
1.27	149	3.21	172, 173, 248	5.27	244	6.44f.	185f.
1.29	161, 164, 173,	3.26	126, 127	5.28f.	140, 162	6.45	186
	187	3.27	125–7, 128	5.28–30	136	6.46	156

INDEX OF APOCRYPHAL AND PSEUDEPIGRAPHIC SOURCES

INDEX OF NAMES

Made in the USA
Coppell, TX
17 April 2023

15736708R00157